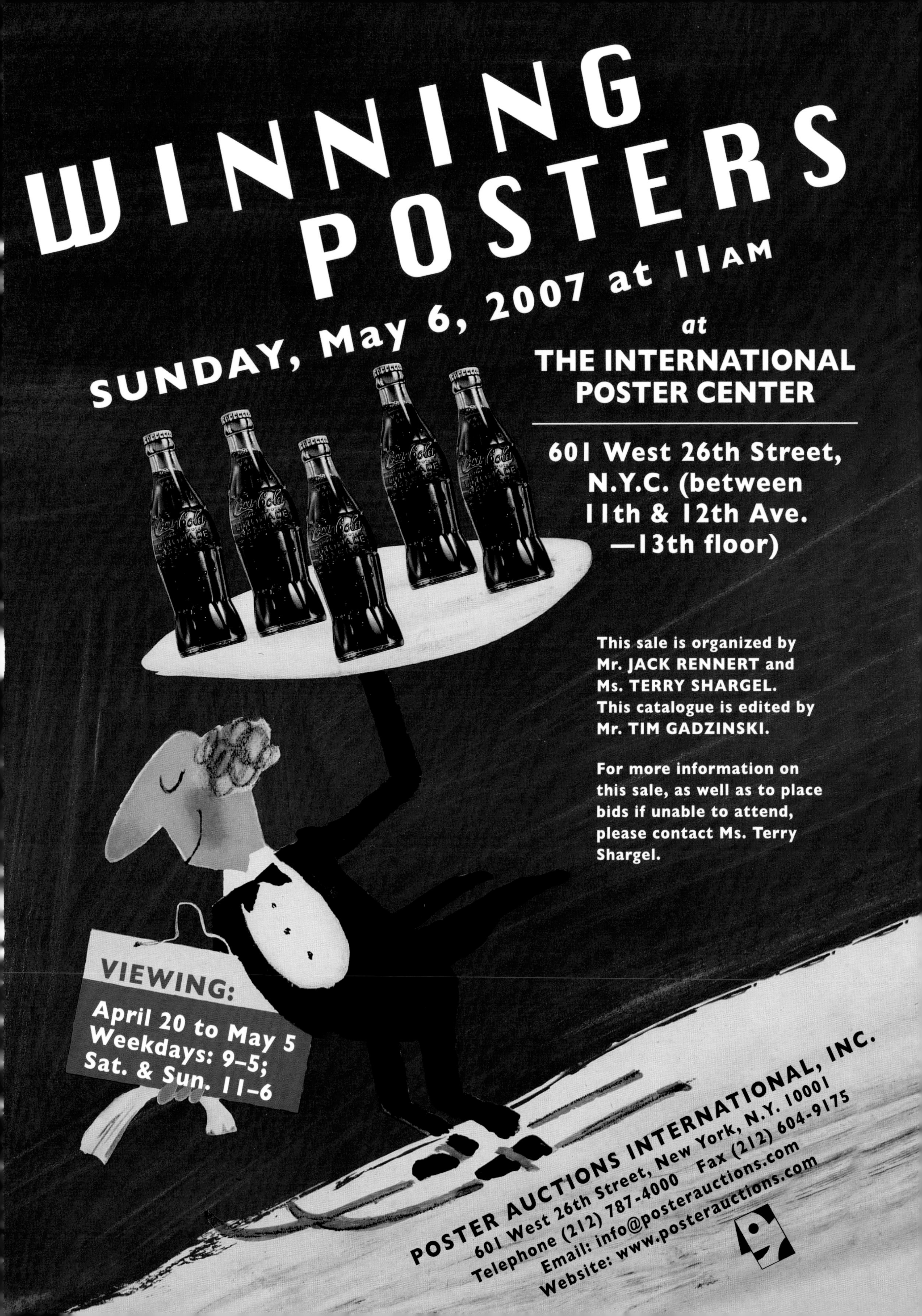
WINNING POSTERS
SUNDAY, May 6, 2007 at 11AM
at
THE INTERNATIONAL POSTER CENTER
601 West 26th Street, N.Y.C. (between 11th & 12th Ave. —13th floor)
This sale is organized by Mr. JACK RENNERT and Ms. TERRY SHARGEL. This catalogue is edited by Mr. TIM GADZINSKI.
For more information on this sale, as well as to place bids if unable to attend, please contact Ms. Terry Shargel.
VIEWING:
April 20 to May 5
Weekdays: 9–5;
Sat. & Sun. 11–6
POSTER AUCTIONS INTERNATIONAL, INC.
601 West 26th Street, New York, N.Y. 10001
Telephone (212) 787-4000 Fax (212) 604-9175
Email: info@posterauctions.com
Website: www.posterauctions.com

# CONTENTS

---

# ACKNOWLEDGMENTS

I am most grateful to the many individuals who have given their full support and assistance to us in the preparation of this WINNING POSTERS sale. First and foremost, our thanks to the 78 consignors in 16 states and 10 foreign countries who entrusted their finest works to us for this very special occasion.

Our staff has been materially helpful in all aspects of this auction, and I wish to especially single out the work of my associate, Ms. Terry Shargel. Our editorial department was headed once again by Mr. Tim Gadzinski, who is responsible for the lively and incisive text in this book. Helping with many of the administrative aspects were Ms. Sarah Sternick, Ms. Julie Press and Mr. Xavier Serbones. Mr. John Greenleaf and Mr. Edward Haber handled all computer and internet-related matters. And finally, a special personal note of thanks to Barbara Rennert, who helps and encourages in countless ways.

We take great pride in making all of our annotations as complete and accurate as possible, and we are helped enormously in this task by being able to call upon very knowledgeable colleagues throughout the world. Helpful in answering our many questions for this book were Mr. Chester Collins, Mr. Wiliam W. Crouse, Mr. Ronald Keats, Dr. Maura Mansfield, Mr. Jacob Mills, Mr. Dave Oneida, Mr. Howard Sigman and Dr. René Wanner.

In the production of this catalogue, I was again fortunate to be able to call on the talents and devotion of fine craftsmen: Mr. Guenter Knop is our very able photographer; the staff of Harry Chester, Inc. was in charge of design and production, and I especially want to thank Ms. Susannah Ing; all aspects of printing and binding were again handled by Cosmos Communications and I am especially indebted to Ms. Judy Lamm of their large and able staff.

Public relations for this sale have been ably handled by Mr. David Reich.

To all of them and to all the others who offered help, suggestions and encouragement, many thanks.

—Jack Rennert

---

### CONDITIONS OF SALE

We call your attention to the Conditions of Sale printed at the end of the book.
Those bidding at this sale should first familiarize themselves with the terms contained therein.

---

### OUR NEXT SALE

We are pleased to announce that the PAI-XLV sale of rare posters
will be held on Sunday, November 11, 2007.

Consignments are accepted until July 15, 2007.

---

### BID WITH CONFIDENCE—EVEN IF YOU CANNOT ATTEND

If you cannot attend the auction of May 6, please use the Order Bid Form provided.
It should be mailed or faxed to arrive at our office no later than Friday, May 4.
Note that all illustrations in this book are of the item being sold—we never use stock photos.

Jack Rennert—License 0797440

# AUTO RACING POSTERs

## THE MONACO GRAND PRIX

Beyond a shadow of a doubt, the Monaco Grand Prix is the most glamorous Formula One race in the world. And what makes it unique is it's combination of state-of-the-art machines and a picturesque—even quaint—setting: its 100-lap route, unaltered over the years, goes through the ancient streets of the tiny principality, around hairpin turns, along the edges of hair-raising cliffs and along coastal roads, all in amazingly close proximity to the spectators that throng there for the action. Naturally, it's an attraction that has every hotel in Monaco and the surrounding region booked months in advance.

The Automobile Club of Monaco had been holding annual rallies before 1928, but with the success of the inaugural Grand Prix in 1929, they decided to continue the new and exciting race annually, with a single hiatus between 1938 and 1948. And this decision to hold the Grand Prix yearly became the stuff of legend, both in terms of the racing and the posters produced to promote them.

The Monaco Grand Prix posters continue to enthrall today's collector for the same reason the race itself continues to fascinate—it's Mediterranean elegance meeting unbridled speed without an intermediary, two unlikely factors combining to create a product that's more impressive than either of its parts. And considering that both parts are rather impressive to begin with, that's quite an accomplishment indeed.

This assemblage of posters is the most comprehensive array of Monaco Grand Prix designs that we've ever had the pleasure to offer, beginning with the program cover drawing from the initial race and continuing through the thrilling pursuits of the late-1980s. Illustrious races all, illustrated for all time with legendary posters.

PREMIER

GRAND PRIX AUTOMOBILE

DE MONACO

organisé par

l'Automobile Club de Monaco

avec le concours
de l'International Sporting Club et du Journal L'Auto

DIMANCHE 14 AVRIL 1929
à 13 heures 30 précises

100 tours de Circuit, soit 318 kilometres

LISTE DES ENGAGÉS

| | | |
|---|---|---|
| ALLEMAGNE: | CARACCIOLA | Mercédès Benz |
| AUTRICHE: | STUCK | Austro Daimler |
| BELGIQUE: | BOURIANO | Bugatti |
| FRANCE: | DAUVERGNE | Bugatti |
| | DORE | Licorne |
| | DREYFUS | Bugatti |
| | ETANCELIN | Bugatti |
| | LAMY | Bugatti |
| | G.PHILIPPE | Bugatti |
| | DE ROVIN | Delage |
| GRANDE-BRETAGNE: | WILLIAMS | Bugatti |
| ITALIE: | GHERSI | Alfa Roméo |
| | PERROT | Alfa Roméo |
| | RIGAL | Alfa Roméo |
| | SANDRI | Maserati |
| | DE STERLICH | Maserati |
| | ZEHENDER | Alfa Roméo |
| POLOGNE: | BYCHAWSKI | Bugatti |
| SUISSE: | LEPORI | Bugatti |

CIRCUIT DE MONACO
3180

For the incredible history of this race, see *Le Grand Prix Automobile de Monaco* in the Books & Periodicals section.

**1. Premier Grand Prix Automobile de Monaco. 1929.**
Artist: **Anonymous**
12¼ x 19 in./31 x 48.4 cm
*Ink and pencil drawing.* Framed.
The poster that was produced from this drawing—totally unavailable today—contained only the text portion. But here, in what is most likely a program cover design, the circuit that the racers' would traverse is also included at bottom. But even with this inclusion, it's difficult to ignore the humble beginnings from which such memorable future designs would spring. Organized by wealthy cigarette manufacturer, Antony Noghes, in 1929, under the auspices of Prince Louis II through the Automobile Club de Monaco, the Grand Prix was the result of a challenge for the A.C.M., which could be recognized internationally only if it could stage a race in the very limited territory of the principality. The Rallye Automobile Monte Carlo, run by the A.C.M. since 1911, could not be considered as it used the roads of other European countries. The inaugural Grand Prix was won by William Grover-Williams driving a Bugatti Type 35B painted in what would become the famous British racing green.
**Est: $8,000-$10,000.**

**2. Monaco Grand Prix 1930.**
Artist: **Robert Falcucci (1900-1989)**
$30^3/_4$ x $46^3/_4$ in./78.2 x 119 cm
Imp. Monégasque, Monte-Carlo
Cond A.
Ref: Auto Show I, 73; Affiches Azur, 331; Deco Affiches, p. 81; Affiches Riviera, 256;
    PAI-XXXII, 115
One of the best and most dynamic views of the Monaco Grand Prix is this one for
the second running, with a twilit view of Monte Carlo in the background. The winner
that year was René Dreyfus, driving a Bugatti T35B. The multitalented Falcucci—
painter, decorator, illustrator, posterist—began his involvement with auto graphics
at Renault but became best known for his Monaco poster designs of the 1930s.
This is, in fact, the first real poster for this famed race: As stated in the description
for the previous poster, the poster for the first event, in 1929, contained only text.
**Est: $12,000-$15,000.**

**3. Monaco/23 Avril 1933.**
Artist: **Geo Ham (Georges Hamel, 1900-1972)**
31 x $47^1/_4$ in./78.8 x 120.2 cm
Imp. Monégasque, Monte-Carlo.
Cond A.
Ref: Auto Posters, p. 51; Deco Affiches, p.83; Affiches Azur, 333;
    Affiches Riviera, 259; PAI-XXXVI, 348
The 1933 event introduced a new practice, determining starting position by practice
times, rather than randomly by lot. Design pioneer Enzo Ferrari set up what is con-
sidered to be the most distinguished team in Grand Prix racing, the Alfa Romeo group.
This time around, the winner was Achille Varzi in a French Bugatti T51, but Alfa
Romeo took three of the next four places. Design-wise, we detect some of Falcucci's
influence, but Ham, who spent much of his career on paintings and illustrations of
cars and airplanes, obviously knows his craft at least equally well.
**Est: $12,000-$15,000.**

**4**                                                                 **5**

**4. Monaco/2 Avril 1934.**
Artist: **Geo Ham (Georges Hamel, 1900-1972)**
31³/₈ x 46⁵/₈ in./79.5 x 118.3 cm
Imp. Monégasque, Monte-Carlo
Cond A.
Ref: Roberts, p. 109; Ferrari, p. 110; Affiches Riviera, 264; PAI-XXVIII, 30
The brilliant red of the racer is offset by the subdued pastels of the Riviera background in Ham's design. He chose to show Lord Howe in his Maserati, but the 1934 race was dominated by Alfa Romeos; they took three of the first five places, with Guy Moll driving the leading car.
**Est: $10,000-$12,000.**

**5. Monaco/22 Avril 1935.**
Artist: **Geo Ham (Georges Hamel, 1900-1972)**
31³/₈ x 46⁷/₈ in./79.7 x 119 cm
Imp. Monégasque, Monte-Carlo
Cond A.
Ref: Affiches Riviera, 260; PAI-XL, 360
With the Nazi regime now in full sway in Germany, the Mercedes-Benz team arrived with the most powerful cars yet used in the Grand Prix, and earned first prize easily. With Italian driver Luigi Fazioli at the wheel, the 3.99-liter Mercedes W25 model led from start to finish, never seriously challenged by the three Alfa Romeos and the Maserati that took the next four spots. On the poster, Ham puts us right in the action, against the glittering background of sun-drenched Monte Carlo.
**Est: $11,000-$13,000.**

**6. Monaco/11 et 13 Avril 1936.**
Artist: **Geo Ham (Georges Hamel, 1900-1972)**
31 x 46³/₄ in./78.9 x 118.7 cm
Imp. Monégasque, Monte-Carlo
Cond A.
Ref: Affiches Riviera, 261; PAI-XXVIII, 32
For the 1936 Grand Prix, we get two cars battling around a hairpin turn—and in the background, a beautiful view of the bay, sunny, serene, oblivious to all the fuss. The car closest to us is an Auto Union, a German car which, for the first time among racing cars, had its engine in the rear. In 1936 it was a real race again, and in the hard rain; with one car losing oil, cars were spinning all over the place. Chiron, Fagioli and Nuvolari were the casualties; Rudi Caraccioli, driving for the German team, managed to nurse his Mercedes through to win. Auto Union was a joint venture of four German automobile manufacturers—Horch, Audi, DKW and Wanderer—established in 1932 in Zwickau, Saxony, during the Great Depression. Purchased by Volkswagen in 1964, the Auto Union name was dropped and only the Audi brand was used to denote cars manufactured by the Ingolstadt-based company.
**Est: $11,000-$13,000.**

7

8

11

**7. Monaco/16 Mai 1948.**
Artist: **Geo Ham (Georges Hamel, 1900-1972)**
$31^3/8$ x $47^1/8$ in./79.7 x 119.8 cm
Imp. Monégasque, Monte-Carlo
Cond A.
Ref: Affiches Riviera, 263; PAI-XXVIII, 33
The old castle battlements are the background for the 1948 race—the resumption of the Grand Prix after an 11-year hiatus. For reasons that are not altogether clear, Geo Ham signed his works "Geo Matt"—sort of an inversion of his already-shortened last name—during this period.
**Est: $8,000-$10,000.**

**8. Monaco Grand Prix 1956.**
Artist: **Jacques Ramel (1913-1999)**
$31^1/8$ x $46^3/4$ in./79.2 x 118.9 cm
Imp. A.D.I.A., Nice
Cond A-/Unobtrusive tears at edges.
Ref: Ferrari, p. 213; PAI-XXXVIII, 507
Ramel, who contributed several strong designs for the Grand Prix, gives only a hint of the ambience by showing an imposing Monaco structure suspended in space above the racers. The featured driver appears to be the popular Alberto Ascari in his red Ferrari 500; the race was actually won by a Maserati driven by Stirling Moss.
**Est: $6,000-$7,000.**

**9. Monaco Grand Prix 1960.**
Artist: **René Lorenzi**
47 x $61^7/8$ in./119.3 x 157.1 cm
Imp. Monégasque, Monte Carlo.
Cond A-/Very slight tears in upper red background.
Ref: PAI-XXV, 10
For the race's eighteenth running, Lorenzi favors us with a somewhat startling concept, dividing the image horizontally in halves, the top swathed in fiery red. This was the last year of the old 2.5-liter formula, and rear-engined cars were now in full control. The winner was Stirling Moss in a Lotus-Climax.
**Est: $3,000-$4,000.**

**10. Monaco 1962/XXe Grand Prix.**
Artist: **Michel Trublin (1939- )**
$45^7/8$ x $61^1/4$ in./116.5 x 155.5 cm
J. Ramel, Nice
Cond A-/Slight staining and offsetting of red ink in bottom text area.
In Trublin's vision for the twentieth running of the road race, the Formula One has reached such an impressive velocity that its very matter appears to have come undone, transubstantiating for a move into an altogether new dimension of speed. The winner of that year's race was New Zealander Bruce McClaren behind the wheel of a Cooper-Climax.
**Est: $4,000-$5,000.**

9

10

12

13

**11. Gd Prix d'Europe/Monaco. 1963.**
Artist: **Michel Beligond (1927-1973)**
15 x 22³/₄ in./38 x 57.9 cm
Editions J. Ramel, Nice
Cond A.
The sky is achingly blue, the buildings continue to bake in the Mediterranean sun and racers chase one another through the narrow streets with steely intensity and

the sound of Formula One engines fill the air as if the region was being beset by enormous swarms of mechanical bees. All in all, a fairly standard Grand Prix Sunday in Monaco. 1963 would mark the first victory at Monaco for British driver Graham Hill, who would win a total of five races there between '63 and '69, a feat that would earn him the title, "King of Monaco."
**Est: $1,500-$2,000.**

**12. 22e grand prix/10 Mai 1964.**
Artist: **J. May**
15 x 23¹/₄ in./38 x 59.2 cm
J. Ramel, Nice
Cond A.
Ref: PAI-XLIII, 33
The speed of the Formula 1 racer is so extreme that car and driver appear to be more liquid than solid, transformed by acceleration into an entirely different form of velocity-based matter altogether as it heads towards the heart of the principality. Graham Hill won the Grand Prix in 1964 as a member of the British Racing Motor team. Hill, the only driver to win the so-called Triple Crown of motor racing—the Indianapolis 500, the Twenty-Four Hours of Le Mans and the Monaco Grand Prix—described his life behind the wheel thus: "I'm an artist, the track is my canvas, and the car is my brush."
**Est: $1,500-$2,000.**

**13. Monaco Grand Prix 1965.**
Artist: **Michael Turner (1934- )**
15¹/₂ x 24¹/₄ in./39.3 x 61.7 cm
Edition J. Ramel, Nice
Cond A.
Ref: Ferrari, p. 300; PAI-XLIII, 34
A number of the famous Monaco Grand Prix races were brought to pulse-pounding life via the brush of this highly talented draftsman. All show the racers speeding along from a vantage point that displays the way the course wends its way through the city. The 1965 race featured the debut of the Honda team from Japan, and a surprise success of the BRM V8, which won with Graham Hill at the wheel.
**Est: $2,000-$2,500.**

**14**

**15**

**16**

**17**

**18**

## MONACO GRAND PRIX (cont'd)

**14. Monaco Grand Prix 1966.**
Artist: **Michael Turner (1934- )**
15$^1$/$_2$ x 24$^1$/$_8$ in./39.5 x 61.2 cm
J. Ramel, Nice
Cond A.
Ref: PAI-XLIII, 35
Turner keeps the racing excitement revved-up and the location sun-baked and swank in his poster promoting the 1966 Monaco Grand Prix. As was the case the year before, the BRM V8 took the checkered flag, this time piloted by Great Britain's Jackie Stewart.
**Est: $1,700-$2,000.**

**15. Monaco Grand Prix 1967.**
Artist: **Michael Turner (1934- )**
16 x 24$^1$/$_4$ in./40.5 x 61.5 cm
Edition J. Ramel, Nice
Cond A.
Ref: PAI-XLIII, 36
For the twenty-fifth running of the road race held at the independent Riviera principality, Turner contrasts his sleek torpedo-shaped racers off of the city's 19th-century Byzantine-style cathedral, upping the tradition ante without forcing the issue. The race was won by Denny Hulme (1936-1992), who took the wheel for the Brabham Racing Organization, the only Australian team ever to carry a Formula One World Champion to victory.
**Est: $1,500-$2,000.**

**16. Monaco/9-10 mai 1970.**
Artist: **Michael Turner (1934- )**
15$^1$/$_2$ x 23$^1$/$_2$ in./39.2 x 59.8 cm
Imp. Monégasque, Monte Carlo
Cond A–/Slight tears and stains at paper edges.
Ref: PAI-XLIII, 38
The 1970 race provided down-to-the-wire excitement as Jack Brabham led the entire race only to go into the bales two turns from the finish line. He regained control of his vehicle, but not in time to catch Jochen Rindt, who took the checkered flag.
**Est: $1,500-$2,000.**

**17. Monaco/29e Grand Prix 1971.**
Artist: **Steve Carpenter (1943- )**
15$^1$/$_2$ x 23$^7$/$_8$ in./39.2 x 60 cm
J. Ramel, Nice
Cond A.
Ref: PAI-XLIII, 39
The vignettes called upon by Carpenter to illustrate the entire running of a Monaco Grand Prix race come off as somewhat surreal in combination with the more action-oriented aspects of the design. He makes it clear just how perilously close spectators were to the action. The 1971 race was won by Jackie Stewart in a Tyrrell-Ford. Stewart, nicknamed "The Flying Scot," is a three-time Formula One racing champion, well-known in the United States as a commentator of racing television broadcasts where his Scottish accent made him a distinctive presence.
**Est: $1,000-$1,200.**

**18. Monaco/2 & 3 Juin 1973.**
Artist: **Jacques Ramel (1913-1999)**
16$^1$/$_2$ x 25$^1$/$_8$ in./41.9 x 63.2 cm
Edition J. Ramel, Nice
Cond A–/Slight tears at paper edges/P.
In a move that presages the potential perspectives re-created in today's video game consoles, Ramel rolls out four Formula One competitors, craftily gaining in size from top to bottom as they approach the viewer, creating a thrilling sense of motion and speed. The photomontage design includes a panoramic view of Monaco at bottom, but accurately reflects the attitude that—at least on the second and third of June that year—racing took precedence above everything else in the sun-sated principality. Returning from an ulcer that had shortened his season the previous year, the irrepressible Jackie Stewart took First Place at the Grand Prix that year for Team Tyrrell-Ford. Stewart would retire from his illustrious driving career at the end of the 1973 season.
**Est: $1,200-$1,500.**

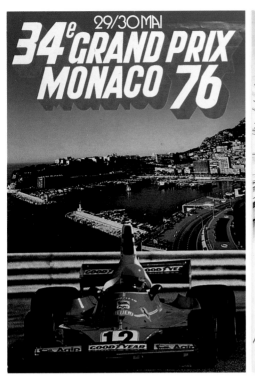

**19**

**20**

**21**

**22**

month that this year's race was run) foreground graphics transport us to a far, far more invigorating reality. South African Jody Scheckter won the '77 race for the Wolf-Ford team before leaving the following year to drive for Ferrari.
**Est: $1,200-$1,500.**

**21. Monaco/37e Grand Prix. 1979.**
Artist: **Alain Giampaoli (1946- )**
15⅝ x 23 in./39.7 x 58.4 cm
A.I.P., Monaco
Cond A.
Ref: PAI-XLIII, 40
The action is so fast-paced in Giampaoli's advertisement for the thirty-seventh running of the Monaco Grand Prix that we only get a rearview of the racer as he enters into a turn like a bat out of hell. Jody Scheckter, a South African driver who rapidly ascended the ranks of Formula One after moving to Great Britain, took first place in the 1979 competition behind the wheel of a Ferrari. He was the last driver to win a driver's championship for Ferrari until Michael Schumacher did so twenty-one years later.
**Est: $1,000-$1,200.**

**22. 38e Grand Prix/15/18 Mai. 1980.**
Artist: **Jacques Grognet (1927- )**
15¾ x 23½ in./40 x 59.7 cm
A.I.P., Monaco
Cond A-/Tears and creasing at edges/P.
Ref: PAI-XLIII, 41
It wasn't the Ferrari driven by South Africa's Jody Scheckter that first crossed the finish line at the thirty-eighth running of the Monaco Grand Prix. Whether that was Grognet's prediction or simply his way of showing the Number One car bearing down on the passerby is left for the viewer to decide. It was, however, Carlos Reutemann who took First Prize for the Williams-Ford team that year. After his racing career came to an end, Reutemann became a prominent politician in the Santa Fe province of his native Argentina.
**Est: $1,200-$1,500.**

**19. Monaco Grand Prix/1976 & 1978: Two Posters.**
Artists: **Robert Cross Martin (1937- )**
**and Alain Giampaoli (1946- )**
Each: 13¾ x 23½ in./40 x 59.7 cm
A.I.P., Monaco
Cond A-/Slight creasing at edges/P.
Photolithography versus contemporary graphic art. It's a win/win situation for the Monaco racing aficionado. For the 1976 running of the event, Bob Martin opted to juxtapose the intensity of a McLaren-Ford vehicle banking through a curve off of the serene Mediterranean enclave above, facilely displaying that speed and sophistication are capable of generating equivalent heat. In addition to supplying the photographs for this poster and designing the text, Martin, an American, was also a member of the Manaco Philharmonic Orchestra. It wouldn't be the Number Twelve car that brought home the glory in 1976, however; that honor belonged to the Ferrari-piloting Austrian, Niki Lauda. Moving two years into the future, we see Giampaoli putting forth

the testosterone-laced notion that speed transforms everything in its immediate vicinity with this quartet of cars that appear to be more in formation than actively competing against one another. The checkered flag for this race went to France's Patrick Depailler, who would hold the lead for a total of thirty-eight consecutive laps on his way to glory.
**Est: $1,000-$1,200.** (2)

**20. 35e Grand Prix Monaco. 1977.**
Artist: **Emile Hugon**
15¾ x 23½ in./40 x 59.7 cm
a-i-p Monaco
Cond A-/Slight creasing and tears at edges/P.
Ref: PAI-XII, 23b
A tremulous dynamic sublimation holds sway in this Hugon promotion for the 1977 Monaco Grand Prix, relegating the architectural details to a blanched silhouette as the somewhat space age (don't forget: "Star Wars" became an international sensation the same

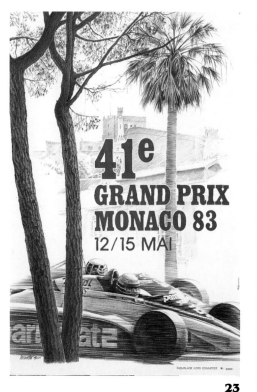

**23**

**24**

42ᵉ GRAND PRIX MONACO 31 MAI-3 JUIN 1984

43ᵉ GRAND PRIX MONACO 85 16/19 MAI

**25**

**26**

45ᵉ GRAND PRIX MONACO · 28·31 MAI 87
CHAMPIONNAT DU MONDE DE FORMULE 1 DE LA F.I.A.

**27**

## MONACO GRAND PRIX (cont'd)

**23. 41e Grand Prix Monaco 83.**
Artist: **Michel Z. Lecomte (1935- )**
15³/₄ x 23¹/₂ in./40 x 59.7 cm
A.I.P., Monaco
Cond A/P.
Considering that ultraviolet is beyond the visible spectrum at its violet end, we'd have to say that an ultraviolet tone dominates this Lecomte advertisement for the forty-first Monaco road race, with a touch of supra-red thrown in for good measure in order to cover both ends of the don't-blink-or-you'll-miss-something gamut. With a bit of lithographic wishful thinking, Lecomte casts home-country favorite Jacques Lafitte in the role of the race's dominant force (Lafitte, *malheureusement*, wouldn't even finish the competition thanks to gearbox issues), but it would be Finnish driver Keke Rosberg that would prove to be the ultimate force to be reckoned with in Monaco that year.
**Est: $800-$1,000.**

**24. Monaco/42e Grand Prix/1984.**
Artist: **Pierre Bérenguier (1934- )**
15¹/₂ x 24¹/₈ in./39.4 x 61.3 cm
A.I.P., Moncao
Cond A.
Even though the speed of the oncoming car makes it appear as if virtually everything in the Bérenguier poster is rushing towards the viewer—the result of a velocity-induced vacuum, no doubt—the element that's perhaps the most striking is the frightening nearness of the background's race official to the on-road action, an inclusion that's shockingly accurate. The depicted vehicle would not be the victor of that year's race—the Niki Lauden driven McLaren-TAG would spin off the track during the seventeenth lap. However, Lauden's teammate, Alain Prost, would take the checkered flag. The now-retired driver held the record for most Grand Prix victories from 1987 to 2001, after which that accomplishment was bested by the legendary Michael Schumacher.
**Est: $800-$1,000.**

**25. 43e Grand Prix/16/19 Mai. 1985.**
Artist: **Jacques Grognet (1927- )**
15⁵/₈ x 23¹/₂ in./39.7 x 59.7 cm
A.I.P., Monaco
Cond A-/Creasing and tears at edges/P.
Ref: PAI-XLIII, 42
As opposed to the somewhat slick futuristic angle seen in some of the Monaco race designs, Grognet takes a more photo-inspired approach in his promotion for the 1985 running of the Monaco Grand Prix, an approach that one can't help but notice helps to accentuate the

corporate sponsorship of the vehicle. France's Alain Prost (the first French Formula One World Champion, incidentally) took the checkered flag that year driving for the Marlboro McLaren International team.
**Est: $1,200-$1,500.**

**26. 44e Grand Prix/8-11 Mai 86.**
Artist: **Jacques Grognet (1927- )**
15³/₄ x 23¹/₂ in./40 x 59.7 cm
A.I.P., Monaco
Cond A-/Slight creasing at top left corner/P.
Ref: PAI-XLIII, 43
Apart from the vehicle shaking off the shackles of gravity, Grognet stays relatively close to the formula he utilized the previous year in order to promote the forty-fourth Monaco Grand Prix, keeping the vehicle realistic and the Marlboro sponsorship conspicuous. And even though he graphically prognosticated that

Keke Rosberg would dominate the race, it was once again Alain Prost, Rosberg's Marlboro McLaren International teammate who would win at Monaco for the second year running.
**Est: $1,000-$1,200.**

**27. 45e Grand Prix/Monaco 87.**
Artist: **Alain Borgheresi (1960- )**
15³/₄ x 23¹/₂ in./40 x 59.7 cm
A.I.P., Monaco
Cond A-/Slight creasing at edges/P.
Borgheresi clearly illustrates that, even though Monaco's no backwater podunk, everything takes a backseat when Grand Prix time rolls around. Traditionally, the number of competitors permitted in this Grand Prix was lower than at other circuits due to the tight, twisty nature of the track. Originally set at sixteen, the field was increased to a full grid of twenty-six in 1987. Crit-

# 46e GRAND PRIX DE MONACO

12-15 MAI 1988

**FORMULA 1 WORLD CHAMPIONSHIP**

BRESIL 26 MARS
SAN MARINO 23 AVRIL
MONACO 15 MAI
MEXIQUE 29 MAI
U.S.A. 4 JUIN
CANADA 19 JUIN
FRANCE 9 JUILLET
GRANDE BRETAGNE 16 JUILLET
ALLEMAGNE 30 JUILLET
HONGRIE 13 AOUT
BELGIQUE 27 AOUT
ITALIE 18 SEPTEMBRE
PORTUGAL 24 SEPTEMBRE
ESPAGNE 1er OCTOBRE
JAPON 22 OCTOBRE
AUSTRALIE 5 NOVEMBRE

47e GRAND PRIX DE MONACO 4~7 MAI 1989

**PROGRAMME**

JEUDI
DE 8 h 00 A 9 h 00
SEANCE D'ESSAIS
PREQUALIFICATIFS DE F1
DE 10 h 00 A 11 h 30
1ère SEANCE D'ESSAIS DE F1
NON CHRONOMETRES
DE 13 h 00 A 14 h 00
1ère SEANCE D'ESSAIS DE F1
CHRONOMETRES

SAMEDI
DE 10 h 00 A 11 h 30
2 e SEANCE D'ESSAIS DE F1
NON CHRONOMETRE
De 13 h 00 A 14 h 00
2 e SEANCE D'ESSAIS DE F1
CHRONOMETRES

DIMANCHE
DE 11 h 00 A 11 h 30
ESSAIS LIBRES
NON CHRONOMETRES DE F1
A 15 h 30 DEPART DU
47e GRAND PRIX
AUTOMOBILE DE MONACO

**28**

team manager, Ron Dennis, that his lead was safe, Senna slowed down. This was to be his downfall, as on lap sixty-seven he lost concentration and spun into the barrier at Portier, meaning that the race was won, for the fourth time in five years, by Alain Prost. But don't be too disappointed for Senna: this would prove to be the Brazilian's only loss between 1987 and 1993. He would garner victory the following year for which the following poster was executed. Though ostensibly a promotion for the entire 1989 Formula One season, the focus is placed firmly on the Monaco Grand Prix, with the uncredited designer placing the gauzy race graphics betwixt his towering "F1" black block font. Senna's life would be tragically cut short at the age of thirty-four after suffering severe head trauma in a crash at the 1994 San Marino Grand Prix at Imola, Italy.
**Est: $800-$1,000.** (2)

### 29. Monaco Grand Prix/"Mercédes".
**Artist: Jean Massé**
38³/₄ x 23¹/₂ in./98.5 x 59 cm
*Hand-signed watercolor painting; foxing and water stains at edges.* Framed.
Though no driver's name is attached to this fast-paced Grand Prix artwork, several factors lead us to believe that it's none other than Manfred von Brauchitsch (1905-2003) behind the wheel. First off, the Mercedes Benz team only won three Monaco Grand Prix races, consecutively during a three year stretch between 1935 and 1937. Secondly, the automobile on display is definitely a "Silver Arrow," a Nazi state-backed vehicle that was in the race only during 1936 and 1937 (the Grand Prix wasn't run between 1938 and 1947). And lastly, von Brauchitsch would have been the only person racing for Mercedes-Benz who was famous enough to commemorate in a painting. Despite winning forty-five races over a six-year span in the 1930s, von Brauchitsch was nicknamed "Der Pechvogel" (roughly translated: "Mr. Bad Luck") for the races he lost, his hard-driving impetuosity and his imperious Prussian officer-class mien. When he died at the age of ninety-seven, he was the last surviving winner of a prewar Grand Prix.
**Est: $2,500-$3,000.**

ics of the move said that the increase was brought about in order to reduce the number of non-qualifiers to appease team sponsors (it's hard to ignore the poster's endorsement-laden vehicle), but the Fédération Internationale du Sport Automobile (or FISA) insisted that the change was made to bring Monaco in-line with other Grand Prix events. Nigel Mansell led the race until lap thirty when he retired with a loss of turbo boost. This handed first place to Ayrton Senna, who dominated the rest of the race, making a pit stop without losing the lead and setting fastest lap on the seventy-second lap behind the wheel of a Lotus.
**Est: $1,000-$1,200.**

### 28. Grand Prix de Monaco/1988 & 1989: Two Posters.
**Artists: Jacques Grognet (1927- ) and Anonymous**
1988: 15³/₄ x 23¹/₂ in./40 x 39.8 cm
1989: 16¹/₂ x 23¹/₄ in./42 x 59 cm
A.I.P., Monaco
Cond A/P.
In the first of these two posters, Grognet takes a step back from photo-inspiration, turning to a more animation-influenced style. His design piles vehicle, vegetation and stronghold one atop another, the end result of which produces Formula One cars with a fairly insectile appearance. The McLaren team had dominated qualifying in 1988, with Ayrton Senna gaining pole position and leading from the start. Reassured by McLaren-Honda

30

31

## 30. Rallye Automobile/Monte Carlo/Janvier 1931.
Artist: **Robert Falcucci (1900-1989)**
31³/₈ x 47 in./79.7 x 119.4 cm
Imp. Monégasque, Monte-Carlo
Cond A.
Ref: Affiches Azur, 328; Affiches Riviera, 255;
    PAI-XXXII, 117
*There sometimes seems to be a bit of confusion as to whether or not the Monte Carlo Rally and the Monaco Grand Prix are separate races. They are, in fact, two different races with a very clear distinction—the Rally, which predates the Monaco race, was never granted full national Grand Prix status because the event is not held wholly within the principality boundaries, taking place primarily on the roads of other European countries. The Monaco Grand Prix, on the other hand, is raced completely within Monaco.*

Falcucci's imaginative approach to the 1931 Monte Carlo Rally is a strange futuristic design—a geometric/geographic fantasy with map course lines and rivers on a globe, and a car backlit by a setting sun that encompasses its own small silhouette of Monte Carlo's famous bay.
**Est: $7,000-$9,000.**

## 31. 24 Heures du Mans. 1954.
Artist: **Geo Ham (Georges Hamel, 1900-1972)**
15⁵/₈ x 22⁷/₈ in./39.6 x 58.2 cm
Imp. A.A.T. Thrivillier, Paris
Cond A.
The town of Le Mans was the home of the first major Grand Prix race in 1906. The name had been used

before at Pau but the Grand Prix de l'Automobile Club de France was the first big circuit race. The international fame of Le Mans was not to be based on Grand Prix racing, however, but rather on the 24 Heures du Mans, which was held for the first time in 1923. A far less literal interpretation of the at Circuit de la Sarthe than the Belligond promotion for the twenty-four hour endurance race executed four years later (*see* No. 32), this Ham poster gives us a tailgating line of drivers making their way through a powdery midnight-blue landscape as time ticks away, reminding the viewer that the true competition at Le Mans is man and machine versus the clock. Not surprisingly for the mid-1950s, Ferrari came away with First Place at the 1954 event.
**Est: $2,500-$3,000.**

## 32. 24 Heures du Mans. 1958.
Artist: **Michel Beligond (1927-1973)**
11¹/₄ x 15¹/₈ in./28.7 x 38.4 cm
A.A.T. Thivillier
Cond A.
Characterized by periods of torrential downpour and brilliant sunshine, the 1958 24 Hours of Le Mans found the Ferrari team scoring a resounding victory over Aston Martin and Jaguar. The winning team covered 2,548 miles, almost exactly 100 miles more than the runner up. Interestingly, Beligond's evocatively streaky nighttime scene features the #24 car, a Peerless Motors car entered in the 2-litre GT class, which, against all odds, won its class over the likes of the mighty Ferrari empire.
**Est: $1,400-$1,700.**

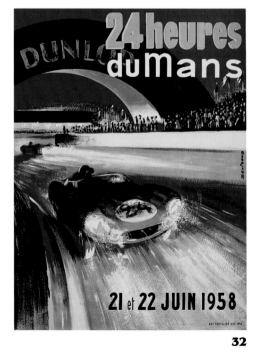

32

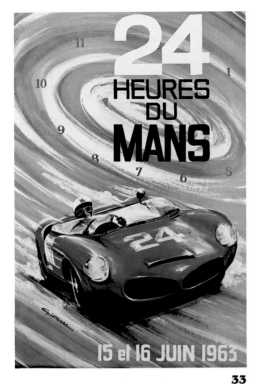

**33**
**34**
**35**

**36**
**37**

**33. 24 Heures du Mans. 1963.**
Artist: **G. Leygnac**
15¹/₂ x 22³/₄ in./39.3 x 57.9 cm
Imp. Thrivillier
Cond A.
A swirling vortex of time, from which no Le Mans driver can truly escape, once more calls the clock-racing nature of the rally to the public's attention. The thirty-first running of this race drew more than 300,000 spectators to the track to see Lorenzo Bandini and Ludovico Scarfiotti of Italy cover nearly 4,562 kilometers on their way to victory behind the wheel of a Ferrari 250 P.
**Est: $1,200-$1,500.**

**34. 41eme Gd. Prix de L'A.C.F./Reims. 1954.**
Artist: **Geo Ham (Georges Hamel, 1900-1972)**
15³/₄ x 23 in./40 x 58.5 cm
Imp. Taivillier, Paris
Cond A.
Ref: PAI-XIII, 20 (var)
A great Ham design, with white, blue and red racers coming straight at us down the course, advertises a race at Reims. It's interesting to note that the larger format

version of this poster (*see* PAI-XIII, 20) bears a "d'après" designation, while this smaller format does not.
**Est: $1,700-$2,000.**

**35. Pau/Grand Prix Automobile. 1952.**
Artist: **Geo Ham (Georges Hamel, 1900-1972)**
15³/₈ x 22⁷/₈ in./39 x 58.1 cm
Chabrillac, Toulouse
Cond A.
The Grand Prix de Pau was first held in 1901 and started running regularly in 1933, with a race being held more-or-less every year since, excluding the duration of World War II. Run around a circuit laid out on the streets of the French town—in many ways similar to the more famous Monaco Grand Prix—it was the first race to ever be called a Grand Prix. The winner of the Pau Grand Prix on this Pentecost weekend was Alberto Ascari for Team Ferrari. Apart from the last two years of the decade, Italian cars dominated at Pau—Ferrari, Maserati and Gordini. The straight-away action in the poster is actually the work of an unnamed artist working from a design originally conceived by Ham, and is thus marked "d'après."
**Est: $1,400-$1,700.**

**36. Grosser Preis von Deutschland. 1967.**
Artist: **Michael Turner (1934- )**
23⁵/₈ x 33 in./60 x 83.7 cm
Druckerie Will und Rothe, Mainz
Cond B+/Unobtrusive folds.
Turner directs his speed-tweaked talents from the sunny Mediterranean climes of Monaco to Germany's legendary Nürburgring race track for the 1967 German Grand Prix without losing a beat, placing the viewer directly in the path of oncoming competitors while perfectly capturing the tough, demanding character of the course. None of the drivers portrayed in the poster, however, would claim victory that day—that distinction belonged to Denny Hulme. Hulme won that year's Monaco Grand Prix as well, a race for which Turner also created the publicity (*see* No. 15). Coincidence? It's interesting to note that this race was the first in Formula One history to be broadcast in color television in Germany.
**Est: $1,200-$1,500.**

**37. Nürburgring/Porsche. 1967.**
Artist: **Weitmann**
32¹/₄ x 44 in./82 x 111.5 cm
Printed in Germany
Cond A.
An airborne Porsche six-cylinder 910 creates an indelible image for Porsche superiority in this photomontage design for the 1967 ADAC (Allgemeiner Deutscher Automobil-Club) 1000-kilometer race at Nürburgring. Weitmann's photo serves as an ideal allegory for Porsche, who was determined to surpass Ferrari as the leader of international sports prototype racing. Building faster and faster cars with every season, Porsche was quickly closing the gap. But after this year's 1,000 twisting, turning and undulating kilometers through the German countryside, Porsche was not just first in class, but first overall! The dawn of a new era was had broken. Known simply as "The Ring" by motorsport enthusiasts, Nürburgring—built in the 1920s around the village and medieval castle of Nürburg in the Eifel mountains—is widely considered to be one of the toughest and most demanding race tracks in the world.
**Est: $1,700-$2,000.**

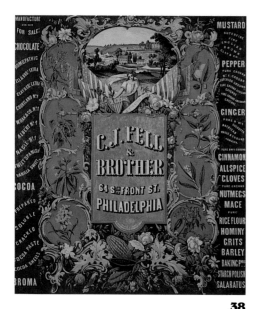

**38**

**39**

## ANONYMOUS

**38. C. J. Fell & Brother.** ca. 1850.
15³/₄ x 18¹/₂ in./40 x 47 cm
Herline, Philadelphia
Cond A–/Slight creases.
Ref: PAI-XXXII, 1
A design reminiscent of 18th-century wallpaper advertises the offerings of a Philadelphia spice manufacturer. Beautiful botanic illustrations in curved moldings frame the company name, with a scenic medallion on top and an emblematic arrangement of some exotic pod at the bottom. Along with the familiar spices—mustard, pepper, ginger and nutmeg—there are some we've never heard of: broma, salartes and starch polish. And the whole reminds us of the beauty that can accrue to the most everyday items. Edward Herline came from Germany to set up his printing plant in Philadelphia in 1848; he remained at the 2 North 6th Street address shown on this poster until 1856. Peters indicates his firm was "responsible for considerable very creditable work" (p. 215).
**Est: $1,200-$1,500.**

**39. Le Napoleon.** ca. 1865.
35⁵/₈ x 25³/₈ in./90.5 x 64.5 cm
Lith. Decan, Paris
Cond B/Restored tears, largely at edges.
The Montgolfier brothers made the first human aerial voyage in history on June 4, 1783, in a balloon made of linen coated with alum to reduce the risk of combustion from the burning straw that provided the lift inside the base of the balloon. Within weeks, other innovators, such as Jacques Charles and Nicolas Robert, were taking to the sky in hydrogen-filled models. Balloons became all the rage, both for their transportation potential and their military implications. Napoléon Bonaparte himself recognized the reconnaissance possibilities of the inflatables and used them in his campaigns. Perhaps this balloon was named "Le Napoleon" for nostalgic reasons rather than militaristic, seeing as the rendered event appears to be transpiring for fun and little more. It's interesting to note that parachutes, both in large and small scale, appear to have played a part in this particular launch.
**Est: $1,200-$1,500.**

**40. Ambassadeurs/Dasca's Family.** 1877.
15¹/₂ x 23¹/₈ in./39.4 x 58.6 cm
Imp. E. Levy, Paris
Cond B+/Slight stains at top paper edge.
Ref: Spectacle, 887; Cirque, 186
Either the paternal cornerstone of the acrobatic and tightrope walking Dasca troupe worked with diminutive family members or he was huge. Regardless of proportions, the entertainment value dealt-out by the Dascas was doubtlessly humongous seeing as mischief appears to have played an equal part of their well-balanced

**41**

antics. The Ambassadeurs café-concert on the Champs-Elysées was so named for its proximity to the Hotel Crillon, which used to house foreign ambassadors. In its belle epoque heyday, the café presented music hall stars from Yvette Guilbert to Aristide Bruant.
**Est: $1,400-$1,700.**

**41. Le Fétiche.** 1890.
25⁵/₈ x 32⁵/₈ in./65.2 x 82.8 cm
Lith. F. Appel, Paris
Cond A.
Ref: Spectacle, 457
What's your fetish? Hopefully, it's operetta posters from the late-19th century! It's difficult to determine whether the title of this Roger-composed piece that played itself out at the Théâtre des Menus-Plaisirs is referring to an object to which extreme superstition has been attached or to a fixation with a specific physical attribute—the un-

credited posterist simply gave us too many details to choose from and not enough historical information exists on the operetta to say for sure. The cavalcade of hints, however, is fascinating—military eccentricity, martial pulchritude, seemingly summoned bugs (you can't convince me that the creepy gent in the top hat with the flute doesn't have something to do with the arrival of the flying menace) and a decidedly insectile bride.
**Est: $1,000-$1,200.**

**42. Les Boggio.**
30¹/₂ x 39 in./77.5 x 99 cm
Affiches Louis Galice, Paris
Cond B/Slight tears at folds and paper edges.
While the central panel and portraits of the Boggios are more than enough to convince the viewer of the duo's "elegance," it's the cameos that border the design like lithographic ivy that proves that they are "classical dancers." Every dip, every swirl, every split, every lift is put to the page in order to present their command to the public in this stock poster and the results are satisfyingly spry.
**Est: $1,000-$1,200.**

of bringing the firm's tea to the forefront of the market. However, the rationing of tea during World War II struck a serious blow to the company and after their industrial complex was destroyed in an air raid, Mazawattee never recovered, declining throughout the 1950s and disappearing from the shelves altogether by the mid-1960s.
**Est: $1,400-$1,700.**

### 44. IVme Centenaire de Christophe Colomb Exposition. 1892.
$28^1/4$ x $39^5/8$ in./71.8 x 100.7 cm
Cond B/Slight tears and stains near folds and edges; possibly missing bottom margin.
With talents ideally suited to present historical pageantry, the skills of this unnamed posterist are abundantly evident in an advertisement for a Genoa exposition celebrating the 400th anniversary of Columbus' discovery and promotes Italian-American relations in the process. Columbus, landing on the shores of a distant land, looks to the heavens with open-faced thanks for their arrival as his crew revels euphorically about him. And though they just may be ecstatic to be on dry land, they're active participants in the dawning of a new age. And on the far-less reverential side, it's rather impossible to ignore the "discreet" allegorical symbolism of the Old World greeting the New.
**Est: $1,400-$1,700.**

### 45. La Mode du Petit Journal.
$22^3/8$ x $33^3/4$ in./56.8 x 85.8 cm
D. Cassigneul, Paris
Cond B/Slight staining in background and top text area.
From previous posters, we know that Le Petit Journal published its share of serialized novels and did its best to popularize aviation (*see* PAI-XXVII, 98A) during its nascent days. However, as the sprightly newsie seen here can attest, "The Little Newspaper" also appears to have had a vested interest in fashion, with a full-color supplement appearing weekly within its pages, complete with patterns from which readers could stay couture *au courant* without the expense of patronizing trendy boutiques.
**Est: $1,200-$1,500.**

### 43. Mazawattee Tea.
30 x $39^3/8$ in./76.2 x 100 cm
Stafford & Co., Netherfield
Cond A.
Clearly the unknown artist who designed this poster must have been somewhat familiar with the product because their beautiful creation has the same soothing effect on the psyche as a luscious cup of tea enjoyed in a garden setting. With an arboreal scene as civilized as this, could there be any doubt that Mazawattee Tea was "The Most Delicious Tea in the World?" I say "was" because the brand that was known throughout Britain and the Commonwealth has been discontinued for approximately forty years and is now mostly forgotten. Mazawattee Tea can be traced back to the early-1850s,

when John Boon Densham, a chemist in Plymouth, started selling loose leaf teas from India and China. The temperance movement was gaining momentum, and many considered tea to be the ideal alternative to alcohol. The slogan "The cup that cheers but does not inebriate" became fashionable. The name of the tea itself is derived from an exotic combination of the Hindi word *mazatha*, meaning "luscious," and the Sinhala word *watte*, or "garden." The strange linguistic hybrid proved to be remarkably popular. People were fascinated by this unusual name, and so it achieved the objective

**49**

"THE FAREWELL"

**46**

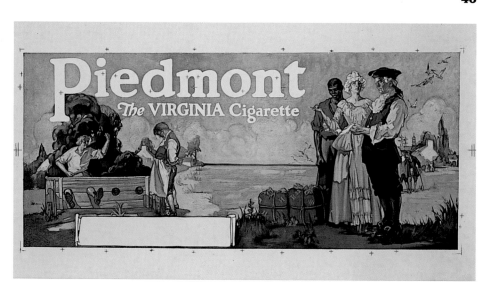

**47**

**48**

## ANONYMOUS (cont'd)

**46. Fogg's Ferry/"The Farewell".** ca. 1892.
$41^1/2$ x 28 in./105.4 x 71 cm
The Enquirer Job Printing Co., Cin, O
Cond A–/Restored tear in window at left.
A popular touring show in the late-19th century, "Fogg's Ferry" left behind few plot specifics apart from what can be pieced together from the surviving evidentiary lithographs, all of which appear to have been printed by the Enquirer Company of Cincinnati. The one plot detail that pops up consistently is that the ragamuffin in the blue polka-dot apron is no mere tomboy, but the daughter of an influential, wealthy judge, though for some unexplained reason people seem to believe that she's an orphan. How this detail figures into the rendered "Farewell" seen here is anyone's guess, though it certainly would appear as if it wasn't the fondest of affairs.
**Est: $1,000-$1,200.**

**47. Piedmont Cigarette.**
$29^3/4$ x 16 in./75.6 x 40.5 cm
Cond A.
Ref: PAI-XXXVII, 117
The American Tobacco Company began manufacturing Piedmont cigarettes in 1893 and continued production until 1980. Made from tobacco grown in the Piedmont District of Virginia, the corporation's pack graphics retained their decorative lettering, unchanged for the

**48. Continental Fire Insurance Co. of New York.** 1895.
30¹/₂ x 24¹/₂ in./77.5 x 62.2 cm
J. Ottmann Lith. Co., N.Y.
Cond B/Tears at corners. Framed.
Ref: PAI-I, 74 (var)
A previously seen version of this design (*see* PAI-I, 74) came with this central panel flanked by the Brooklyn and Manhattan offices of the promotion-minded insurance company. Here, however, the Native American encampment stands on its own, evocative and stirring —and slyly humorous as well. If you look at the right-hand side of the design, you'll notice that the teepee there is insured by the Continental Insurance Company. The message is perfectly clear—even though these indigenous people may lose everything to the approaching wildfire, Continental has them covered. Originally housed at 46 Cedar Street, the company today is headquartered at 180 Maiden Lane, just a couple of blocks away. *In original period frame.*
**Est: $2,000-$2,500.**

**49. Othie del Rio.** 1894.
24³/₄ x 69³/₄ in./63 x 177 cm
Affiches Americains Ch. Levy, Paris
Cond B/Slight tears at folds and paper edges.
Leggy Othie del Rio didn't leave behind a trail of career accomplishments, but her in-all-likelihood unremarkable time in the spotlight is survived by this wondrous anonymous appearance poster. Apart from the delicate loveliness with which he renders del Rio as she reaches for the stars, the unnamed designer did a superlative job of recreating her costume, whose central rill of sequins is recreated with such care that it takes on a decidedly three-dimensional appearance.
**Est: $1,400-$1,700.**

**50. Gil Blas.** ca. 1892.
37³/₈ x 51³/₈ in./95 x 130.6 cm
Imp. ƒmile Lévy, Paris
Cond A.
Ref: PAI-XL, 194
The Parisian weekly, *Gil Blas*, promotes itself with roguish, nearly misogynistic swagger, which is somewhat peculiar considering that they bill themselves the "most literary" journal available. Perhaps reading wasn't

such a passive pastime at the turn-of-the-twentieth century. You can't argue with the well-rounded contents of the publication however, with a complete listing of all featured writers, theatrical reviews, literary excerpts, sports coverage, articles on the social scene and much, much more, including an underfoot mention of illustrated supplements. Though the work bears a strong resemblance to that of Choubrac, the lack of a signature or a specific reference keeps this the work of Anonymous.
**Est: $2,000-$2,500.**

**51. A la Place Blanche.** 1896.
46⁵/₈ x 62³/₄ in./118.4 x 159.5 cm
Imp. Th. Dupuy, Paris
Cond B+/Unobtrusive tears and stains at folds.
Impressionistically pretty pictured poise promotes the new summer line of women's fashions available at the Place Blanche emporium, with an airy silk ensemble specially called to the attention of the public in the at-bottom text.
**Est: $1,700-$2,000.**

**52. Tournée Réjane-Baron.**
31¹/₂ x 44³/₈ in./77.5 x 112.7 cm
Imp. Charles Verneau, Paris
Cond B/Recreated left margin; slight tears, largely in upper text area.
A proven success on the Parisian theatrical scene, Réjane takes her act on the road in this touring production, promoted with not only a lovely poster portrait, but a set of cameo cards that show-off a few of her characters that audiences could look forward to seeing (most intriguing: Germinie Lacerteux, a character, one has to imagine, that despite her calm exterior was somewhat tightly wound). "Born Gabrielle Réju (1857-1920), Réjane sang in cafes at 15, won second prize at the Conservatoire at 17, and made her way into theater, where she became a celebrated audience favorite. She tackled all kinds of roles, from light comedies to classic dramas, but proved to be at her best in playing passionate women: 'Madame Sans-Gène,' 'Zaza' and 'Sapho.' As the creator of the original *Madame Sans-Gène*, she also played her in the first film version of the Sardou classic, shot in 1911 for Le Film d'Art" (Cappiello/Rennert, p. 56).
**Est: $1,000-$1,200.**

nearly hundred years Piedmont was for sale while their poster advertising mined historical nostalgia, primarily in the form of colonial or Wild West scenery. This particular press proof before text insertion and removal of registration marks shows the once-common occurrence of the delivery of tobacco to market. The most interesting feature of the poster, however, is the disturbed gentleman shaking his fist in the stocks at left. One has to wonder what offense landed him there, since in today's health conscious society, one has to suspect that he might receive such a punishment for lighting up in a non-designated area.
**Est: $1,000-$1,200.**

**53**

**54**

**55**

**56**

## ANONYMOUS (cont'd)

**53. Chat Noir.** ca. 1896.
15³/₈ x 11 in./39 x 28 cm
*Oil-on-canvas painting.* Framed.
*In original period wooden frame.*
The full moon may be happy as a clam, but he doesn't appear to be shedding all that much illumination on Montmartre. But then again, he may be smiling because he knows just how much mischief one can find there under the cover of darkness. So who is he to spoil the fun? A definite "on-the-prowl" dynamic pervades the brushwork of this uncredited artist, who, apart from luna-gold, executes his painting in ever-deepening shades of nighttime-blue. And, of course, who better to oversee the lascivious doings than the ebon tomcat whose very name calls forth images of the after-hours Montmartre debauchery perhaps more effectively than any other. *For Steinlen's take on this cabaret, see No. 465.*
**Est: $3,000-$4,000.**

**54. The Miracle Workers of Asmara.** ca. 1901.
37¹/₂ x 78¹/₄ in./95 x 198.6 cm
Lith. Adolph Friedlander, Hamburg
Cond A.
The exploits of these Native-American show-stoppers play themselves out in spectacular fashion on this astonishing 3-sheet Friedlander-produced (#2453) masterwork, from fire walking to magical mayhem to "The Burlesque Buffalo," whose hilarity apparently included being shot repeatedly with arrows. It's not clear what connection "The Miracle Workers of Asmara" have with the capital city of the Ethiopian highlands with which they share a name. Most likely it's nothing more than an exotic-sounding textual conjuring. Regardless of the ambiguity, what sets the poster apart is the superlative Friedlander design, rich in detail and sumptuously executed for maximum promotional impact.
**Est: $5,000-$6,000.**

**55. Elixir Mondet.** ca. 1900.
42³/₄ x 55¹/₄ in./108.6 x 140.4 cm
Imp. Moullot, Marseille
Cond A.
Ref: Alpes, 126
Though the hale-and-hearty lass that's crested this hill with her binoculars on her hip doesn't appear to need a nip of Elixir Mondet—the "King of Tonics and Digestives" made from yellow Alpine bitterwort and "Phos-

phated Kola"—her fellow Alpine hiker might just need a swallow of the restorative if he hopes to keep up. A wondrous promotional vista from an uncredited designer, who includes a bilingual product container that points out that this "Most Wonderful French Tonic Compound" is "a marvelous blood purifier." As if there was any question!
**Est: $1,500-$1,700.**

**56. "The Queen."** 1903.
24¹/₂ x 40¹/₄ in./62.3 x 102.2 cm
McCorquodale & Co., London
Cond A–/Sight tears at folds.
Built by the South Eastern & Chatham Railway, the "Queen" was the first turbine steamer to be constructed specifically for a cross-Channel route, entering service between Dover and Calais in June 1903. The uncredited designer commissioned to create this promotion took a rather interesting tack: the seas are choppy to say the least and the old-fashioned schooners of the background are being pitched to and fro. However, aboard the *Queen,* the crossing is so smooth that nary a passenger appears to be affected in the least. In 1914, during the early part of World War I, the *Queen* helped

to evacuate refugees from Ostend, after which she became a troop transport. Later that year, she rescued over 2,000 refugees from the French vessel "Admiral Ganteaume," which had been torpedoed whilst bound from Calais to Le Harve. On October 26, 1916, the *Queen* was attacked by German destroyers and sunk.
**Est: $1,500-$1,800.**

**57**

**58**

**59**

one fine summer's day in 1884 . . . Aubrespy was eating lunch with some friends in a restaurant in Paris. At the next table a mother and her young child were finishing their meal. Tiring of his desert, the young boy looked longingly at his mother's plate and started, lisping impishly: 'Mummy, I z'en (I want some)! Mummy, gimme z'en (give me some).' No sooner said, but the name of the product 'Zan' was born . . . Glycyrrhiza glabra, whose popular name is licorice, is one of the ligneous-stemmed plants that was cultivated in Asia Minor, then in the Mediterranean region. The rhizome and its roots contain glycyrrhizin and its derivatives are used in medicine . . . Glycyrrhizin . . . the sweet matter obtained from the licorice root, is also used to make soft drinks, and to mask the disagreeable taste of certain pharmaceutical preparations. It is commonly used to make candy in the form of sticks (as shown in the poster) suckers and chews that have been enjoyed by generations of schoolchildren" (Health Posters, p. 17). And from the look of this healthful lass, could there be any doubt as to the efficacy of the product? **Est: $1,700-$2,000.**

**58. Trianon/Pas de Chiqué.** 1899.
33¹/₂ x 48¹/₄ in./85.6 x 122.6 cm
Imp. Chaix, Paris
Cond B/Restored tears at folds and edges.
Even in the days before professional wrestling referred

to their activities as "sports entertainment," the organizers of this Montmartre wrestling tournament want the public to know that there will be "No Fakes" in their matches. Clearly, it's the "Grand Hurtling Challenge" being used to draw spectators to the Trianon, the immensely popular Élysée-Montmartre café-concert. And though there's no slathered-on war paint, pyrotechnics or soon-to-be-dented folding chairs on display—only gentlemanly athleticism will do here—it's hard not to crack a smile when you see that one of the grapplers was also known as "The Terrible Coachman."
**Est: $1,500-$2,000.**

**59. Cafés Gilbert.**
39³/₈ x 59 in./100 x 150 cm
Imp. J. Naudeau, Redon, Portiers
Cond A–/Slight stains at paper edges.
Ref: PAI-XXXVIII, 151
Calling upon a person or place of exotic origin is certainly one way to attract a caffeine-enamored public's attention to one's coffee. Cafés Gilbert, however, takes a rather different approach, demonstrating that a touch of domestic sexiness can be just as effective an angle. Not present in today's hot beverage market, the text makes it clear that this "Good Coffee" was once "On Sale Everywhere."
**Est: $1,200-$1,500.**

**57. Zan.**
31¹/₈ x 45³/₄ in./79.2 x 116 cm
Imp. H. Laas, Paris
Cond A.
Ref: Health Posters, 13 (var)
"Paul Aubrespy (1850-1928) founded the 'Réglisses Zan' (Zan licorice) company . . . The story goes that,

**60**

**61**

**62**

**63**

## ANONYMOUS (cont'd)

**60. "Cirtu".**
45$^1$/$_2$ x 63$^1$/$_8$ in./115.6 x 160 cm
Affiches Gaillard, Paris
Cond A–/Unobtrusive folds.
Whether or not the task of shoe polishing can ever be called a "pleasure" remains in question. However, what's indisputable is the clever craft on display in this anonymous creation for Cirtu, a study in contrasts —toothless boot black meets high-fashion footwear— set against a swirling vortex apparently put into motion by a certain buffing voracity. Also, it's hard to ignore the fact that the name of the pure turpentine polish is very close to the word "surtout"—French for "above all" —which would seem to imply the polish's superiority over any other brand on the market. Though the scrawl of an artist's signature appears to the right of the polisher, we have been unable to determine specific identification.
**Est: $1,400-$1,700.**

**61. Bitter Bianchi.** ca. 1910.
16$^3$/$_4$ x 26 in./47.5 x 66 cm
Cond A.
The hills are alive with the sound of drinking! In all fairness, who wouldn't want a little nip to warm them up in the midst of an Alpine hike. And what better nip to sip than Bitter Bianchi, the heavily-decorated Swiss liqueur. The anonymous artwork is as panoramic as it is amusing, with the female hiker captured for all eternity somewhere between "Yes! Thank You!" and "Oh, I don't know if I really should!"
**Est: $1,500-$1,800.**

**62. Fukui Festival.**
21 x 30$^3$/$_8$ in./53.2 x 77.2 cm
Shoken Printing Co., Tokyo
Cond B+/Slight tears, largely at folds.
The city of Fukui is, naturally enough, the capital of Japan's Fukui Prefecture. Its most famous landmarks

are the Maruoka Castle—the oldest castle still standing in Japan—and Eiheiji—a Zen temple of a sect established in the 1200s—as well as the nearby cliffs of Tojimbo facing the Sea of Japan. Of course none of these things are shown in this anonymous poster as it advertises a week-long July exhibition of local commerce. The never-before-held event doubtlessly focused on the traditional crafts that made Fukui famous, such

as cutlery, lacquerware, traditional Japanese paper, agate and, most especially, the area's thriving textile business, a fact emphasized by the bolts of linen being unfurled by two of the poster's three doves as they soar above the Daiwa Department Store. No mention is made of eyewear, however, which is somewhat interesting seeing as Fukui is the eyeglass capital of Japan.
**Est: $1,200-$1,500.**

**63. Bled/Jugoslavija.**
26⁷/₈ x 38³/₄ in./68.2 x 98.3 cm
Sirec, Nosan
Cond A–/Slight tears at edges.
Bled's scenery is almost impossibly romantic, with a
little white church on an island in the center of an
emerald green mountain lake, Bled Castle perched
high above and the peaks of the Julian Alps all around.
Consequently, the resort is often packed with honey-
mooning couples and others who intend to strike a
romantic spark. However, this poster isn't precisely
angling for the honeymoon crowd; rather, the locale is
looking to entice anyone interested in a little rest and
relaxation in Slovenian splendor. And the carefree,
cartoon-esque execution works spectacularly.
**Est: $1,000-$1,200.**

**64. Caux.**
29 x 45³/₈ in./73.5 x 115.2 cm
Lith. Art. Hubacher, Berne
Cond A–/Very slight tears at edges.
Ref: PAI-VI, 292 (var)
Oh, the stop-action civility of it all. It's hard to imagine
that this well-composed volleyer ever broke a sweat
during his time on the court, but how well you look is
easily as important as how well you play in this tony
vista promoting the spring season at Caux's Palace
Hotel. When it opened in 1902, the Palace Hotel was
the largest and most luxurious hotel in Switzerland,
playing host to such celebrities as John D. Rockefeller,
the Maharajah of Baroda and Rudyard Kipling, not to
mention numerous celebrities from the entertainment
world. *This is the English-language format.*
**Est: $7,000-$9,000.**

**65. F. Hirschberg/Winter-Sport-Kleidung.**
27³/₄ x 38¹/₄ in./70.6 x 97.2 cm
H. Stürtz, Würtzburg
Cond A.
Textually, the winter sports apparel being offered by
this Munich clothier are snow, wind and waterproof.
But that doesn't even begin to describe their trendy
Russian-inspired appearance which, thanks to an un-
credited posterist, is given full play with this earnest
spin around an outdoor skating rink.
**Est: $1,700-$2,000.**

**66. Franco-British Exhibition.** 1908.
25 x 39³/₄ in./63.3 x 101 cm
Hill, Sifken & Co., London
Cond B+/Slight tears at folds.
Ref: PAI-XXII, 119 (var)
Although the poster makes no mention of it, the exhibition it advertises is clearly being held in conjunction
with the fourth Olympiad at London's Shepherd's Bush.
The modern games, still in their infancy, attracted
twenty-two nations, more than 2,000 participants and
took a marathon three-month span to complete. The
fledgling organization could muster only an illustrated
program; the only known poster (*see* PAI-XX, 339) was a
cooperative effort of the French and British Railways.
This poster—a design also shared by French and British
(*see* PAI-XXII, 119) rail concerns—with its draped figure
representing "Peace & Progress" stands alongside
the Union Jack and French tricolor, celebrating the
alliance between the two European nations. *This is
the French- and English-language version.*
**Est: $1,200-$1,500.**

**66**

67

68

## ANONYMOUS (cont'd)

**67. Mele/Mode e Novitá.** ca. 1910.
22$^1$/$_2$ x 36$^3$/$_4$ in./57.2 x 93.3 cm
De Luca & Bardelloni, Napoli
Cond B-/Restored tears at folds.
Come Carnaval, it's important that one is as able to dish out the tomfoolery as one is able to take it. But above all, it's inconceivable that one would appear in the center of such an unbridled melee without looking one's best. And thanks to the maximum quality available at the Mele department store, this cinch-waisted beauty succeeds on both levels: her golden get-up is *commedia dell'arte*-inspired perfection and thanks to the store's novelties selections, she's able to block a flurry of confetti with a fan in one hand while the other strews a multicolored paper whirlwind at some less prepared individual who didn't have the foresight to shop at Mele.
**Est: $2,500-$3,000.**

**68. Amilcar.**
15$^3$/$_8$ x 23$^1$/$_2$ in./39 x 59 .5 cm
*Hand-signed gouache and crayon maquette.* Framed.
Be it city or country driving that occupies the bulk of your time behind the wheel, Amilcar is the perfect car for either environment. And though the artist's signature is less than legible (his scrawl appears under the driver's side front tire) his succinct split-screen graphics sum up the situation with exceptional clarity in a manner somewhat reminiscent of Paul Colin. Amilcar was a company launched by two Paris businessmen, Emil Akar and Joseph Lamy, in 1921. It started with a small car that became progressively larger. The company could not escape the worldwide Depression, however, and went out of business in 1939.
**Est: $2,000-$2,500.**

69

**69. Chelovek Bez Imeni (The Man Without a Name).**
1923.
28¹/₄ x 35³/₄ in./72 x 90.9 cm
Cond B+/Slight tears at folds and edges.
With a mask-wearing, dashing silhouette and an apparent fat-cat caught in some form of a pickle, you'd imagine that the plot of "The Man Without a Name" would involve quite a bit of shadowy intrigue. However, the poster for the Russian release of the 1921 German

film *Der Millionendieb* (*Thief of Millions*) doesn't reveal that the film is actually a rather off-center, extremely far-fetched bit of cinematic fun that was based on an old novel and redone at least four times in Germany. In the movie, an heiress nearing her twenty-first birthday decides to take all of her money out of the bank for a madcap fling. But guess what: the bank doesn't have her millions in cash on hand. So when a bank clerk that knows of her plans finds out about the lack of funds (a clerk who, as you might expect, is madly in love with the heiress), he offers to pose as a thief that has made off with the money, thus avoiding a scandal for his employer. A series of chases across a few scenic sections of the world ensues until the bank can bolster its cash reserves and the poor shlub can return to his blameless life and job. Not surprisingly, he wins the affections of the heiress for his efforts, complete with the presumed millions. Though an artist's mark does appear in the down-left inverted triangle—revealing a portion of the designer's name—no precise identification could be made.
**Est: $1,500-$2,000.**

**70. Adastra.**
19¹/₂ x 25¹/₂ in./49.5 x 64.8 cm
Gebr. Fretz, Zürich
Cond A–/Slight stains at top edge.
With a wingspan that's as far-reaching as the name of the airline is lofty—"To the Stars" in Latin—an Ad Astra plane makes its way serenely above a frozen landscape, snow-blanketed from its mountains to its rolling plains—in short, a terrain best flown over than traveled through. Little is known with regard to the Swiss air transport company other then that it, along with Balair, were merged to create the now-defunct Swissair. The artist's "LH" monogram appears down-right, but no further identification could be made.
**Est: $1,700-$2,000.**

**71. Freudenstadt/Hotel Christophsaue.**
23 6/8 x 41⁷/₈ in./67 x 106.4 cm
Kornsand, Frankfurt
Cond B/Restored tears in pants and paper edges.
Lying on a high plateau at the east edge of the north Black Forest, Freudenstadt is well-known for its fresh air, a climatic health resort of international renown that has played host to an array of notable personalities ranging from King George of England to Mark Twain. With its many hotels, guest houses and haute cuisine, Freudenstadt remains a popular vacation spot. However, hardly any of that matters in this anonymous destination design, which affixes our attention to the skiing and sledding opportunities that the locale affords. And though the poster places the frigid fun front and center, it's interesting to note that the text at the skier's feet guarantees that there will always be clear footpaths leading back to the Hotel Christophsaue for when it's time to get inside.
**Est: $2,000-$2,500.**

**72. Lutra.** ca. 1930.
39¹/₂ x 59 in./100.4 x 150 cm
Goyet, Paris
Cond A–/Unobtrusive fold; slight stains at edges.
Electrical appliances to make your home hum! The company, perhaps best known for their Birum-Lutra floor polisher and vacuum cleaner (deftly included at the bottom of the design), was always very gender-conscious in their advertising. Essentially, they wanted to present industrial advancement without defeminizing the women likely to be their primary clientele. And that promotional predisposition holds true here, where the up-top woman appears to simply love the array of Lutra products spread out before her, products that can be found at their spiffy and spacious Art Deco showroom shown below.
**Est: $1,000-$1,200.**

**74**

**75**

**73**

## ANONYMOUS (cont'd)

**73. Treno Camioni.** 1924.
27³/₄ x 39¹/₂ in./70.3 x 100.3 cm
N. Moneta, Milano
Cond B+/Slight tears at folds.
What better way to make the Italian citizenry aware of the superiority of their railway service than with a rail-traveling trade fair lasting ninety days with seventy-six total stops. It's an ingenious concept and the promotion for the event rises to the challenge, incorporating allegory, technology and destination information in a splendidly harmonious pastiche.
**Est: $1,500-$1,800.**

**74. Think "I".** 1925.
36 x 48 in./91.5 x 121.8 cm
Mather & Company, Chicago, Ill
Cond A–/Slight creases.
A byproduct of the industrial system has been the use of the poster to urge workers to extend themselves to the fullest for the good of the company. Although still published today, none have had the graphic appeal of the ambitious undertaking published by the Chicago firm of Mather & Co., titled "Constructive Organization Posters." One notion about these posters that must be immediately dispelled: they were not government sponsored; they are a call for the best of free enterprise by a very free-enterprising publisher and printer. This poster comes from the extremely rare first Mather series (#72), created in 1925. And though the sentence "There's no 'I' in team" has become almost comically cliché (especially since "team" clearly contains the letters to form the word "me"), this Mather poster—showing a climber struggling solo against a harsh, vertical terrain while the trio behind him scales to the summit with relative ease—comes across as a breath of fresh air. And between "No man can succeed alone" and "Help others and they help you," the message couldn't possibly be any clearer.
**Est: $1,400-$1,700.**

**75. Philips.**
28¹/₂ x 41³/₈ in./73 x 105 cm
Cond A–/Unobtrusive tears at folds.
In a previously seen poster for Philips light bulbs executed by designer Orsi, the company promoted itself as "The Sun Under Your Roof" (*see* PAI-XLII, 22) when it came to indoor use of its product. Here, an anonymous posterist takes us from the inside out, placing a Philips half-watt into the empyrean—with apparently ecliptic results—as a roadster equipped with Philips headlights cuts an incandescent swath through the night below. Evocative, concise and spectacular.
**Est: $2,000-$2,500.**

**76. Vincerel/Reale Federazione di Canottaggio.**
1941.
27¹/₄ x 39¹/₄ in./69.3 x 99.6 cm
Carabellin, Venezia
Cond A–/Unobtrusive tear at upper paper edge.
No more than a single word is needed sum up the philosophy of this competition organized by the Imperial Rowing Federation: Win! And it appears as if this wiry sculler is well aware of just what's at stake. And amidst all the races being held during the two-day August event, it's interesting to note that one of them is the "Fire Brigade National Championship." Though no specific year is indicated on the poster—credited to an "R.S" in the lower right corner—the "XIX" next to the event dates indicates that the races took place during the nineteenth year of Benito Mussolini's fascist regime, or 1941.
**Est: $2,500-$3,000.**

**77. Sun Valley/Idaho.**
23⁵/₈ x 35 in./60 x 89 cm
Cond A.
Gitty-up to Sun Valley, y'all!! In the late 1930s, Averell Harriman developed Sun Valley as a show stop for the Union Pacific railroad, intended to rival the luxury of St. Moritz. Rooms at the lodge were offered free to

celebrities, glamour-seekers followed, and the spot quickly became the country's hottest winter-sport playground. (A 1937 *Life* cover sealed its fame with a photo of its ski lift—the world's first.) But the resort wants the public to know that it's no one-trick pony—it's chock-full of summertime fun, too. And this photomontage creation shows us just about every activity in which a sporty li'l filly would care to partake.
**Est: $1,200-$1,500.**

**76**

**78**

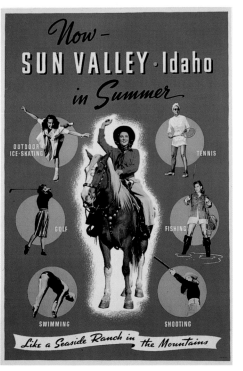

**77**

**79**

## OTTOMAR ANTON (1895-1976)

**78. Hamburg-Amerika Linie/"St. Louis" und "Milwaukee".** ca. 1929.
23¹/₂ x 32³/₄ in./60 x 83.2 cm
Mühlmeister & Johler, Hamburg
Cond A.
When last we saw the "Milwaukee" in an Anton design, the ship was unobtrusively tucked into the horizon (*see* PAI-XXXI, 131). But here, alongside her Hamburg-Amerika Line-mate, the *St. Louis*, the "Largest German

Motorships" leave little room for anything else save the golden expanses of sea and sky and a few representative red lines. The impressive Art Deco execution renders both boats with black hulls (the *Milwaukee* would be painted white after her conversion for greater passenger occupancy in the mid-1930s) from the time when they provided the most sizable Caribbean service for Hamburg-Amerika. In less proud times, the *St. Louis* was involved in one of history's most shameful footnotes—

setting sail from Hamburg carrying 900 Jewish emigrants fleeing Nazi tyranny, the ship was turned away by callous officials of both Cuba and the United States. Anton was a native of Hamburg who started working for a local agency there, but from 1921 on, had his own studio where he produced a large body of work for Hapag, the big transatlantic conglomerate. Later, he became an art instructor at the Bremen High School of Art.
**Est: $1,400-$1,700.**

81

82

80

83

## JOHN ARMSTRONG (1893-1973)

**79. Theatre-Goers Use Shell.** 1938.
44³/₄ x 30¹/₈ in./113.8 x 76.5 cm
J. Weiner Ltd., London
Cond A−/Slight paper loss at lower left corner.
Ref: PAI-XLIII, 527
This charming design—part of the famous series that focused on the various types of folks that "Use Shell" —stresses snob appeal, right down to the blasé facial expressions. In fact, these three "theatre-goers" are so striking in their appearance that they might very well be actors taking a bow on stage. Armstrong himself was a one-man "These People" series: law student, soldier in World War I, then painter, posterist, set and costume designer, and muralist. Eight of his murals decorated Shell headquarters.
**Est: $2,000-$2,500.**

## JANE ATCHÉ (1880-1937)

**80. Job.** 1896.
27¹/₂ x 36¹/₈ in./69.8 x 91.8 cm
Cond A.
Ref (All Var but PAI): DFP-II, 24; Reims, 208;
    Abdy, p. 149; Wine Spectator, 101;
    Masters 1900, p. 26; PAI-XIII, 82
*Rare proof before letters in the smaller format!*
"We know just enough about Jane Atché to be intrigued. She was born in Toulouse, worked in lithographic prints—at first in black and white only, later in color— and earned an honorable mention at the Salon of the Société des Artistes Français in 1902. Her scarce posters all disclose that Mucha was obviously (a strong influence)" (Wine Spectator, 101). Abdy, in fact, considers Atché one of Mucha's two best followers in France (p. 100). Of her half dozen known posters, this one for the cigarette paper firm is her most spectacular.

We get the lyricism of Art Nouveau in the handling of the green dress and the smoke, combined with a compelling Lautrec-esque management of the solid black cape as it slashes through the design. On all levels, it succeeds completely.
**Est: $4,000-$5,000.**

## PAUL BALLURIAU (1860-1917)

**81. Margot la Jolie.** 1897.
57⁵/₈ x 42⁵/₈ in./146.5 x 108.3 cm
Imp. Caby & Chardin, Paris
Cond A.
Ref: DFP-II, 35 (var)
If you listen closely enough, you can hear the bodices ripping as you gaze upon Balluriau's gauzy, romance-and-desperation artwork for "Margot la Jolie," a serialized novel being offered by a publication whose name has yet to be added to the design. Sadly, the romantic

85

86

87

### 84. Cirque de Paris. 1923.
76¹/₂ x 12³/₄ in./194.4 x 32.4 cm
Cond A–/Slight stains at folds.
A fold-out souvenir from the Cirque de Paris in which Barrère craftily captures all the fun and diversionary mayhem of the spectacular entertainment. From the derring-do of aerial acrobats and gymnasts to the rush of observing wild animals in barely-contained close proximity, from the physical prowess of horsemen to the unbridled—and sometimes rather violent—antics of clowns, Barrère skillfully allows the viewer to bring the circus home with them. All without the unpleasant odors or the overpriced cotton candy.
**Est: $1,000-$1,200.**

### 85. Professeurs à la Faculté de Droit. 1909.
35¹/₈ x 17⁷/₈ in./89.4 x 45.5 cm
Cond A.
Ref: Bibliothèque Nationale, Vol. I, p. 337, #2
Previously, we've seen Barrère casting a rather cynical glance unflinchingly in the direction of the medical profession in a series of panels that depicted these professors of the Faculté de Médicine as men barely able to conceal the vices in which they indulged (see PAI-XLI, 96) or as little more than jarred specimens on display (see PAI-XLI, 97). Here, he turns his caricaturistic eye to another group of upper-echelon professionals, namely the learned faculty of the Law School. And though his gaze isn't nearly as caustic towards the legal professionals as it is to the medical, there's really only one word to describe this assemblage of law professors: serious, right down to the down-right remarque. *This is one panel in a series of two.*
**Est: $1,200-$1,500.**

### 86. Polin. 1913.
46¹/₈ x 61³/₄ in./117 x 156.7 cm
Imp. Hervé & Maignon, Paris
Cond B–/Restored tears and stains at folds.
Ref: Spectacle, 1660; PAI-XXVIII, 139
For over forty years, café-concert legend Polin (the stage name of singer Pierre-Paul Marsalés (1863-1927)) reigned supreme over the musical halls of Montmartre and the Champs-Élysées. Making his debut in 1886 at *Concert de la Pépinière*, he would go on to to delight audiences well into the next century with the timid sincerity and naive charm of the character he created. As he did for so many other luminaries of the Paris cabaret, Barrère immortalizes the performer, seen here from the twilight years of his career, still twinkling with impish delight and decked out in his trademark ill-fitting uniform, his beloved handkerchief tucked securely into his back pocket. *This is the larger format.*
**Est: $1,500-$1,800.**

### 87. 1ère Exposition d'Insectes Vivants de Poissons d'Ornament et d'Oiseaux Volière. ca. 1920.
23¹/₄ x 31 in./59 x 78.6 cm
Affiches d'Art Robert, Paris
Cond A.
Though no regard is paid to the atmospheres in which these disparate life forms thrive, Barrère's artwork for the First Living Insect, Ornamental Fish and Aviary Bird Exposition at the Jardin d'Acclimentationis is stupendous, an eye-popping panoply of oft-overlooked life forms. By integrating the bugs, birds and fish into a single environment, Barrère contrasts species off one another for which he wouldn't necessarily otherwise find an opportunity. And the exotic menagerie is truly awesome, from the eclectus parrot to the in-flight stag beetle. And, in a surprise move, the artist shows a tarantula feasting on a hummingbird, an utterly accurate—if somewhat icky—portrayal as the arachnid is a burrow-based hunter.
**Est: $1,700-$2,000.**

antics of "Pretty Margot" weren't unique enough to have survived for a present-day summation. Balluriau, a regular contributor to *Gil Blas*, executed several of the posters to promote the former chief's lurid tales in *Le Journal*. As evidenced in his work exploring the seamier side of Paris, many of the artist's later posters are imbued with the colors and dramatic appeal of his colleague Steinlen.
**Est: $2,500-$3,000.**

### 82. Le Journal/La Tournée des Grand-Ducs.
ca. 1899.
60³/₄ x 44⁵/₈ in./154.5 x 113.3 cm
Imp. Paul Dupont, Paris
Cond B+/Slight tears at folds.
Ref: PAI-XXXIX, 120
The elegant woman with her magnificent fur-lined coat is the centerpiece of this scene for a novel being serialized in *Le Journal*. She and her noble friends seem a bit out of place in what appears to be a debtors' prison.
**Est: $2,500-$3,000.**

## ADRIEN BARRÈRE (1877-1931)

### 83. Scala/Marguerite Deval
23¹/₈ x 31¹/₄ in./58.7 x 79.5 cm
Imp. Ch. Wall, Paris
Cond B+/Horizontal fold; slight tears at edges.
Ref (Both Var): Wine Spectator, 116; PAI-XLI, 95
Deval (1868-1955) was born in Strasbourg and entered show business at the age of sixteen. She ran the gamut of operetta, revues, vaudeville and music hall, finally landing in films at the age of sixty-four—where she then enjoyed a seventeen-year career! Her last appearance came in 1949's "Eve et le Serpent." In this poster, seen here before the addition of text, the sassy redhead makes an appearance in a Scala production of a saucy little diversion entitled "When There's Enough For Two." And with the background shenanigans on display, it's doubtful that the title is referring to an especially tasty soufflé.
**Est: $2,000-$2,500.**

**88**

**89**

## ADRIEN BARRÈRE (cont'd)

**88. Théâtre de Grand Guignol/Le Baiser dans le Nuit.**
$45^1/_2$ x $61^3/_4$ in./115.7 x 156.7 cm
Imp. R. Philippe de Girard, Paris
Cond B+/Slight tears along folds.
The usual Grand Guignol lineup went something like this: slapstick, light drama, comedy, horror, and—finishing up—a farce. Regardless of stylistic thrust, however, the darkness of the Guignol became the point of the plays: virtue and kindness weren't rewarded. Rather, these were plays where the criminals got away, nice people got disfigured and innocence was eternally exploited. In short, everything that appears to be on display in this Barrère promotion for a piece titled "The Kiss in the Night." There's absolutely no doubt that someone got screwed over during the course of this production.
**Est: $2,000-$2,500.**

**89. Grand Guignol/Le Sorcier.**
$43^3/_4$ x $61^1/_8$ in./111 x 155 cm
Imp. Hervé & Maignon, Paris
Cond B/Slight tears at folds.
Barrère allowed himself to crack open the door to his artistically darker side in the posters that he created for the Grand Guignol and the results are phenomenal —gritty, violent, debauched, sleazy and, as we see here, downright creepy. Apparently, the title character in this production was able to transform itself into a terrifying vulture/human hybrid. And heaven help the poor soul that was in the vicinity of "The Warlock" when it was feeding time. Yikes! Barrère is best known for his portraits of French stage personalities ca. 1900-1910. As seen in these examples, his caricature-like treatments and flat colors yielded witty, spirited designs.
**Est: $1,700-$2,000.**

## OTTO BAUMBERGER (1889-1961)

**90. Gotthard.** 1919.
$35^1/_4$ x $50^1/_4$ in./89.5 x 127.6 cm
Wolfsberg, Zürich
Cond A.
Ref: Baumberger, 73; PAI-XXII, 199
The imposing massif of the Alpine peaks dwarf the Swiss

**90**

village huddled in the valley, with the beige of the walls the only break in the grey grandeur of the mountains.
**Est: $1,700-$2,000.**

**91. Hotel St. Gotthard/Zurich.** 1915.
$35^7/_8$ x $50^1/_4$ in./91.2 x 127.6 cm
J. E. Wolfensberger, Zürich
Cond A.
Ref: Baumberger, 53; Schweizer Hotel, 102; PAI-XLII, 120
Here, to emphasize the dignified atmosphere of the famous hotel, Baumberger puts a still life of fine cuisine into a tasteful gold frame. By the standards of 1915 or 2007, it's still one of the best image-building posters any establishment could hope for. A native of Zurich,

**91**

Baumberger regarded himself primarily as a painter, creating posters merely to generate some income. Nonetheless, he produced a magnificent body of more than 200 posters, distinguished not by a style, but by stylistic diversity—each perfectly suited to the clients' needs.
**Est: $1,200-$1,500.**

**92. Durol.** ca. 1923.
$35^1/_4$ x 50 in./89.5 x 127.2 cm
A. Trüb, Aarau
Cond B/Vertical tear extending through length of image.
Ref: Baumberger, 103; Auto Posters, p. 36 (var); PAI-XXVII, 33
The ever versatile Swiss master utilizes bright, primary hues and simplified outlines against a flat black back-

**92**

**94**

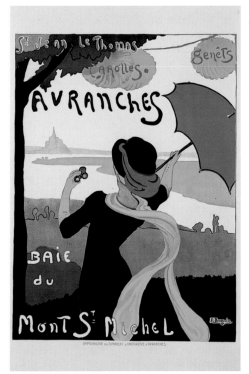

**95**

**93**

## EUGENE BEAUDOIN (1898-?) & MARCEL LODS (1891-1978)

**94. Paris 1937/Exposition Internationale.** 1936.
24¹/₈ x 39 in./61.2 x 99 cm
Imp. Jules Simon, Paris
Cond A.
Ref: Purvis, p. 84; PAI-XLIII, 157
The skywriting, the night scene, the hint of futurism, all contribute to the sense of romance and excitement in this most effective design. The milky azure image with its shimmering pink and white flashes of light won first prize in a poster competition held by the French Ministry of Commerce for the Paris 1937 World's Fair. Its co-creators were architects who were involved in several construction projects together around Paris, including the overall design for the upcoming 1937 World's Fair; they entered the competition on a whim, and regrettably, never produced another poster. After a partnership that extended from 1925 to 1940, Beaudoin left to become director of architectural studies at a school in Geneva, while Lods stayed in private practice in Paris. *This is the medium format.*
**Est: $1,700-$2,000.**

## ALBERT BERGEVIN (1887-1974)

**95. Avranches.**
31¹/₄ x 47¹/₄ in./79.3 x 120 cm
Imp. du Syndicat d'Initiative d'Avranches
Cond A.
Ref: PAI-XLI, 109
A French travel poster for the coast of Normandy. The "Baie du Mont. St. Michel" is touted here with its phenomenal buttressed abbey seen in the background and the names of surrounding coastal towns lettered charmingly on Japanese lanterns. It's the strong forms of the tourist and her richly-colored accessories, however, which attract our attention. Bergevin knew the area well; Avranches is the town where he was born and died.
**Est: $3,000-$4,000.**

**93. Davos.** 1932.
25 x 40 in./63.4 x 101.5 cm
Orell Füssli, Zürich
Cond A.
Ref: Baumberger, 175; Alpes, p. 89; PAI-XL, 75
Although Davos is most frequently associated with winter sports, here it's a picturesque summer scene that's used to entice the potential visitor.
**Est: $1,700-$2,000.**

ground to advertise Durol motor oil, which, if you believe their promotional slogan, is "without rival." Placed in the foreground of the design, the oil canister is the focus of both viewer and illustrated personages, the entire composition ingeniously tied together through the colorful utilization of Durol's triple-pronged icon. *Rare!*
**Est: $3,000-$4,000.**

## PAUL BERTHON (1872-1909)

**96. Le Livre de Magda.** 1898.
17¹/₈ x 24¹/₂ in./43.5 x 62.2 cm
Imp. Chaix, Paris
Cond A. Framed.
Ref: DFP-II, 66; Berthon & Grasset, p. 97;
    Timeless Images, 29; PAI-XLIII, 167
An advertisement for a book of poetry by Armand Silvestre. One may doubt whether the poems themselves were as lyrically lovely as Berthon's ethereal, Art Nouveau illustration of a nude forest nymph, who seems—her hair especially—part of the landscape. "Berthon's small but characteristic body of work . . . epitomizes the Art Nouveau style on paper" (Berthon & Grasset, p. 8).
**Est: $2,000-$2,500.**

**97. Folies-Bergère/Liane de Pougy.** 1898.
23³/₄ x 61¹/₂ in./60.2 x 156 cm
Imp. Lemercier, Paris
Cond B+/Slight tears at folds and edges.
Ref: Berthon & Grasset, checklist #1; DFP-II, 63;
    Folies-Bergère, 24; Reims, 230; PAI-XXXIII, 204
To Berthon, the search for the beautiful was what art was all about and he felt that decoration was "one of the highest forms of all art." And he sought to inject the decorative element into all his work, whether purely decorative panels, or more utilitarian objects such as book covers and posters. He was a tireless exponent of Art Nouveau. His subjects are all quite aloof, his designs full of softness and pastels, but he can invoke a romanticism and even a sensuousness that is all his own. This is Berthon's very first poster, advertising Liane de Pougy's appearance in "L'Arraiganée d'Or" (*The Golden Spider*) at the Folies-Bergère in October, 1896. The design is quite different from his later work, but, as a poster, a superior accomplishment.
**Est: $3,500-$4,000.**

## R. BERTRAND

**98. Argentina.** 1935.
12¹/₄ x 19¹/₈ in./31 x 48.5 cm
*Hand-signed gouache maquette with metallic silver highlights.* Framed.
Apart from a first initial, no specifics regarding Bertrand could be unearthed. Though there are several artists with the last name "Bertrand" that share the initial first "R," none of them matched up stylistically. Which is rather disappointing as this Bertrand was clearly a posterist with a distinct, visually engaging style. This maquette for the Spanish dancer, Argentina (Encarnacion Lopez, 1898-1945), gains added luster thanks to a liberal use of metallic silver ink. "A finished musician, actress and brilliant technician, she mastered the various types of Spanish dancing to the complete satisfaction of the discriminating Spanish audiences" (Dance Encyclopedia, p. 19). In 1938, impresario S. Hurok signed her for a tour of the United States.
**Est: $1,700-$2,000.**

**99. Bugatti.**
9¹/₄ x 12¹/₄ in./23.3 x 31 cm
*Hand-signed gouache and ink maquette.* Framed.
With head-on framework and a fully-realized manifestation of hill-climbing excellence, Bertrand facilely and fully conveys Bugatti's speed and elegance. Ettore Bugatti built some of the most fabulous automobiles in history. Though they were quite expensive, what set Bugatti apart from other designers was his unique ability as an artist—his automobiles were like sculptures, his engines like jewels. As an engineer, he was imperious, and yet, an incredible aesthete. After creating cars for de Dietrich, Deutz and Hermes, Bugatti opened a factory of his own in 1909 in an unoccupied dyeing works in Molsheim, Germany.
**Est: $1,700-$2,000.**

**100. Eglises Romanes/Reseau de l'Etat.**
17⁵/₈ x 23³/₈ in./45 x 59.4 cm
*Hand-signed gouache and ink maquette.* Framed.
Romanesque architecture meets the steam-and-steel of modern technology to startling ends in this Bertrand artwork for the state rail network. Executed practically in separate styles, the church and the locomotive make an unlikely pairing, and yet their symbiosis generates a strikingly persuasive tourism proposition.
**Est: $2,500-$3,000.**

96

101

## GEORGES PIERRE BEUVILLE

**101. Botot.** 1925.
45⁷/₈ x 62¹/₂ in./116.5 x 158.7 cm
Deschizeaux, Le Mans
Cond B+/Slight tears in black robe.
Ref: Health Posters, 230
"Born in Calvados, Georges-Pierre Beuville participated in the Salon d'Automne of 1922. This poster . . . is an inspired piece of design, both in conception, and in an economy of realization. By an equal division of space into black and white he achieves a strikingly convincing portrait of Diafoirus, a larger-than-life blend of facetious craftiness. Using rigorous horizontal symmetry, the five letters of the brand are perfectly balanced in the upper half . . . The vermilion tinting of the cheeks and lower lip echoes the color of the bottle held up next to the doctor's face. Any comic overlay in the portrait is held in check by the serious overtones, as in the message in the lower section that endorses the product, with the seal of the approval from the Medical Faculty of Paris" (Health Posters, p. 177).
**Est: $1,200-$1,500.**

97

## MAURICE BIAIS (ca. 1875-1926)

**102. Scala.** 1901.
32 x 47³/₄ in./81.3 x 121.4 cm
Imp. J. Minot, Paris
Cond A.
Ref: Spectacle, 1329; PAI-XXIX, 226
Biais was a self-taught illustrator, lithographer and posterist. Though talented, Biais certainly wasn't an angel—he was a gambler, a drinker and a heavy smoker —and is almost as well-remembered for his affinity for the Montmartre nightlife as for his creative output. After marrying the dancer Jane Avril—no angel herself —he prepared some posters for her, and thereafter was asked to execute several other theatrical posters. This café-concert scene is a masterpiece of composition, comparable to some of the best works of the better-known Toulouse-Lautrec. The promotion for the Scala concert hall focuses more on what's going on in the audience than it does to what's transpiring on-stage. We're given an image of an elegant woman watching the performance who in turn is being ogled by a lecherous fellow with a cigarette pursed insouciantly between his lips—who is likely Biais himself! Rarely has watching and being watched been given such equal play. How spectacularly voyeuristic!
**Est: $6,000-$8,000.**

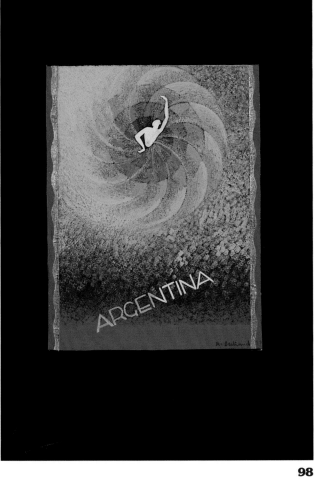

98

99

100

102

**103**

**107**

**104**

**105**

## ARMIN BIEBER (1892-1970)

**103. Ilco Schuhe.** ca. 1925.
35¹/₄ x 49³/₄ in./89.6 x 126.5 cm
Kümmerly & Frey, Bern
Cond A–/Restored slight tear at top paper edge.
In all seriousness, this has to be the only poster ever
to come our way to feature the sport of curling as the
athletic activity of choice! But it's nice to know that
once you're done sweeping and delivering the rock,
there's a quality pair of Ilco shoes to slip into when
you step off of the ice. On a completely trivial side
note, it's interesting to note that curling is the only
Olympic sport that directly prohibits drinking and
smoking in its rules of play.
**Est: $2,500-$3,000.**

## PETER BIRKHÄUSER (1911-1976)

**104. Argo.**
35¹/₂ x 50¹/₈ in./89.5 x 127.4 cm
Wasserman, Basel
Cond A/P.
If an artist is going to create an object poster, is there
really any better object to focus on than a shapely pair
of female legs? Granted, that may sound slightly chau-
vinistic, but realistically speaking, if we're talking in
terms of generating sales for stockings, it's pretty much
advertising perfection—it appeals to female vanity and
male voyeurism. Birkhäuser's Argo promotion works in
precisely this manner, and makes note of the fact that
the product is "elastic" and "solid" as well. Birkhäuser
studied in his native Basel and apprenticed in the studio of the man he bested in the 1934 PKZ contest. He
went on to a career in advertising and fine art. "In his
illustrations he mixed illusionistic objectivity with
visionary and psychological imagery" (Plakat Schweiz,
p. 186). Kellenberger refers to his "rich and abundant
production" (Affiches Suisses, p. 12).
**Est: $800-$1,000.**

**105. Bata.**
35¹/₂ x 50 in./90 x 127.2 cm
Grafica A.-G., Basel
Cond A/P.
Who knew that a single shoe and an accompanying
sock put under the lithographic microscope could be
so appealing? Birkhäuser's poster for the Swiss shoe
manufacturer may not be as sexy as his Argo design,
but it's certainly no less objectively efficacious, executed with clarity and near-photographic precision.
**Est: $800-$1,000.**

## BOBRI (Vladimir Bobritsky, 1898-?)

**106. Pan Am/Europe.** 1960.
27⁷/₈ x 41⁵/₈ in./70.8 x 105.8 cm
Printed in USA
Cond B/Minor restorations in background.
Bobri puts the squeeze on the earth for Pan American
Airlines, cleverly compressing the world at large to
cheekily demonstrate how their "7 magic jet hours"
service from New York to Europe is so easily achieved.
Bobritsky, who signed the majority of his work "Bobri,"

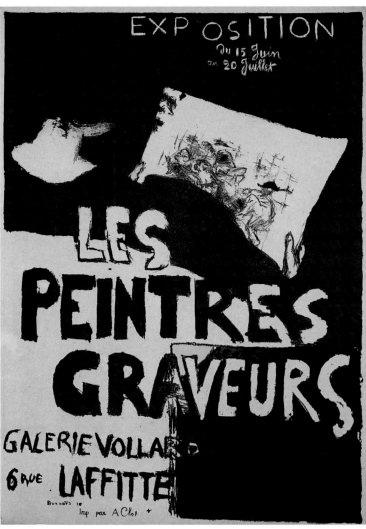

**108**

**109**

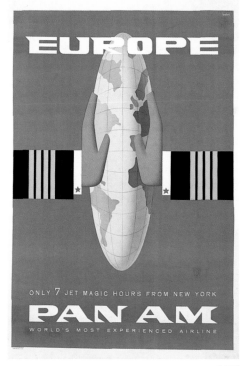

**106**

was born in Kharkov, the Ukraine. Because of the turbulent events of the Revolution, he fled Russia in 1917, never to return. He passed safely into Turkey, supporting himself by designing sets and costumes for the Russian ballet in Istanbul, producing movie posters and creating iconographic paintings in a monastery. He even made an important historical find in Anatolia, Turkey, when he discovered a Byzantine mural in an abandoned Turkish mosque while engaged in archaeological work. He emigrated to New York in 1921, establishing himself as a fashion illustrator. At the peak of that career in the 1930s and '40s, Bobri was a leading artist in New York's burgeoning advertising world—working on such prestigious accounts as Saks Fifth Avenue and Hanes—and was a frequent contributor to the *New Yorker*, *Vogue* and *Harper's Bazaar*. His drawing style was bold, yet elegant, marked by technical refinement and an excellent use of space.
**Est: $1,200-$1,500.**

### PIERRE BONNARD (1867-1947)

**107. La Revue Blanche.** 1894.
23$^1$/$_8$ x 30$^3$/$_8$ in./59 x 77 cm
Imp. Edw. Ancourt, Paris
Cond B/Slight tears, largely at edges. Framed.
Ref: Marx, 32; Bouvet, 30; DFP-II, 77; Maitres, 38;
    Word & Image, p. 26; Modern Poster, 8;
    PAI-XLII, 130
Bonnard's best-known and most enigmatic poster advertises the monthly *La Revue Blanche*, published by the Natansons, who befriended and encouraged him. The significance of this image eludes us today and seems not to have been all that clear when published. Maindron admitted that he could not understand it, but found that "nonetheless it's quite curious." Bouvet gives it a stab: "the strange form (at right) apparently following the young woman, is in fact a man, seen from behind, an opera hat on his head and coat collar turned up, reading the poster for the *Revue* on the wall" (p. 36).
**Est: $8,000-$10,000.**

**108. Les Peintres Graveurs.** 1896.
18$^3$/$_4$ x 25$^7$/$_8$ in./47.6 x 65.7 cm
Imp. A. Clot (Paris)
Cond A–/Slight tears and stains at edges.
Ref: Marx, 40; Bouvet, 38; Ives, 23; DFP-II, 78;
    Modern Poster, 8; Gold, 184; PAI-XXXVI, 176
We look over the shoulder of a prospective buyer in this poster advertising an exhibition at Vollard's gallery—twenty-two prints by artists from the group that called themselves the Nabis, including Vuillard, Vallotton and Bonnard himself. The exhibition was staged to publicize the portfolio "Album des Peintres-Graveurs," which contained the same prints and was simultaneously issued in a small edition of 100 sets by Vollard.
**Est: $2,500-$3,000.**

**109. Le Figaro.** 1894.
16$^1$/$_8$ x 21 in./41 x 61 cm
Imp. Chaix, Paris
Cond A–/Slight tears at paper edges.
Ref: Marx, 70; Bouvet, 78; DFP-II, 81; Fit to Print, 19;
    PAI-XXXVI, 175
Bonnard was primarily a printmaker, illustrator and painter; his poster output is few, but never fails to engage the viewer's interest. This one announces the serialization of a new novel in the pages of *Le Figaro*. Bonnard's signature is placed, rather oddly, on the back of the man's chair.
**Est: $2,500-$3,000.**

**110**

**113**

**111**

**112**

## MARIO BORGONI (1869-1936)

**110. Monte-Carlo.** 1899.
35¹/₂ x 48¹/₂ in./90 x 123.4 cm
Imp. Richter & Co., Naples
Cond B+/Restored tears.
Ref: Affiches Riviera, 96
After attending Naples' Institute of Fine Arts, Borgoni
dedicated himself to lithographic production, collabo-
rating with the Richter firm to create a remarkable
number of posters. Working in many styles yet specializing in tourism posters, Borgoni frequently used the
feminine figure to lure the viewer's eyes to his designs.
Another element to be found in his works is the use of
a frame to open a window onto voluptuous landscapes.
Borgoni uses both of these enticing devices from his
artistic bag of tricks to promote Monte-Carlo, though
truth be told, it's his sunset—not the casino or the
lovely women who flock there—that steals the show.
**Est: $4,000-$5,000.**

## FIRMIN BOUISSET (1859-1925)

**111. Vincent Fils.** 1894.
47³/₄ x 73¹/₄ in./121.2 x 186 cm
Affiches Camis, Paris
Cond B/Restored paper loss at edges.
Well, this Bouisset promotion for Vincent Sons baby
carriages is just adorable, isn't it? And thematically
timeless, because quite honestly, all you need to do
is update the clothing and change the stroller to a
Maclaren and the scenario still plays itself out around
the world on surely an almost daily basis. Bouisset
achieved commercial success by featuring children in
his advertisements as a way of capturing the public's
attention, most notably with his poster for Chocolat
Menier (see PAI-XLIII, 174), a creation with such long-
lasting appeal that we co-opted it as the cover art for
our latest price guide, Poster Prices VIII.
**Est: $1,500-$2,000.**

## HENRI BOUTET
(Louis Maurice Henri Boutet de Monvel,
1851-1919)

**112. Madame Chrysanthème.** 1893.
24 x 31¹/₄ in./60.7 x 79.3 cm
Choudens, Paris
Cond A-/Slight tears and stains at edges.
Ref: DFP-II, 94; Reims, 248; PAI-XXIX, 232

*Madame Chrysanthème* "was based on the 1887 novel
by Pierre Loti which may have furnished at least the
germinal idea of both Jones's *The Geisha* and Puccini's
*Madama Butterfly*. It had continuous music and is not
an operetta; by the time of its New York premiere in
1920, with the Japanese Tamaki Miura in the title role,
the intense popularity of the Puccini favorite made
unflattering comparisons with the Message work in-
evitable" (*Operetta: A Theatrical History*, by Richard
Traubner, p. 224). Operatic loyalties aside, one cannot
overlook the pastel allure of the Monvel design, with
the title character materializing from the paper like a
woodblock mirage.
**Est: $1,000-$1,200.**

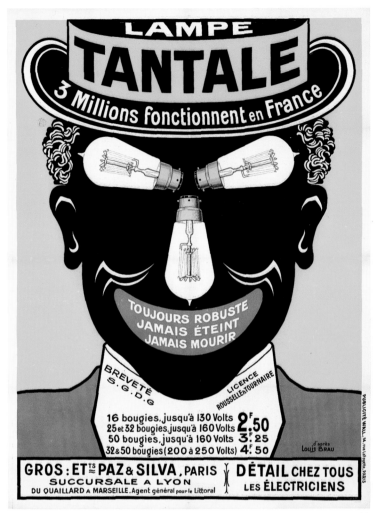

**114**

**116**

**115**

### WILLIAM H. BRADLEY (1868-1962)

**113. Collier's Weekly/Out Door Number.** 1900.
10¹/₈ x 15¹/₄ in./25.8 x 38.7 cm
Cond A–/Slight stains.
Ref: PAI-XLIII, 176
In his advertisement for the "Out Door Number" of
*Collier's Weekly*, Bradley sets down a bit of cyclic
horseplay, demonstrating in the process one of the
best reasons to get out of the house and get some

exercise—because it's fun. Cleverly making this a more-
than-one sport cover is the fully-loaded golf bag at top.
Will Bradley was an innovative, influential typographer,
designer and publisher. The international Art Nouveau
movement found its American expression in the delicate and ornate work of this genius. In 1895, Bradley
moved from Chicago to Springfield, Massachusetts,
where he established The Wayside Press, a publishing
and graphic arts venture whose main product was
*Bradley: His Book*, an art magazine appearing monthly.
**Est: $1,400-$1,700.**

### LOUIS BRAU

**114. Lampe Tantale.** ca. 1910.
46³/₄ x 62³/₄ in./118.6 x 159.2 cm
Publicité Wall, Paris
Cond B/Restored tears.
What do you get when you combine one part minstrel
with three parts light bulb? Clearly you arrive at a somewhat unsettling electrified bust, something more akin
to a sci-fi robot than an actual human. Which would
make sense seeing as this flat-black-faced golem with
incandescent lamps for eyes and a nose has a sales
pitch literally coming out of his mouth, promising that
Tantale bulbs are always robust, never need to be
turned off and will never die. Much like a robot. It's a
queer promotional angle, but the uncredited artist
working from Louis Brau's original artwork (the poster
bears the appropriate "d'après" designation) pulls off
a creation that burns itself into the mind's eye of the
viewer as surely as the product's tantalum filaments
burn bright, night or day.
**Est: $1,500-$2,000.**

### ROGER BRODERS (1883-1953)

**115. Jura/Lac de Malbuisson.** ca. 1930.
24³/₄ x 39³/₈ in./63 x 100 cm
Imp. Lucien Serre, Paris
Cond A.

Ref: Broders, p. 51B; Broders/Travel, p. 50; PAI-XIX, 216b
Vibrant hues highlight this PLM Railroad poster for
motor coach service to the village of Malbuisson, situated on the four-mile long St. Point Lake, the largest
body of water in the Jura mountains. In the period between the wars, Roger Broders was the finest designer
of French travel posters bar none. Many, including many
of his best, were for the French Railways—in fact, the
majority were for a single company: the Paris-Lyon-
Méditerranée. He used three distinct approaches in his
travel and tourism posters. One highlighted the fashionable sorts of people who frequented the advertised
resorts and hotels. The second approach was the impressionistic rendering of the scenery alone. The third
was Art Deco influenced stylization of the scenery into
areas of flat color and boldly graphic, near-geometric
pattern. He was especially masterful at setting up his
compositions—often elevated to provide some panoramic sweep, and always framing the view so as to focus
interest just where it was desired. The result was always
an engaging, effective design—one doesn't just view
the scene, one comes upon it.
**Est: $1,200-$1,500.**

**116. Vichy/Comité des Fêtes.** ca. 1926.
28⁷/₈ x 41 in./73.4 x 104.1 cm
Lucien Serre, Paris
Cond B+/Restored tears at edges. Framed.
Ref: Broders, p. 55; Broders/Travel, p. 55;
    Deco Affiches, p. 93; PAI-XLIII, 178
A nighttime scene on the shores of a lake—with a float-
ing stage on which a ballet is in progress, glittering
boats on the water and a land-based audience in evening dress beneath colorful lanterns—makes a strong
case for attending the Vichy Festival. As always, Broders
places us at just the right vantage point to catch all the
action. *Without a doubt, one of the most spectacular
travel posters of all time.*
**Est: $12,000-$15,000.**

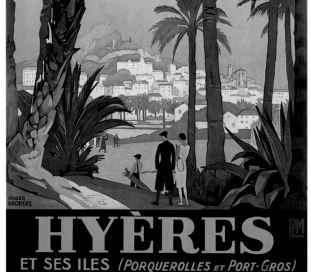

## ROGER BRODERS (cont'd)

**117. Hyères.** ca. 1931.
24$^1$/$_4$ x 39$^1$/$_8$ in./61.6 x 99.4 cm
Lucien Serre, Paris
Cond B+/Restored tears along right paper edge.
Ref: Broders, p. 83; Broders/Travel, p. 21; Golf, p. 13;
PAI-XXXI, 319
The text boasts that Hyères is "the Côte d'Azur's most southerly resort" and Broders reinforces this message by framing his view with a canopy of palms. Their deep cool shadows set off the hot sun on the yellow stucco walls of the Mediterranean town and make the lush green golf course most inviting. "Contemporary to Cannes-Mandelieu and Saint-Raphael, this course has disappeared. The club was chaired by Viscount Noailles whose famous cubic style villa designed by Le Corbusier attracted the jet set of those times . . . Broders . . . managed to recreate the atmosphere of a sport practiced by elegant people at that time highlighting the old town of Hyères hiding at the bottom of the foothills in the background" (Golf, p. 13).
**Est: $2,000-$2,500.**

## GEORGE REITER BRILL (1867-1918)

**118. The Philadelphia Sunday Press: Two Posters.**
1896.
Each Approx: 14$^1$/$_2$ x 21$^1$/$_4$ in./36.7 x 54 cm
H. I. Ireland, Philadelphia
Cond A–/Slight tears and stains at edges.
Brill's illustrations appeared in many leading periodicals and almost all his posters were for newspapers, the largest number being for the *Philadelphia Sunday Press.* He had the distinction of having the largest number of posters on display at the 1896 Reims exhibition of any American artist. Of his forty-two total posters there, thirty-one were those executed for this

Philadelphia newspaper. In line with the bulk of his work, these designs affix their winsome appeal to the turn-of-the-century covergirls that sweep us along with them. The June 28th promotion revels in family fun, offering a promotional handheld toy merry-go-round "With all the Animals Flying round the Circle" for the boys and girls, hoping to secure their parent's patron-

age with unapologetic progeny pressure. And though Brill doesn't typically give way to textual influence in his *Sunday Press* designs, it seems rather likely that his illustration for the November 1st edition is an example of the "Extremes of Our City's Life: The Best and the Worst Sides Graphically Pictured."
**Est: $1,500-$1,800.** (2)

**122**

**123**

**121**

**120**

## ALEXY BRODOVITCH (1898-1971)

**119. Donnet Zedel.** 1925.
47¹/₂ x 58³/₄ in./120.6 x 149.2 cm
Imp. H. Chachoin, Paris
Cond B+/Unobtrusive tears at folds.
Ref: PAI-XXXII, 106
The handsome yellow Donnet is silhouetted against a blue Mediterranean sky as it climbs a road above the Côte d'Azur. It is, as the slogan punningly tells us, "The car that climbs, the brand that's climbing."
**Est: $3,000-$4,000.**

## DONALD BRUN (1909-1999)

**120. Meccarillos.**
35¹/₂ x 50¹/₄ inj./90.1 x 127.7 cm
Säuberlin & Pfeiffer, Vevey
Cond A/P.
Big Chief Nicotine no smoke 'um peace pipe, he smoke 'um Meccarillos. Without a doubt the laws of political correctness would never allow this sort of statement to be uttered today, but taking into consideration that prolific Swiss designer Brun created his poster before the world became obsessed with such folly, that's exactly what he's graphically implying. I mean, the poster's Native American smoker loves the product so much that he's painted his teepee to match the Meccarillos packaging, for the love of Pete!
**Est: $800-$1,000.**

## GASPAR CAMPS (1874-1931)

**121. Cordial-Médoc.**
12³/₄ x 27 in./32.6 x 68.7 cm
Imp. F. Champenois, Paris
Cond B+/Usual silk tears. Framed.
Ref: PAI-XLII, 149
A luscious Art Nouveau design, executed with most meticulous workmanship and printed in exceptionally rich colors on silk, for a well known liqueur. Note how the peacock's feathers make an ideal decorative addition to the woman's ensemble. All of Camps' subtle indulgences are lushly highlighted in this silk printing, creating a warmth and richness not attainable with mere paper.
**Est: $2,000-$2,500.**

**122. Lilac Allure.** ca. 1904.
13¹/₄ x 28 in./33.6 x 71 cm
Imp. F. Champenois, Paris
Cond B/Creasing. Framed.
Ref: PAI-XXXVIII, 215
*Printed on silk.*
A blonde sylph draped in lavender diaphany—though stock-still gives the illusion of imminent flight grace of a flock of kaleidoscopic fowl posed flittingly about her gown's skirt—poses prettily in front of a carved wall lush with lilacs. A strong argument for the necessity of beauty for beauty's sake, printed on silk for additional luster.
**Est: $1,700-$2,000.**

**123. Indio Rosa.**
14³/₈ x 20 in./36.5 x 51 cm
Cond B+/Unobtrusive tears at upper right corner.
Camps, a Spaniard who spent most of his career in France, was one of a number of artists hired by the Champenois printing house to fill the void when Mucha left for America in 1904. Creating both advertising and decorative works, Camps eventually found his own groove—less graphic than Mucha and more akin to oil painting, marked by soft edges and shadings, as well as loads of sentiment. In this promotion for Indio Rosa rolling papers, his nicotinic señorita—luxuriantly and flirtatiously robed, an ornate bauble with flawless skin and expertly-applied cosmetic excess—facilely overshadows the Native American with whom she shares a preferred addiction.
**Est: $1,400-$1,700.**

**124. Putting Pretty.**
6¹/₄ x 14 in./16 x 35.5 cm
Cond A-/Slight stains. Framed.
The first words to pop to mind upon seeing your typical Camps female aren't "physically active." The majority of them certainly appear to be ladies of leisure, decorative works in their own right meant to be gazed upon rather than put into motion. But this and the following design prove that every once and a while these flappers liked to get out for a bit of physical activity. Fashionable physical activity to be sure, but forms of exercise nonetheless. Set against a splendiferous kaleidoscopic matrix, a thoroughly-modern golfer distractedly lines up her putt. Perhaps she's more interested in who's stepping up to tee-off on the next hole than making par herself. Focus, my dear. Focus.
**Est: $1,400-$1,700.**

## GASPAR CAMPS (cont'd)

### 125. Downhil Demoiselle.
6$^1$/$_4$ x 14 in./16 x 35.5 cm
Cond A–/Slight stains. Framed.
Set nearly into the nadir of an Art Deco sunburst, this comely downhiller appears to be creating quite a ruckus on the slopes. In fact, if we're not mistaken, she's caused the background sled-full o' gents to lose control of their ride. But who can blame them—when a well-togged stunner such as this decides to make her way down an Alpine track or two, distraction becomes a part of the plan for any male with a pulse in her immediate vicinity.
**Est: $1,400-$1,700.**

## LEONETTO CAPPIELLO (1875-1942)

### 126. Cervezas la Cruz del Campo. 1906.
46$^1$/$_2$ x 62$^1$/$_8$ in./118 x 157.8 cm
Imp. Vercasson, Paris
Cond A–/Slight tears at folds.
Ref: Cappiello/Rennert, 98; Cappiello, 274
"An interesting recurring motif in Cappiello's work is the jolly, rotund gourmand. He seems to be presented not so much as a comic figure—although it's sometimes difficult not to have a chuckle or two at his expense—but more as a model consumer: He knows what's good, and is quite unabashedly savoring every morsel or drop of the product at hand. And although gluttony is regarded as one of the Seven Deadly Sins, individual connoisseurs of the good life were sometimes admired: in mythology, Bacchus; in history, such as King Henry VIII; and in literature, such as Falstaff. It is likely that these precedents inspired Cappiello to make frequent use of the sybaritic characters. The idea is to persuade you that such experts at high living wouldn't recommend anything but the very best. Who could doubt, for example, that the satisfied brew master in the Spanish poster for la Cruz del Campo beer is immensely satisfied with the product?" (Cappiello/Rennert, p. 89). *Rare!*
**Est: $10,000-$12,000.**

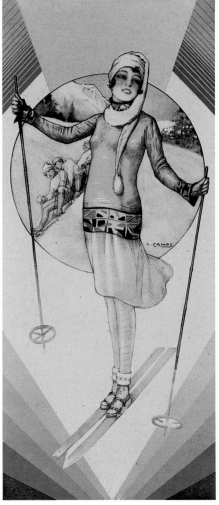

**128**

**129**

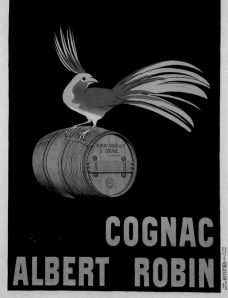

**130**

**127. Docteur Rasurel/"Sous Vêtements Hygiéniques".** 1906.
45¹/₂ x 61¹/₄ in./115.4 x 155.5 cm
Imp. Vercasson, Paris
Cond A–/Unobtrusive tears along folds.
Ref: Cappiello/Rennert, 107; Health Posters, 26;
  Gold, 123; PAI-XXXIX, 172
"Docteur Rasurel was a trademark for a line of thermal underwear, union suits and other warming textile products for the home . . . 'The dynamic of the design is based, on the one hand in the contrasted colors, the

plain black background freeing the text and the figures from any superfluous detail, and, on the other, on the unity of movement and posture displayed by the three figures, which forms a perfectly harmonious ensemble. The whole poster evokes an impression of vitality and energy . . . The comfortable benefits of wearing Rasurel underwear seems to be confirmed by the contented expressions of the three figures shown' (*Posters of Health*, by Marine Robert-Sterkendries, p. 29)" (Cappiello/ Rennert, p. 94).
**Est: $5,000-$6,000.**

**128. Vittel.** 1912.
29³/₈ x 40³/₄ in./74.6 x 103.7 cm
Imp. Vercasson, Paris.
Cond A–/Slight creasing.
Ref: Cappiello/Rennert, 213; PAI-XXXI, 341
In Cappiello's second creation for Vittel, the "poster reveals the personified source of the spring water, as Cappiello puts a face to this flourishing French spa. This textual variant touting the Eastern Railways makes it clear that they provide rapid transport to the mineral springs from both Paris and, with the help of connecting service, London" (Cappiello/Rennert, p. 146).
**Est: $2,500-$3,000.**

**129. Longines.** ca. 1911.
35 x 50¹/₄ in./89 x 127.8 cm
Imp. Vercasson, Paris
Cond A–/Slight crease and tears near bottom text area.
Ref: Cappiello/Rennert, 195; PAI-XXXI, 340 (var)
"An appreciation for the Longines poster, showing Father Time himself endorsing it as 'the best of precision watches,' appeared in an essay by F. Bouvet de Monvel in the December 13, 1913 issue of *Le Monde Illustré*: 'Enthroned on clouds like those blissful saints

in church windows who are as majestic as God, and blasé in the face of the world's old age. At his feet, the homely hourglass that kept time for our ancestors is casually tossed in a golden ray of sunlight. Farewell, old relic! . . . You're obsolete and Father Time no longer has any use for you. Just like everyone else, he uses a watch. But his can't be like everyone else's. It's a 'Longines' that he has chosen. In a triumphant gesture, as if he's relieved of a great sadness, he raises it above his head. His watch shows ten-thirty-and you better set yours'" (Cappiello/Rennert, p. 139). This edition of the poster—put out by Vercasson eleven years after their initial printing—is the smallest version of all known formats and changes the bottom text to inform the public that Longines timepieces are available "at fine watchmakers."
**Est: $2,500-$3,000.**

**130. Cognac Albert Robin.** 1906.
47¹/₄ x 63 in./120 x 160 cm
Imp. Vercasson, Paris
Cond A–/Tears near top paper edge.
Ref: Cappiello/Rennert, 97; Cappiello, 267;
  Wine Spectator, 169; PAI-XLII, 152
"The Cognac Albert Robin firm was established by none other than Albert Robin in 1860 and the business has been in the family ever since. It produces fine cognac and pineau wine. Cappiello's representative bird of choice is more a fanciful rendering than an actual robin. Seeing as he was certainly more interested in stopping the viewer with a red-breasted, fiery-plumed bird than churning out an accurate reproduction of avian life, this should come as little surprise" (Cappiello/Rennert, p. 89).
**Est: $1,700-$2,000.**

**131**

**132**

LA PRINCESSE
DE
*BABYLONE*

Par Mons. de VOLTAIRE

A PARIS

JAVAL ET BOURDEAUX
*52*, AVENUE VICTOR HUGO

1928

**133**

**CAPPIELLO (cont'd)**

**131. Chiseled Pneumatic.**
4$^1$/$_2$ x 6$^1$/$_4$ in./11.5 x 16 cm
*Hand-signed gouache and crayon drawing.* Framed.
The rubber doesn't precisely meet the road in Cappiello's preliminary drawing for an unspecified tire promotion, but the rendering is stirring all the same. And the two conclusions that one can draw from the artwork are both equally persuasive: either the tire has been chiseled by some mythological smithy (which makes it all-but-indestructible) or the manufacturers have produced a pneumatic of such magnitude that even Vulcan himself couldn't puncture it. Brilliantly simple.
**Est: $2,000-$2,500.**

**132. Au Restaurant.** 1899.
18$^3$/$_4$ x 18$^1$/$_4$ in./47.5 x 46.4 cm
*Watercolor, gouache, ink and pencil artwork on paper.* Framed.
Certainly there's an element of "there to be seen" in this early Cappiello artwork—in all likelihood intended for the pages of *Le Rire*—but this charming blonde certainly seems as if she would attract the attentions of more than a single waiter. And from the way she's proffering an unneeded plate, it appears as if she's come to suspect that she'll be dining alone even though that hadn't been part of her original plan. Perhaps she should get together with the gentleman in the background who doesn't seem all that thrilled to be flying solo either. A wonderful scenario from the artist that proves that he's as keen an observer of the ebb and flow of daily life as he is a master of creative incongruity.
**Est: $7,000-$9,000.**

**133. La Princesse de Babylone, by Mons. de Voltaire.** 1928.
*Illustrated by Leonetto Cappiello.*
10 x 12$^7$/$_8$ in./25.5 x 32.6 cm
Published by Javel et Bourdeaux
Ref: Cappiello/Rennert, p. 13; PAI-XLIII, 603
In mint condition!
*One of a deluxe limited edition of forty copies printed on Japon Impérial vellum. The deluxe copy is the "Exemplaire imprimé spécialement pour Monsieur Robert Coulouma" and hand-signed by Cappiello. Comes with a separate folder containing four additional suites: one in color, one in two colors, one in blue and one in black-and-white. Leather cover*

**134**

**135**

**136**

lonian princess of the title. It's interesting that Voltaire chose a mythic love story to explore the precepts of an intellectual movement that advocated reason as a means to establishing an authoritative system of aesthetics, ethics, government and logic, which would in turn allow objective truths about the universe to reveal themselves. Though fantastical, the story provided the author with an open discourse to explore the wisdom of Eastern philosophy vis-à-vis the oppression of Occidental Inquisition.
**Est: $3,500-$4,000.**

**135. Aurore.**
$47^1/_4$ x 63 in./120.2 x 160 cm
Imp. Devambez, Paris
Cond A.
Ref: Cappiello/Rennert, 484; PAI-XXXIX, 200
"No doubt Aurore shoes are the Number One brand of quality footwear, but what convinces us most of all is the spring in the woman's stride. She's the one that persuades us that this is the brand that solves the problem of pedestrian comfort" (Cappiello/Rennert, p. 299).
**Est: $4,000-$5,000.**

**136. L'Oie d'Or.** ca. 1930.
$62^1/_2$ x $45^7/_8$ in./158.5 x 116.5 cm
Imp. Devambez, Paris
Cond A.
Ref: Cappiello/Rennert, 483; PAI-XLII, 483
Goose liver pâté gets the royal treatment: the golden goose wears a crown, and so does the open tin of the product, and the background is pure imperial scarlet. But, after all is said and done, what other design choice could be deemed appropriate for à brand that claims to be "The Queen of Foie Gras"?
**Est: $4,000-$5,000.**

Several Cappiello-illustrated books can be found in the Books & Periodicals section.

*design by Lorrain. In lavish presentation case.*
Voltaire's philosophical tale—originally published in 1752—gets a facelift in this 1928 special edition, thanks to Cappiello's fifteen color engravings. The results are first-rate, with Cappiello, free of commercial constraints, celebrating his artistic freedom with an even broader palette clearly brought about by a narrative utterly devoid of product placement.
**Est: $5,000-$6,000.**

**134. La Princesse de Babylone.** 1928.
$6^1/_4$ x $8^1/_2$ in./16 x 21.6 cm
*Hand-signed watercolor, pencil and ink artwork.*
Framed.
Perhaps it's not the lion lying down with the lamb, but it's pretty darn close. The assuaging artwork, intended as an illustration for Voltaire's French Enlightenment philosophy-laced novel, introduces us to Amazan, the shepherd vying for the hand of Formosante—the Baby-

**137**

**138**

## CAPPIELLO (cont'd)

**137. Champagne Vicomte de Castellane.** 1922.
47 x 62³/8 in./119.3 x 158.5 cm
Imp. Devambez, Paris
Cond A–/Unobtruaive folds.
Ref: Cappiello/Rennert, 362; PAI-XXXI, 346
"Florent de Castellane, a genuine viscount, founded the champagne company bearing his name in 1895; the business, now owned by the Laurent-Perrier group, survives to this day. Other than making wine, the viscount had another passion—collecting Cappiello posters. They have been retained by his estate and are occasionally shown to the public in traveling exhibitions. This pumpkin-pantalooned courtier, wearing the champagne's label as a breastplate, is a charming nod to the origin of the effervescent intoxicant" (Cappiello/Rennert, p. 231).
**Est: $8,000-$10,000.**

**138. Everyday Nude.** 1920.
18¹/4 x 27¹/4 in./46.4 x 69.2 cm
*Crayon drawing.* Framed.
In a day and age where breast augmentation and elective surgery have become something of a national obsession (not to mention practically the norm rather than the exception), it's refreshing to catch a glimpse of this Cappiello nude—a normal, mature woman, far from the "ideal" that's forever been perpetuated by youth-obsessed advertising and entertainment, but one who's clearly comfortable in her own skin all the same. Of course, none of this would be as powerful without Cappiello's great artistry—minimal, rough crayon strokes providing a soft and sensuous manifestation, a palpable sensuality that eases itself across the page with confident maturity, both on the part of the artist and his model.
**Est: $5,000-$6,000.**

**139**

**139. Buvez du Vin.** 1933.
15⁷/8 x 23¹/2 in./40.2 x 59.6 cm
Imp. Devambez, Paris
Cond A.
Ref: Cappiello/Rennert, 508; PAI-XXIX, 262
The French hardly need to be told to "drink wine and live happily," but here the French wine industry reminds them anyhow. (Another version of the poster—*see* PAI-IX,

**140**

107—adds the notion of the happiness that comes from drinking wine with fish.) And, indeed, we see happiness—in human form—emerging from a France-shaped mass of grapes. With at least 100 posters for wines and spirits to his credit, Cappiello was the logical choice for this commission—and the right choice as his brilliant solution proves. *This is the smaller format.*
**Est: $2,000-$2,500.**

141

143

142

## 140. Cognac Monnet. 1927.
51¹/₈ x 78¹/₂ in./130 x 199.5 cm
Imp. Vercasson, Paris
Cond A–/Unobtrusive tear in Monnet's "M."
Ref: Cappiello/Rennert, 443; PAI-XLIII, 207
"'Sunshine in a glass' is the company slogan of Cognac Monnet, and Cappiello, with a charming literal-mindedness, depicts exactly that—and, of course, the pure black background makes it stand out prominently. The cognac firm was founded in 1905 by Jean Gabriel Monnet, and is today part of the Hennessy Corporation" (Cappiello/Rennert, p. 275).
**Est: $4,000-$5,000.**

## EMIL CARDINAUX (1877-1936)

### 141. Palace Hotel/St. Moritz. 1922.
35³/₄ x 50¹/₄ in./89.9 x 127.6 cm
Wolfsberg, Zürich
Cond A–/Slight tears at paper edges.
Ref: Cardinaux, 74; PAI-XXXVII, 181
Cardinaux had a special talent for landscapes that could easily pass for fine paintings; he never lost the painterly touch in all his graphic work. This is clearly shown in this resort poster: a great impressionistic scene of a golfing party against the impressive alpine panorama. A native of Bern, Cardinaux went to Munich at the age of twenty-one to study law, but the bohemian atmosphere of the town got to him and he turned to art instead. He came under the influence of Franz van Stuck and Ferdinand Hodler, important symbolist painters, and started painting mountain landscapes in their style. But back in Bern, from about 1905 on, he turned to applied graphics as a means of livelihood and eventually became one of Switzerland's most honored posterists.
**Est: $10,000-$12,000.**

### 142. Schweiz/Bade und Luftkurorte.
25¹/₈ x 40¹/₈ in./63.8 x 101.9 cm
Wolfsberg, Zürich
Cond A–/Unobtrusive stain at bottom margin.
Ref: Cardinaux, 90 (var)
For the network of climactic and hydrothermal Swiss spas, from Lausanne in the southwest to Zurich in the northeast, Cardinaux unleashes this monumental design for the one means of travel certain to get you to any healthful getaway you please—the Swiss Railway. And though the focus is dominated by foreground classicism, it's important to note that tennis, musical entertainment and socialization are also given a nod, albeit only as background attractions.
**Est: $2,000-$2,500.**

### 143. Bally/Schuhe für Berg- und Wandersport. 1924.
35¹/₈ x 50¹/₈ in./89.3 x 127.4 cm
Wolfsberg, Zurich
Cond A–/Unobtrusive folds.
Ref: Cardinaux, 97 (var): PAI-XLII, 172
Cardinaux designed several posters for Bally between 1924 and 1936. Here, a stylish, but practically dressed group is cleverly arranged on an embankment with their legs dangling so that their Bally hiking boots fall to the center of the poster.
**Est: $2,500-$3,000.**

**Herbst in derSchweiz**

KENNEN SIE DEN ZAUBER DER SCHWEIZERSEEN, DIE MAJESTÄTISCHE
SCHÖNHEIT DER ALPEN IM HERBST?
(S.B.B.) FÜR JEDE AUSKUNFT ÜBER REISEN UND DEN AUFENTHALT IN DER (S.B.B.)
SCHWEIZ WENDE MAN SICH AN DIE SCHWEIZERISCHE VERKEHRSZENTRALE IN ZÜRICH
ODER LAUSANNE, SOWIE AN ALLE REISEAGENTUREN DER GANZEN WELT.
„WOLFSBERG-ZURICH"

**144**

**147**

## CARDINAUX (cont'd)

**144. Herbst in der Schweiz.** 1921.
$25^3/_8$ x $400^3/_8$ in./64.5 x 102.5 cm
Wolfsberg, Zürich
Cond A–/Slight ceasing near edges.
Ref: Cardinaux, 79 (var); PAI-XLI, 155
"Come to know the charm of the Swiss lakes, the
majestic beauty of the Alps in the autumn." The tender
sentiment expressed in this text seen at the bottom of
this Cardinaux design is more than adequately expanded
in the artist's painterly treatment seen above, its impressionistic style eliciting both the bittersweet languor
of seasonal transition and the splendor of autumnal
serenity. This is a part of a series in which Cardinaux
utilized all four seasons to promote ideal year-round
travel in Switzerland (for "Winter," *see* PAI-XI, 156).
**Est: $1,700-$2,000.**

## ALOIS CARIGIET (1902-1985)

**145. Frigor.**
$35^1/_2$ x $50^1/_4$ in./90.1 x 127.7 cm
Wolfsberg, Zürich
Cond A–/Unobtrusive tear at bottom paper edge.
Cappiello used a polar bear to advertise Caillier's
Frigor chocolate (*see* PAI-IX, 79) and Carigiet utilizes
a young Eskimo woman in order to promote the company's big chocolate taste. What conclusion can we
draw from this frigid association? Why, quite obviously
Frigor's so delicious that it gives you chills. Cailler is
one of Switzerland's oldest and most traditional brands
of chocolate, created in 1819. 1898 saw the construction of the very first chocolate factory in Broc and the
Frigor bar was introduced to the public in 1923. The
distinctive milk taste is still a unique feature of Cailler
chocolate, which is today a member of the Nestlé
family. Carigiet was trained as a decorator and house
painter, but in 1923 went to work at an ad agency and
drifted into poster design, theater decor and mural
painting. He later also gained some fame as an illustrator of children's books.
**Est: $1,400-$1,700.**

**145**

**146. Olympic Winter Games/St. Moritz 1948.**
$25^1/_4$ x $40^1/_2$ in./64 x 102.8 cm
Eidenbenz-Seitz, St. Gall
Cond A.
Ref: Olympics, p. 57; PAI-XXVIII, 466
A skier, rendered in bold crayon strokes, invokes vic-
tory as he stands at the top of his run with the Alps
spread out before him like a white-robed audience.
**Est: $1,700-$2,000.**

**146**

## A. M. CASSANDRE
## (Adolphe Mouron, 1901-1968)

**147. Le Nouvelliste.** 1924.
$46^5/_8$ x $62^3/_8$ in./118.5 x 158.4 cm
Hachard, Paris
Cond A–/Slight stains in borders; unobtrusive folds.
Framed.

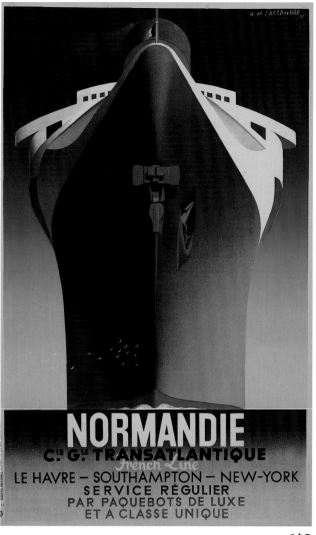

**148**

**149**

**150**

the news from on-high and the tricolored nationalistic sky transmits more than a few abstract notions. But one thing is perfectly clear: *Le Nouvelliste* is precisely the order for keeping up with the events of the day. *Rare!*
**Est: $8,000-$10,000.**

**148. Statendam.** 1928.
$30^5/8$ x $40^1/4$ in./77.7 x 102.2 cm
Nijgh & Van Ditmar, Rotterdam
Cond B/Slight tears, largely in margins. Framed.
Ref: Cassandre/BN, 18; Mouron, 104, Pl. 13;
    Brown & Reinhold, Pl. 12; Cassandre/Suntory, 20;
    PAI-XLII, 181
A dramatic arrangement of ventilation cowlings and funnels creates a powerful impact. In contrast with the rigid geometry of the ship's lines, the wavy trail of smoke provides the feeling of three-dimensional plasticity. A masterly poster by any standard. Typically when this poster appears in one of our auctions, it does so with the wide grey border having been trimmed-off (*see* PAI-XXX, 319). However, here it is in its full, complete form—just as Cassandre intended it to be seen. *With full grey border!*
**Est: $10,000-$12,000.**

**149. Normandie/Service Regulier.** 1935.
$24^1/2$ x 39 in./62.2 x 99 cm
Alliance Graphique/L. Danel, Paris
Cond A–/Slight tears in margins. Framed.
Ref: Cassandre/BN, 89; Mouron, 56;
    Brown & Reinhold, 53; Cassandre/Suntory, p. 91;
    Weill, 345; Deco Affiches, p. 33;
    Moderno Francés, p. 194; Musée d'Affiches, p. 65;
    PAI-XLIII, 234

Ref: Cassandre/BN, 2; Mouron, Ill. 5; Cassandre/Tokyo, 4;
    Cassandre/Suntory, p. 175; PAI-XXXI, 367
One of Cassandre's earliest works for a Lyonaise political daily. The stylized geometric design functions almost like an Art Deco Rorschach test, the combination of the archfully descending bird, beak-delivering

An advertisement for the *Normandie* and her "First Arrival in New York City on June 3 (1935)" touted that "The arrival in New York Harbor of the gigantic superliner *Normandie* will inaugurate a new era of transatlantic travel. She will set new standards of luxury and speed, steadiness comfort and safety . . . not merely the largest liner afloat (79,280 tons) . . . but in almost every respect *a new kind of liner!*" And in almost every respect, this Cassandre masterpiece was a new way of selling the glamour and excitement of ocean liner travel. A deceptively simple, but impressive design with the ship towering above us, a flight of small birds at bottom giving the image as much scale and strength as the imposing hull itself. The classic design appeared with several variants of text at the bottom; this is the version with the ship's name emblazoned over its ports of call.
**Est: $10,000-$12,000.**

**150. Philips Television.** 1951.
$12^1/8$ x $16^3/4$ in./30.7 x 42.5 cm
Smeets, Weert (not shown)
Cond A/P.
Ref: PAI-XVI, 196
An unusual, rare design by Cassandre used as a window card or point-of-purchase display by Philips, the Dutch electronics firm. It's a very intriguing first impression of television—Philips didn't even start producing sets until 1950. The only place where this poster is reproduced is in a Dutch book published to celebrate the 100th anniversary of the Philips company; even they didn't have recourse to a copy of the design, reproducing it instead from a promotional book of the printer, Smeets, in which it was included. It's doubtful that it was ever printed as a full size poster.
**Est: $2,500-$3,000.**

## A. M. CASSANDRE (cont'd)

**151. L'Oiseau Bleu.** 1929.
24¹/₄ x 39¹/₂ in./61.5 x 100.4 cm
Imp. L. Danel, Lille
Cond A–/Slight tears at edges.
Ref: Cassandre/BN, 29; Mouron, 18;
   Brown & Reinhold, 46, Pl. 10;
   Cassandre/Suntory, 56; Train à l'Affiche, 263;
   Affiche Réclame, 81; PAI-XXXVII, 184
"Speed is the theme (of this poster) with its cloud of
smoke swirling around the checkered red-and-white
signal—the only fixed point in the image—standing
out against a background of converging telegraph
wires. In a highly effective metaphor for speed, a pur-
ple martin (*oiseau bleu*) is substituted for the express
train hurtling past at full steam" (Mouron, p. 64).
**Est: $7,000-$9,000.**

**152. Pathé.** 1928
15¹/₂ x 23¹/₄ in./40 x 59.1 cm
Alliance Graphique, Paris
Cond A.
Ref: Cassandre/BN, 67 (var)
In his poster for an unspecified Pathé model, Cassandre "materializes the sound with an image of waves.
But here the concentric circles originate at a rooster,
the emblem of the firm, while the Pathé signature,
which is equally characteristic, is registered in the foreground: the arrangement of the letters guides the
reading, making the mark's graphics the focal point of
the message or, at least, of our immediate perception"
(Cappiello/BN, pp. 88 & 90). And in the presence of
Cassandre's hypnotic minimalism, it's rather difficult
to believe anything other than that the best wireless
receivers are manufactured by Pathé, which in this
case, can be found at Deshairs in Grenoble. *Rare!*
**Est: $4,000-$5,000.**

**153. L'Intransigeant.** ca. 1925.
29¹/₂ x 15³/₄ in./75 x 40 cm
Email Ed. Jean
Ref (All Var): Cassandre/BN, 5; Mouron, 21, Pl. 6; Cas-
   sandre/Suntory, p; PAI-XV, 194
*Enamel sign; overall excellent condition.*
Printed on both sides, this enamel sign—advertising
classified ads to be printed in the pages of the newspaper—reproduces Cassandre's classic image not only
once, but twice per side. "For the daily newspaper
*L'Intransigeant*, which bore 'the largest circulation of
any evening newspaper' as a subtitle, Cassandre
relates in *L'Affiche*, in December 1926, that his silent
partner had only given him the sole instruction of han-

dling the theme of information and left him alone after
that, embracing the project immediately, without asking for alterations. Refined, the composition directs
one's attention to the ear—towards which run tele-
graphic wires—the open mouth—which suggests a cry,
speech—and the eye—to which the blue pupil and
intensity are clearly attached. This profile becomes an
allegory of the newspaper: what is heard and what is
seen is immediately said, loud and clear. The framing,
while cutting-off the name of newspaper, restores its
popular name, *L'Intransigeant* being usually shortened to *L'Intran*" (Cassandre/BN, p. 43). *Rare!*
**Est: $8,000-$10,000.**

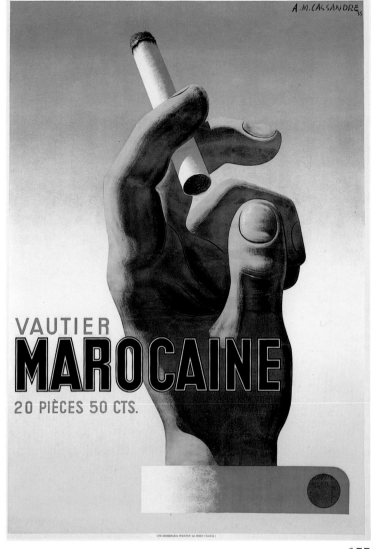

**154**

**155**

**156**

**154. Réglisse Florent.** 1925.
39¹/₄ x 59 in./99.7 x 150 cm
Imp. Hachard, Paris
Cond A.
Ref: Cassandre/BN, 6; Mouron, Pl. 5;
    Brown & Reinhold, 4; Cassandre/Suntory, 10;
    Moderno Francés, p. 154; PAI-XLIII, 238
To advertise a licorice pastille, Cassandre turns to
the "object poster," the new rage from Germany and
Switzerland. A big close-up of the product helps lodge
the label in the consumer's mind and produces a
simple, strong circle-based design.
**Est: $3,500-$4,000.**

**155. Marocaine.** 1935.
35¹/₈ x 50¹/₈ in./89 x 127.2 cm
Lith. Sauberlin & Pfeiffer, Vevey
Cond B+/Recreated borders.
Ref: Mouron, Ill. 181; PAI-XV, 201
In 1935, Cassandre created four tobacco posters that
were printed in Switzerland. One was for Pacific cigarettes (*see* PAI-XL, 284), one for Cesar cigars (*see*
PAI-XVII, 9), another for Kisroul pipe tobacco and this
one for Marocaine cigarettes. It's the rarest of the
four, a bold stroke: the hand at center, in natural skin
tones, gives us a sculptural effect, as if Cassandre
wanted to build a monument to this brand.
**Est: $5,000-$6,000.**

## HENRI CASSIERS (1858-1944)

**156. Ostende/Dover.** ca. 1900.
24¹/₄ x 39⁷/₈ in./61.6 x 101.4 cm
O. De Rycker & Mendel, Bruxelles
Cond B+/Unobtrusive tears at folds and top text area.
Ref: DFP-II, 1002; PAI-XL, 173 (var)
Fine detailing, both in the sympathetic portrayal of the
peasants and in the accurate depiction of the boat
and ship, acknowledges Cassiers as a fine draftsman,
as well as designer. In this German-language version of
the poster, the Belgian State Railway and Steamship
departments advertise thrice-daily, three-hour channel
crossings from Ostend to Dover aboard an apropos
trio of their ships: the *Princesse Elisabeth*, the *Jan
Breydal* and the *Pieter de Coninck*. A distinguished
Belgian painter and magazine reporter/illustrator turned
posterist, Cassiers became an aquarellist of note at
an early age, placing his work at many exhibitions and
earning various kudos. In the 1890s, he traveled as a
roving magazine contributor. In poster work, he stays
with his painterly style, most frequently depicting a
folksy scene to which text is added.
**Est: $1,400-$1,700.**

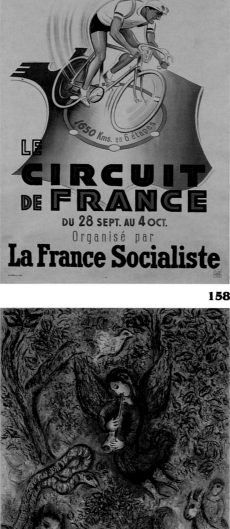

**158**

**159**

**160**

**157**

**161**

## E. CELOS

**157. Aperitif Clacquesin.** ca. 1910.
17¹/₈ x 31³/₄ in./43.5 x 80.6 cm
Imp. Chambrelent, Paris
Cond B+/Slight tears at folds and edges.
Everyone looks pretty thirsty in this Célos poster, so it would seem as if the Clacquesin delivery truck hasn't made its way to this hamlet a moment too soon. The locals don't seem to care all that much that the beverage is promoted as being "The Healthiest of the Aperitifs." They just want their Clacquesin and they want it now! And in case you're unfamiliar with this particular drink, allow me to point out that Clacquesin is a wood tar liquor, made with the resin of a pine tree. To each his or her own.
**Est: $1,000-$1,200.**

## CELLO

**158. Le Circuit de France.** 1944.
46⁵/₈ x 62¹/₂ in./118.4 x 158.8 cm
Imp. Bédos, Paris
Cond A-/Slight tears at edges.
The Tour de France is the most famous and prestigious road bicycle race in the world, held annually since 1903. However, during the years plagued by both World Wars, the race was suspended for obvious reasons. During World War II, the invading Germans wanted "normalcy" in their occupied territories and France without the Tour certainly wasn't normal. They asked Jacques Goddet—the editor of *L'Auto*, which owned and ran the Tour, and Tour de France director—to restart the race, offering to open the border between German-occupied France and Vichy France in order to make it happen. Goddet refused, but several other truncated stage races were held during that period, the most notable of which were the Grand Prix du Tour de France and the Circuit de France. Sponsored by *La France Socialiste*, the Circuit ran a total of 1,650 kilometers over its six-stage running. And though a World War II censorship stamp is clearly visible in the lower right corner, Cello's nationalistic vigor and spirit is unapologetically on display for all to see.
**Est: $1,400-$1,700.**

## MARC CHAGALL (1887-1985)

**159. Nice/Soleil, Fleurs.** 1962.
24¹/₄ x 39¹/₄ in./61.5 x 99.7 cm
Mourlot, Paris
Cond A/P.
Ref: Sorlier, p. 38; PAI-XL, 288
A mermaid with a bouquet characterizes the two aspects of Nice of interest to the ministry of tourism which commissioned the poster—the seaside and its exotic flora.
**Est: $1,500-$1,800.**

**160. Die Zauberflöte/Metropolitan Opera.** 1966.
25¹/₂ x 39¹/₄ in./64.7 x 99.7 cm
Mourlot, France
Cond A. Framed.
Ref: Sorlier, p. 107; PAI-XLII, 204

This is one of two posters for the opening season of the new Metropolitan Opera at Lincoln Center. It advertises the opening of February 19, 1967: Mozart's "Magic Flute" with sets and costumes by Chagall. Like its companion poster, it borrows a detail from "The Triumph of Music," one of the two large decorations by Chagall that flank the entrance to the opera house. A native of Vitebsk, Russia, Chagall arrived in Paris in 1910 and soon made a name for himself in art circles with his somewhat surreal, poetic vision that seemed best suited for illustrating dreams. Almost all his posters are taken from paintings and prints that were not originally created as posters, but many of them, because of their bold images and bright colors, turn out to make fine posters nonetheless.
**Est: $1,500-$2,000.**

**163**

**164**

**162**

**161. Metropolitan Opera/Opening September 1966.**
25$^1$/$_4$ x 39 in./64 x 99 cm
Mourlot, Paris
Cond A. Framed.
Ref: Sorlier, p. 109; Lincoln Center, 14;
    Theaterplakat, 223; PAI-XLII, 205
The second poster for the inaugural season of the Metropolitan Opera at Lincoln Center, New York, in 1966. According to Sorlier, the subject is the opera *Carmen*, and it's Rudolf Bing, the Met's director and the man who commissioned the Chagall works, who is represented as the central character.
**Est: $2,000-$2,500.**

## ROGER CHAPALET (1903-1995)

**162. Transatlantique/Linea Francesa.**
23$^1$/$_2$ x 39$^1$/$_2$ in./59.6 x 100.4 cm
J.A.D., Paris
Cond A.
Chapelet makes a pitch to Spanish-speaking potential cruisers—specifically potential male cruisers—with his swank Art Deco promotion for the Compagnie Generale Transatlantique where the skies are cloudless, the seas are calm and the boat is ninety-seven percent populated by half-dressed women. Permission to board! Chapelet was active primarily during the late-1950s/early-1960s.
**Est: $2,000-$2,500.**

## LOUIS CHARBONNIER (1874-1935)

**163. La Muse du Montmartre.**
33$^1$/$_2$ x 53$^3$/$_4$ in./85.2 x 136.5 cm
Imp. Caby & Chardain, Paris

Cond A–/Unobtrusive tears at folds.
You certainly didn't expect "The Muse of Montmartre" to be a bony spinster, fond of needlepoint and unguents, did you? No, no. Charbonnier's carefree fairy is definitely more along the lines of the mystical creature you'd expect to see serving as an inspiration to the residents of the hilltop commune in Paris' 18th arrondissement—lyrical, ethereal and fairly unconcerned with her state of dress (or, more appropriately, undress). Though the details of the poster would seem to indicate that the emporium in the shadow of the Moulin Rouge specialized in musical instruments and supplies, no definitive answer can be given as no history of the store appears to exist. However, in today's Paris, the Grand Hotel de Turin is the establishment that currently operates at 6 Rue Victor Massé.
**Est: $3,000-$4,000.**

## JEAN CHASSAING

**164. Aurore.**
45$^7$/$_8$ x 62$^3$/$_8$ in./116.5 x 158.5 cm
Imp. Daudé Frères, Paris
Cond A.
Ref: PAI-XL, 290
Chassaing puts forth a far more fashionista vision than Cappiello (*see* No. 135) in his promotion for Aurore shoes. The inexplicable, yet undeniable feminine quest for the perfect pair of shoes—which for the sake of argument could easily be dubbed "The Cinderella Syndrome"—is magnificently detailed in this spectacular Art Deco design for the inimitable line of Aurore footwear.
**Est: $2,500-$3,000.**

**165**

**166**

## JULES CHÉRET (1836-1932)

**165. Au Grand Turenne.** 1875.
33³/₄ x 47 in./85.6 x 119.4 cm
Imp. Jules Chéret, Paris
Cond B+/Unobtrusive folds.
Ref: Broido, 786; Maindron, 663; Célébrités, 74
"Many prosperous and highly respected clothing and fabric stores were located between the current place de la République and the rue du Louvre. For the firm 'Du Grand Turenne', situated on the corner of the Boulevard du Temple and the rue Charlot, the proximity of the street named Turenne after the famous Marshal of France (Henri de la Tour d'Auvergne, Vicomte de Turenne, 1611-1675) who fought against then served Louis XIV until his death, had to be a determining factor in the choice of this corporate name" (Célébrités, p. 52).
**Est: $2,000-$2,500.**

**166. A Voltaire/Cadeaux.** 1876.
34¹/₈ x 48 in./86.8 x 121.9 cm
Imp. Jules Chéret, Paris
Cond A–/Unobtrusive folds.
Ref: Broido, 758; Maindron, 637; Reims, 542;
   PAI-XXII, 263
Between 1875 and 1881, Chéret executed ten posters for this emporium promoting children's clothing and gifts. Here, the tots and their toys take center stage while a bust of Voltaire hovers benignly in the background.
**Est: $2,500-$3,000.**

**167. L'Horloge/Le Pékin de Pékin/Suiram.** 1877.
15⁵/₈ x 22⁷/₈ in./39.6 x 58.2 cm
Imp. Jules Chéret, Paris
Cond B+/Unobtrusive folds; slight stains at edges.
Ref: Broido, 153; Maindron, 133
Political correctness takes a back seat in this Chéret advertisement for "The Peking from Peking," a theatricality put together by a performer named Suiram. Though his career wasn't quite the stuff of legend, the poster presents Suiram as a flexible, bandy-legged virtuoso, no doubt intending to display that his gymnastic abilities were on par with the famed acrobats of China.
**Est: $2,000-$2,500.**

**168. La Fille du Meurtrier.** 1883.
34 x 48 in./86.2 x 121.8 cm
Imp. Chaix, Paris
Cond A.
Ref: Broido, 647; Maindron, 534
Though the legend of his graphic output may firmly be based in his bevy of colorful, lighter-than-air *Chérettes*, the fact of the matter remains that before he became the "go-to" posterist of Paris, Chéret had to worry about paying the bills, too. And one such way was to produce the promotional materials for the pulpy serialized novels that regularly appeared in the city's many publications. A task for which, as you can see for yourself in this seat-of-your-pants poster for "The Murderer's Daughter" (it could also translate as "The Murderer's Whore" if you were so inclined), he was no slouch either. Xavier de Montépin may not be an immediately recognizable literary name, but he did collaborate with Alexandre Dumas, père—author of *The Count of Monte Cristo, The Three Musketeers* and *The Man in the Iron Mask*—on a novel titled "Le Tour de Saint-Jacques."
**Est: $1,700-$2,000.**

**169. Hippodrome/Saison Equestre.** 1883.
16¹/₄ x 22¹/₄ in./41.2 x 56.5 cm
Imp. Chaix, Paris
Cond A–/Slight tears and stains at paper edges.
Ref: Broido, 404; Maindron, 326
1883 may be singled-out textually as an "Equestrian Season" here, but Chéret makes it abundantly clear that the Hippodrome is no one-trick pony, offering everything from acrobats to lion tamers. In all, Chéret created more than forty posters for the establishment between 1878 and 1888.
**Est: $1,400-$1,700.**

**170. Aux Buttes Chaumont/Jouets et Objets pour Etrennes.** 1885.
68¹/₄ x 47¹/₄ in./173.3 x 120 cm
Imp. Chaix, Paris
Cond B+/Slight tears and stains at folds.
Ref: Broido, 699 & Pl. 29; Maindron, 582

**168**

Not only is this rocking horse riding little lady spoiled-child-joy personified, she's the primary 2-sheet beneficiary of the largesse of an overindulger wise enough to shop for toys and gifts at the Aux Buttes Chaumont department store, vendors of everything from bowling sets to bugles and miniaturized livestock to sailboats. *One of the rarest of Chéret's posters!*
**Est: $6,000-$8,000.**

167

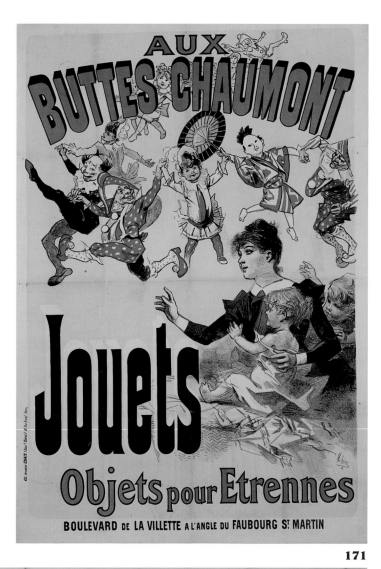

171

169

170

**174**

**175**

## JULES CHÉRET (cont'd)

**171. Aux Buttes Chaumont/Jouets.** 1886
48$^5$/$_8$ x 69$^1$/$_8$ in./123.5 x 175.6 cm
Imp. Chaix, Paris
Cond B/Slight tears at folds.
Ref: Broido, 700; Maindron, 583; Reims, 282;
    PAI-XXVII, 336
Toys are being promoted in this poster for Aux Buttes Chaumont department store, and Chéret's indulgent mom is willing to buy her fortunate children any of the delightful dolls their hearts desire.
**Est: $2,000-$2,500.**

**172. La Salamandre.** 1886.
34$^1$/$_4$ x 48$^1$/$_4$ in./87 x 122.5 cm
Imp. Chaix, Paris
Cond B+/Slight tears at folds.
Ref: Broido, 974 (var); Maindron, 804 (var);
    PAI-XXXVII, 208
The "Salamander" advertised here is a portable fire-place which "burns day and night without going out." The little girl's mother, or perhaps her governess, effortlessly brings the heater over for her benefit, and both are bathed in its warming glow in this Chéret domestic wonder. *This is the rare, 1-sheet format.*
**Est: $1,700-$2,000.**

**173. L'Écho de Paris/Courte & Bonne.** 1888.
34$^1$/$_4$ x 48$^3$/$_8$ in./87.7 x 122.4 cm
Imp. Chaix, Paris
Cond B–/Unobtrusive tears at folds and edges.
Ref: Broido, 657; Maindron, 544; Fit to Print, 5
"Chéret created a poster to advertise the sale of this novel about the pleasures and perils of Parisian high life (*see* PAI-XLI, 185). He followed that up with this poster advertising the serialization of the novel. Unusually, the elegant women are in the background here, while the stark corpse of the hero lies amid the cards and champagne which led him to his demise" (Fit to Print, p. 10).
**Est: $1,500-$1,800.**

**172**

**173**

**174. Théâtrophone.** 1890.
33$^7$/$_8$ x 47$^7$/$_8$ in./86 x 121.6 cm
Imp. Chaix, Paris
Cond B+/Slight tears, largely at paper edges.
Ref: Broido, 271; Maindron, 237; DFP-II, 192;
    Maitres, 33; PAI-XLII, 218

This was the earliest example of live transmission—for a fee, a subscriber could listen to an opera or a recital that was being picked up by a telephone hookup. The young woman doing the listening is one of Chéret's most charming models.
**Est: $3,000-$4,000.**

**178**

**176**

**177**

**179**

**175. Alcazar d'Été/Revue Fin de Siecle.** 1890.
34 x 49¹/₈ in./86.2 x 124.7 cm
Imp. Chaix, Paris
Cond B/Restored tears at folds and margins.
Ref: Broido, 170; Maindron, 150; DFP-II, 189;
PAI-XXXVII, 226
It's plain to see which of the two performers Chéret
prefers—the male is barely visible at left. But take
note of the square monocles that the couple shares,
each in a different eye—a whimsical touch.
**Est: $3,000-$4,000.**

**176. Grands Magasins du Louvre/Jouets, Etrennes
1891.**
34 x 96³/₈ in./86.2 x 245 cm
Imp. Chaix, Paris
Cond A-/Slight tears at folds.
Ref: Broido, 673; Maindron, 560; DFP-II, 203;
PAI-XXXIX, 226
A cascading 2-sheet image of overjoyed children with
the toys and gifts they've received from the Louvre
department store. Infectiously charming.
**Est: $2,500-$3,000.**

**177. Quinquina Mugnier.** 1897.
34¹/₈ x 96³/₈ in./86.7 x 244.6 cm
Imp. Chaix, Paris
Cond A-/Restored tears, largely near paper edges.
Ref: Broido, 882; PAI-XXV, 256
The pert sweet-faced waitress alone is enough to convince us of the merits of the beverage, and Chéret appears to be aware of it, as he leaves out all background
other than shaded blue in this 2-sheet design. The client
was a company started in 1863 by Frédéric Mugnier,
who prepared a potion from a wine base flavored with
blackberries and cherries and started selling it as an
aperitif. At the time this poster was prepared, Mugnier
had one of the largest distilleries in Dijon.
**Est: $1,700-$2,000.**

**178. Jardin de Paris/Champs-Elysées.** ca. 1890.
16³/₄ x 22¹/₂ in./42.5 x 57.2 cm
Imp. Chaix, Paris
Cond A.
Romance and intrigue are implicit—flowers, fans and
clandestine encounters really couldn't be implying
much else—in this straightforward Chéret creation for
the café-concert next door to the Pavillon de l'Horloge.

Joseph Oller, owner of the Moulin Rouge, took over
the Jardin de Paris, which remained a popular nocturnal
destination until it closed in 1914. *Rare!*
**Est: $1,200-$1,500.**

**179. Elysée Montmartre/Bal Masqué.** 1891.
14¹/₂ x 22 in./37.5 x 55.9 cm
Imp. Chaix, Paris
Cond B_/Slight tears; horizontal fold. Framed.
Ref: Broido, 321; Maindron, 261; PAI-XXXVII, 241
"One of the big Paris dance halls advertises by showing a couple enjoying themselves with abandon. One
of Chéret's assets as a posterist was the way he gave
his figures motion; there is a swing and a rhythm in
his revelers that sweeps us right along with them. It's
hard to imagine one of Chéret's figures as a household drudge or seamstress; they seem to exist only
for the moment, heedlessly bound for pleasure alone.
The posters make you forget everything mundane—
and therein lies the master posterist's greatest talent"
(Gold, p. 100). *This is the smaller format.*
**Est: $1,200-$1,500.**

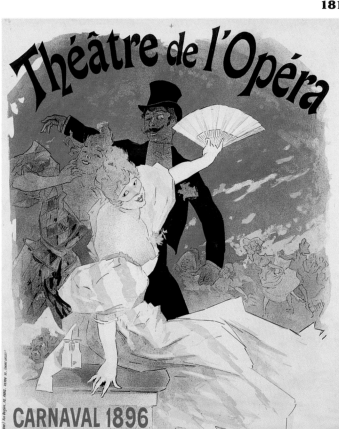

## JULES CHÉRET (cont'd)

**180. Folies-Bergère/Fleur de Lotus.** 1893.
$34^3/_4$ x $48^1/_8$ in./88.2 x 122.2 cm
Imp. Chaix, Paris
Cond A-/Unobtrusive folds.
Ref: Broido, 126; Maindron, 114; Abdy, p. 356; Reims, 366;
     Dance Posters, 27; Wine Spectator, 7; PAI-XXXVIII, 275
"Chéret executed more than 60 posters for the Folies-Bergère between 1874, when the first major expansion of the business took place, and 1897, the very zenith of its success. The names of the revues hardly matter, as all were meant to present beautiful girls in attractive settings, and for *Fleur de Lotus*, Chéret makes a spectacularly exuberant design, a masterpiece of graceful motion and pure joy" (Wine Spectator, 7).
**Est: $7,000-$8,000.**

**181. Pastilles Géraudel.** 1895.
34 x $48^5/_8$ in./86.5 x 123.5 cm
Imp. Chaix, Paris
Cond B+/Slight tears and stains, largely at edges; image and colors
          excellent. Framed.
Ref: Broido, 910; DFP-II, 259; Health Posters, 6; Gold, 32; PAI-XL, 292
Prancing through a blizzard as if she were two-stepping through falling cherry blossoms, this blithe figure is courting a cough that only Géraudel lozenges could fend off. Which stands to reason since their common sense slogan, "'If you cough, take Géraudel Pastilles' appears like a leitmotiv in all the publicity campaigns for the product, whether in France, or as far abroad as China . . . This is one of the most striking examples of the work by Jules Chéret . . . The clarity of the color is astonishing and denotes the influence of Impressionist painting" (Health Posters, p. 14).
**Est: $8,000-$10,000.**

**182. Théâtre de l'Opéra/Carnaval 1896/11 Janvier.** 1895.
$34^1/_2$ x $48^3/_8$ in./87.5 x 123 cm
Imp. Chaix, Paris
Cond B+/Slight stains at paper edges; unobtrusive folds.
Ref: Broido, 293; Maitres, 9 (var); DFP-II, 251 (var); Reims, 528; PAI-XXXI, 393
Like virtually all of the posters Chéret did for the dances at this theater between 1892 and 1897, the design features a profiled woman in a billow-ing dress looking out over her shoulder as a shadowy male figure and other

**183**

**185**

**186**

Cond A–/Unobtrusive folds; slight printer's creases on left side. Framed.
Ref: Broido, 368; DFP-II, 256; Wine Spectator, 19; Gold, 131; PAI-XXXVII, 276
The skater in the red-and-yellow striped skirt is one of the loveliest of the several designs that Chéret created for the Paris ice-skating rink between 1893 and 1900. And with the help of her partner—umbered by an eclipse of radiant beauty—creates a compelling vision of oppositional balance that couldn't possibly be more appealing. *This is the larger format.*
**Est: $12,000-$15,000.**

**185. Palais de Glace.** 1896.
15⅝ x 22 in./39.7 x 56.1 cm
Imp. Chaix, Paris
Cond A–/Slight tears at paper edges.
Ref: Broido, 370; Reims, 454; PAI-XLI, 212
Although the size is identical to the *Courrier Français* format, this is, in fact, a separate printing—seen here with unusually wide borders—and not part of that series. *This is the smaller format.*
**Est: $2,500-$3,000.**

**186. Quinquina Dubonnet.** 1896.
15⅛ x 22¼ in./38.5 x 56.4 cm
Imp. Chaix, Paris
Cond A.
Ref: Broido, 879; PAI-XLII, 233
A charming lass displaying a bottle of the aperitif, as well as her glass, which we can only assume she intends to consume once her moment in the spotlight has passed. This version of the image comes from the series Chéret contributed to the *Courrier Français*, a lively 12-page weekly magazine, started in 1894, which championed the work of many leading posterists. The horizontal crease present in the poster is due to the folding of the magazine for distribution and in no way detracts from the condition.
**Est: $2,000-$2,500.**

revelers dance around her. Chéret would do a single design each winter and it would be repeated with varying text throughout the season. For 1896, the charmer's dress is striped in two shades of green and she gestures to her escort with a fan. It is interesting to see how Chéret, reworking the same visual ingredients, always keeps us interested.
**Est: $5,500-$6,500.**

**183. Parfumerie-Distillerie Monaco/Iris Villa.** 1897.
34⅛ x 48¼ in./86.8 x 122.5 cm
Imp. Chaix, Paris

Cond A–/Slight stains at edges.
Ref: Broido 940; PAI-XLI, 215
The message in Chéret's delicately-handled design is clear: If you use Iris Villa fragrances, you will feel as if you are carrying an armful of flowers.
**Est: $5,000-$6,000.**

**184. Palais de Glace.** 1896.
33¾ x 48 in./85.7 x 122 cm
Imp. Chaix, Paris

**187**

**188**

## JULES CHÉRET (cont'd)

**187. Palais de Glace.** 1900.
$16^1/_8$ x $25^5/_8$ in./41 x 60 cm
Imp. Chaix, Paris
Cond A.
Ref: Broido, 373
In this poster, one of the rarest in the Palais de Glace cycle, the flirtatious auburn-haired temptation in her revealing pink get-up has the undivided attention of the mustachioed gentleman holding her hand. The feasibility of her skating form is obviously not in question. Note that this is the rare, smallest format version of the poster, not a part of the *Courrier Français* series.
**Est: $3,000-$3,500**

**188. Seated Gentleman.**
$7^3/_4$ x $10^3/_4$ in./19.7 x 27.3 cm
*Hand-signed oil painting on board.* Framed.
*Dedicated to Monsieur Jarta; dated "Aout" (August).*
With all of his spectacular poster work, it's easy to forget that Chéret was also a fine painter, as much in command of the palette as the lithographic stone. So to that end, we present you with this stately oil work that facilely whisks-away the notion that Chéret was a single-medium artist. Though his identity is unknown (though we suspect he may very well be the "Monsieur Jarta" to which the painting is dedicated) his bearing —or more importantly Chéret's ability to transfer his bearing to the canvas—indicates an aura of respectability that transcends mere reproduction.
**Est: $3,000-$4,000.**

## ALFRED CHOUBRAC (1853-1902)

**189. Au Joyeux Moulin Rouge.**
$31^7/_8$ x $46^1/_2$ in./81 x 118.1 cm
Lith. F. Appel, Paris
Cond A.
Ref: PAI-XXXIX, 237

**190**

**191**

Simply put, Paris is dancing at the "Cheerful" Moulin Rouge, the hotspot that virtually single-handedly created the cancan craze, opening its doors on October 6, 1889. And if you can't believe a revealing reveler and her well-appointed partner, well then who can you believe? Choubrac was one of the pioneers of French poster art; in 1884, when Maindron published his first article on posters, he listed only nine active posterists known to him, and included the three poster artists whose work made up the first poster exhibition, held that same year in the Passage Vivienne in Paris: Alfred and Léon Choubrac and Jules Chéret.
**Est: $3,000-$4,000.**

**189**

**193**

Josepha enjoyed spicy food, Rosa's tastes were somewhat on the bland side. More peculiarly, Rosa gave birth to a son and both women nursed the infant. Their lives were cut short when at age forty they died in the influenza epidemic of 1918 while appearing in Chicago.
**Est: $1,500-$2,000.**

### 192. Derouville Nancey.
31$^1$/4 x 47$^1$/4 in./79.3 x 120 cm
Atelier Choubrac, Colombes, Seine
Cond A.
Choubrac captures the muscular dynamism of this dancing team's routine, effectively translating their intense movement to the stationary medium of the poster, most especially in the forceful flutter of the woman's golden skirt and her partner's vertical aptitude.
**Est: $1,700-$2,000.**

### 193. Twenty Costume Designs.
Each: 9$^3$/4 x 12$^3$/4 in./25 x 32.5 cm
Ref; PAI-XXXV, 263
*Gouache and ink on boards*; images are excellent; slight stains at edges.
All but six of these costume designs are hand-signed. Choubrac's involvement with theater extended beyond posters and into costume and set designs as well. The same charm and imagination that he brought to bear in posters are evident in these original drawings.
**Est: $1,500-$2,000.** (20)

### 190. Brunin.
36$^1$/4 x 51$^1$/8 in./92.2 x 129.8 cm
Atelier Choubrac, Colombes s. Seine
Cond B+/Tears along folds and edges.
There are people from every entertainment era who like to believe that their generation bore the true innovators, the genuine architects of virtually every diversionary style. But long before "Forbidden Broadway," *Saturday Night Live* or Rich Little popularized celebrity impersonation, Brunin performed on the stages of France, billed, not surprisingly, as a "Comic Original." It's not altogether clear to which gender the performer should be assigned, but one thing is sure—he/she certainly was willing to skewer the signature appearances of the biggest names of their epoch, from Sarah Bernhardt to Loïe Fuller.
**Est: $1,000-$1,200.**

### 191. Theatre de la Gaité/Rosa-Josepha.
31$^3$/8 x 46 in./79.6 x 117 cm
Lith. F. Appel, Paris
Cond A.
Behold Rosa and Josepha Blazek, a truly unique sister/sister team that captivated music hall and vaudeville audiences in the late-19th/early-20th centuries, both in Europe and the United States. Choubrac's poster for their appearance at the Theatre de la Gaité presents the Blazek's unflinchingly—conjoined pygopagus twins that earned a living in the song-and-dance game. Born on January 20, 1879, in Skerychov, Bohemia, the pair that shared a common lumbar region (as well as other more delicate regions) always made it perfectly clear that, despite their attachment, they were very different people—Rosa always walked forward, Josepha always walked backwards; Rosa liked wine, Josepha liked beer;

**194**

**195**

**196**

**197**

double-eagle crown, studded with real amethysts, opals, and turquoises" (Bernhardt/Drama, p. 9).
**Est: $5,000-$6,000.**

## P. R. CLAUDIN

**196. Nancy 1912.**
31 x 46³/₄ in./78.9 x 118.8 cm
Lith. Berger-Levrault, Nancy
Cond A−/Unobtrusive tears at bottom edge.
Ref: Toujours Plus Haut, p. 98; Envolèrent, 98; Looping the Loop, 53; PAI-XX, 9
"Nancy, a town in northeastern France, was the scene of a representative group of exhibition fliers in the spring of 1912. Noted for its university, library, and museum of archeology, Nancy also possessed historical military importance having been occupied by the Prussians in the Franco-Prussian War of 1870 and 1871. Typical of the day, spectators were regaled with various events for speed, altitude, and duration, with a variety of biplanes and monoplanes sharing in the prizes. Speed was king that year. A mile-a-minute was no longer considered exceptional and machines were more rugged in construction, more powerful, and more stable than the relatively uncertain craft of the first few years of flight . . . As indicated by their preponderance in the picture, monoplanes like the Blériot were rapidly coming into their own, rivaling the biplanes of

## CHOUBRAC (cont'd)

**194. Corsets Baleinine Incassables.** ca. 1900.
49 x 35¹/₂ in./124.5 x 90 cm
Imp. Bourgerie, Paris
Cond B+/Slight staining and tears at folds.
Ref: Lingerie, p.16; Gold, 120; PAI-XXX, 75
A captivating design for Corsets Baleinine Incassables. At the turn of the century, all women wore corsets, whether they were generously proportioned or as skinny as the legendary comedienne Polaire, who reputedly used a dog collar for a belt. Here we have a cavalcade of belles in their corsets with stays made out of un-breakable whalebone for "softness, elegance, and long wear." It comes as no great surprise that during the Belle Epoque "the textile industry was humming: After the corset it took a camisole, blouse, petticoats, and ankle-length dress before the wearer was ready to face the outside world" (Gold, p. 83).
**Est: $2,500-$3,000.**

## GEORGES CLAIRIN (1843-1919)

**195. Théodora/Théâtre Sarah-Bernhardt.** ca. 1896.
29³/₈ x 80¹/₂ in./74.6 x 204.5 cm
Imp. F. Champenois, Paris
Cond B+/Slight folds and creases.
Ref: Bernhardt/Drama, p. 139; PAI-XLII, 45
A two-sheet poster by a painter and illustrator who was a close friend of Sarah Bernhardt, but did few posters. He gives us a very sensitive portrait, full of feeling and majesty, of Bernhardt as the famous Byzantine empress Theodora. It is an almost Mucha-like treatment, largely in black and white, with metallic gold in the background. If it lacks Mucha's embellishments and decorative style, it is nonetheless impressive. "The costumes for *Théodora* . . . are among the richest and most thoroughly researched in fin-de-siècle stage design. Setting off the lavishly bejeweled clothing . . . are sumptuous accessories that include Theodora's

**198**

**199**

Henry Farman and his imitators. Air addicts, however, were not yet prepared to decide between one or the other. The main interest of the public lay in the sheer novelty and excitement of watching man navigate the air" (Looping the Loop, p. 81).
**Est: $2,500-$3,000.**

## E. CLÉRISSI

**197. Monaco.**
24¹/₂ x 39¹/₄ in./62.5 x 99.4 cm
Heliochrome Sadag, Bellegarde
Cond B+/Restored borders.
We've seen plenty of images of this principality serving as a backdrop for accelerating vehicles (*see* Nos. 1-28), but here we get a good look at the picturesque Mediterranean destination without having to look past race cars to do so. In order to remind us—as if we'd forgotten—that the PLM railway services the area, Clérissi

sets the viewer in Moneghetti, Monaco's hilly district that overlooks Fontvielle and Monaco-Ville, the capital quarter constructed atop a rocky promontory on the site of a 13th-century Genovese fortress, the towers of which are still present and well-preserved.
**Est: $1,000-$1,200.**

## PAUL COLIN (1892-1986)

**198. André Renaud.** 1929.
46¹/₄ x 62⁵/₈ in./120 x 159 cm
Imp. H. Chachoin, Paris
Cond A. Framed.
Ref: Colin, 39; Colin Affichiste, 74; Art Deco, p. 99; PAI-XLIII, 282
The two pianos that André Renaud simultaneously played look like a double exposure, but, like all the geometric "tricks" of Colin, they are deliberately drawn for maximum effect. And the effect that Colin seeks

here—to overwhelm us with the wizardry of Renaud— is achieved by the sheer mass of the combined pianos.
**Est: $20,000-$25,000.**

**199. Sylvie.** 1928.
43¹/₂ x 60 in./110.5 x 152.5 cm
H. Chachoin, Paris
Cond B+/Unobtrusive tears near upper left corner. Framed.
Ref: Phillips II, 188
Though she may not have achieved the name recognition of other single-moniker performers—such as Charro, Prince or Cher—Sylvie has one thing none of those better-known celebrities have—a promotional poster portrait executed by Colin. Sadly, seeing as Sylvie isn't precisely an uncommon name in the world of French entertainment, none of the specifics of her talent could be uncovered.
**Est: $1,500-$2,000.**

CHAMPS
ÉLYSÉES

MUSIC
HALL

PAUL
COLIN

LES FÉERIES FANTASTIQUES
DE LA LOÏE FULLER

H. CHACHOIN Imp. PARIS. 1925

**200**

## PAUL COLIN (cont'd)

**200. Champs-Elysees/La Loie Fuller.** 1925.
$46^3/_8$ x $62^1/_8$ in./117.7 x 157.8 cm
Imp. H. Chachoin, Paris
Cond B+/Slight tears at folds.
Ref: Colin, 21; Colin Affichiste, 4; PAI-XXI, 145
"Josephine Baker and the Revue Nègre would be a hard act to follow for anyone less noted and less experienced than 'La Loïe,' but the dancer who had captivated Paris for over thirty years was still up to the task. When she came to the Champs-Élysées . . . she was 63 years old. 'Old, but still very interesting,' recalls Colin . . . It was her use of lighting effects and wind machines and other devices, all of which she devised herself in her own laboratory, that turned her appearance into a spectacular, 'psychedelic' light-and-motion show . . . A year later, in 1926, she gave her final performance in London; she died in 1928. And how successfully Colin has caught

the swirling rotating motion of the dancer with this circular design. To hold up this poster to the Loie Fuller designs of Chéret, Lautrec, Orazi and others, is to gain an instant lesson in the history and progress of the poster and to appreciate the fact that Colin ranks with equal stature with these luminaries of the medium" (Colin, pp. 7 & 8). This design is very different from almost all Colin posters in forsaking the figurative and concentrating on form and color.
**Est: $40,000-$50,000.**

**201. Loie Fuller.** ca. 1925.
45 x $59^1/_4$ in./114.3 x 150.5 cm
*Newly-discovered, hand-signed original gouache, watercolor, ink and crayon maquette.* Framed.
Colin indicated that he had to create the poster for Loie Fuller (*see* previous lot) before actually meeting

her, but that thereafter he created another poster. That poster was never printed, but as with the following five other pieces, this artwork was discovered in the office of his art school in Paris. This remarkable modernist vision with surrealist overtones stands on its own as an important document of Art Deco significance. It's interesting to compare the previously seen poster and this masterful maquette—whereas the poster still places the dancer in the eye of a prismatic hurricane, this artwork—doubtlessly enriched by having seen Fuller in-person—casts the dancer as the very flame of pyrotechnic innovation, a flash-and-swirl of conflagrant colors to which no corporeal entity is attached. Colin, in a move that can be described as nothing short of genius, captures the precise spirit of the performer without requiring her presence. Simply and utterly brilliant.
**Est: $30,000-$40,000.**

FÉÉRIES
FANTASTIQUES

LOÏE
FULLER

PAUL
COLIN

## PAUL COLIN (cont'd)

### 202. Comedie des Champs-Elysées. 1926.
42 x 56³/₄ in./106.6 x 144.2 cm
*Hand-signed gouache, ink and crayon maquette.* Framed.
Ref: PAI-I, 292 (var)
Whereas the previously seen version of this artwork contained no text
whatsoever (*see* PAI-I, 292), this maquette places the names of some of
the performers in the waves before the hull of the vessel. The name of the
theater is even specified at bottom of the design. And it's these bits of
information that allow us to specifically identify what this artwork was
intended to advertise. Among the adrift names we find that of Louis Jouvet
(1887-1951), an actor, director, designer and technician, considered by
many to be one of the most influential figures of the French theater in the
Twentieth Century. He served as the director of the Comédie des Champs-
Elysées between 1923 and the mid-1930s and it was during this period
that he would appear in the French adaptation of Sutton Vane's "Outward
Bound" ("Le Grand Large"). The unusual play (originally produced in 1923)
revolved around a group of passengers who find themselves making an
ocean voyage on a ship that seems to have no crew. Slowly they realize
that they are dead and bound for the after world, which is both heaven
and hell. The highly successful play, whose content clearly presages future
twisted tales such as those that appeared on "The Twilight Zone," ran for a
total of 190 performances at the Comédie des Champs-Elysées.
**Est: $6,000-$8,000.**

### 203. Oreum.
26³/₄ x 38¹/₈ in./68 x 97 cm
*Hand-signed gouache, ink and crayon maquette.* Framed.
In colloquial Korean vernacular, the word "oreum" translates as both
"secondary volcano" and "climbing up." And though it's unlikely that
neither Colin nor the owners of this boutique were aware of this fact, it
seems only appropriate that if someone should find themselves with a
sudden upheaval of discretionary income and felt the urge to make an
appropriately social-climbing purchase, they might want to stop into Oreum
for the baubles to match the occasion. Colin's artwork is resplendent, a
tidy Art Deco paean to the good life.
**Est: $8,000-$10,000.**

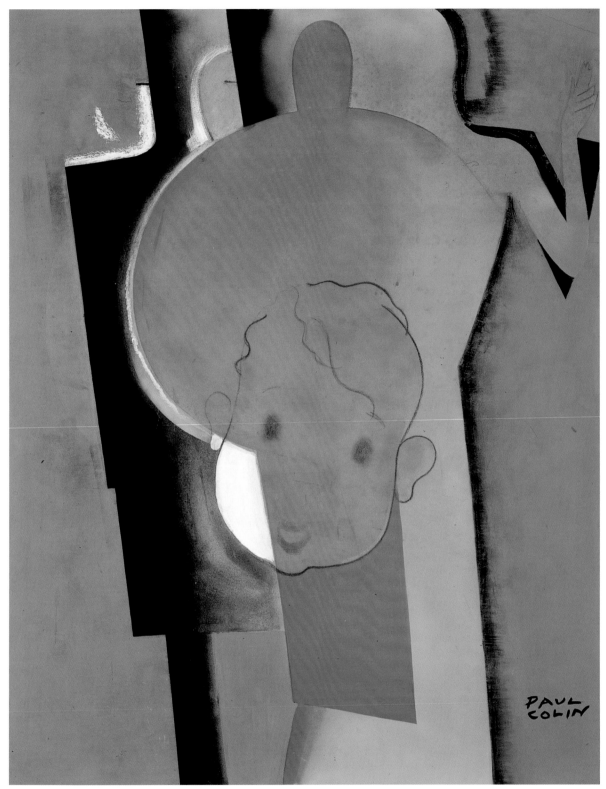

205

**204. Jean-Pierre Aumont.** 1935.
46 3/4 x 62 in./118.7 x 157.5 cm
*Hand-signed watercolor, gouache and crayon maquette; penciled-in instructions to printer upper-right.*
Ref (Both Var): Colin Affichiste, 89; PAI-XV, 332
Colin looks at the actor both objectively and subjectively—in the completed poster (*see* PAI-XV, 232) as in the original artwork on display here. At left, the camera's view; at right, the artistic impression using two shades of yellow—sand and cadmium—and the merest hint of the features that tend to stick in one's mind, such as the eyes and the well-groomed hair. Jean-Pierre Aumont was born in 1909, made his debut in the theater at age twenty and eventually became a big film star in France, appearing on the screen regularly between 1931 and 1976. He even made a few guest appearances in Hollywood productions, such as "Lili" in 1953. During World War II, he fought with the Free French and was decorated with the Croix de Guerre, as well as the Legion d'Honneur.
**Est: $4,000-$5,000.**

**205. Bal des Petits Lits Blancs.** 1930.
41$^1$/2 x 52$^5$/8 in./105.3 x 133.6 cm
*Hand-signed watercolor, gouache and crayon maquette.* Framed.
Ref (Both Var): Colin Affichiste, 119; PAI-XXXII, 275
By the time it made its way to a poster completion, this original artwork promoting the annual Parisian benefit gala may have become a bit more geometrically well-attended (*see* PAI-XXXII, 275). However, one thing remains a constant: helping children in need was the very heart of the event, and the beaming innocence of the central visage—contrasted off the severe angles of the background revelers—delivers the message with poignant simplicity. Colin pulls this off with such breezy nonchalance that it's almost easy to overlook the fact that this avant-garde creation—influenced as much by Cubism and Modernism as it is by Art Deco—isn't merely just a well-crafted maquette: it's one of the top paintings of the period. And to overlook such an accomplishment would indeed be a disservice.
**Est: $13,000-$15,000.**

**206**           **207**

**206. Yvonne Guillet.** 1931.
46¹/₂ x 62¹/₄ in./118 x 158 cm
*Hand-signed watercolor, gouache and crayon*
*maquette.*
Ref: Colin, 54 (var)
Apart from a tonal shift away from golden to a more
profound pink, this original artwork for Colin's Guillet
design has changed little—if at all—in its journey to
poster fruition. Yvonne Guillet first sang operettas in
the outskirts of Paris. She had a lead in the revue "'Nu,
Nu, Nunette' (Nude, Nude, Nunette) at the Concert
Mayol in 1926 (to tie-in with the 'No, No, Nanette' triumph over at the Mogador) and was also featured in
'Quel beau nu!' (What beautiful nudity!) and 'La revue
des femmes nouvelles' (The revue of the new women),
all of which exalted the beauty of minimally-dressed
women. In 1930 she became a star of Henri Varna's
revue 'Très exitante' at the Concert Mayol, with Doris
Stroeva. She retired from the stage shortly after and
married the playwright and writer of revues, Pierre
Varennes. As with . . . so many (other designs) by Colin,
the central figure stands straight and the background
provides the dance or other movement. There is little
hint of her earlier roles here: She is so very proper
and formal that one is tempted to call it a put-on"
(Colin, p. 9).
**Est: $6,000-$8,000.**

**207. Jane Marnac/Au Temps des Valses.** 1930.
13¹/₂ x 20 in./36 x 50.8 cm
*Hand-signed gouache and ink maquette on paper.*
Framed.
Ref (All Var): Colin, 52; Colin/Affichiste, 15;
    PAI-XLII, 242
"She has been called the most Parisian of all stage stars
and in her 90 active years (1886-1976) Jane Marnac
played hundreds of roles in the theatre and sang in
numerous operettas. Colin met her at the Apollo, where
he was kept busy with decors, programs, advertisements and posters. It was there she created the French
version of the celebrated 'Trial of Mary Dugan,' and,
in 1930, starred in the Noel Coward operetta, 'Waltz
Time,' titled 'Au Temps des Valses' in Saint-Grenier's
adaptation for the French stage" (Colin, p. 9). Apart
from a slightly smaller size and a gown that's a paler
shade of green, the artwork seen here remained virtually intact upon poster completion.
**Est: $5,000-$6,000.**

**208. Le Nouveau-Né.**
44³/₄ x 61 in./113.5 x 155 cm
Imp. Bedos, Paris
Cond B/Tears, largely at folds and paper edges.
Just as a seedling needs proper care to grow into a
flower in full bloom, so does an infant require loving

**210**

**208**

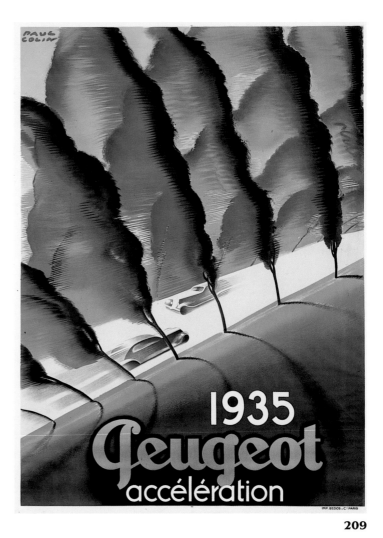

**209**

**211**

care and appropriate accouterment to mature into a fully-realized being. And so the shop with a name that doesn't mince words (could there possibly be a more direct appellation than "Newborn" when it comes to a store that specializes in the needs of babies) commissioned Colin to trot out there wares in an appropriate family-friendly fashion. And the result is fantastic—practical, cute and endearing. Rare!
**Est: $2,000-$2,500.**

**209. Peugeot.** 1935.
46⁷/₈ x 62³/₈ in./119 x 158.5 cm
Imp. Bedos, Paris
Cond A–/Unobtrusive slight stains.
Ref: Modern Poster, 173; Auto Show I, 79;
    Art & Auto, p. 181; PAI-XLI, 234
Stately poplars lining country roads like green sentinels are commonplace in France, and Colin makes them appear to bend and sway to the swift passage of the car zipping past them. Does it give us any technical information about Peugeot? No, but we can practically hear the rustle of the leaves stirred up in the car's wake, and that's a much more effective way to convince us of the car's merits.
**Est: $12,000-$15,000.**

**210. Paris.** 1945.
24¹/₂ x 39¹/₄ in./62 x 99.7 cm
Imp. Art et Tourisme, Paris
Cond A.
Ref: Colin Affichiste, 180; Colin, 72; PAI-XXXV, 292
"The war was over; it was a time for rebuilding and reminding Frenchmen, as much as visitors from abroad, that Paris was still there, in all its magnificence. This poster, commissioned by the French National Railways (S.N.C.F.) appeared in all the provincial railroad stations. Three of the capital's most important and enduring symbols are represented—the Arch of Triumph, the Cathedral of Notre Dame and the Eiffel Tower—with doves circling above them and the outlines of the city" (Colin, p. 10).
**Est: $1,000-$1,200.**

**211. Vichy/Mai-Octobre.** 1948.
24⁵/₈ x 38⁷/₈ in./62.6 x 98.8 cm
Imp. Wallon
Cond B+/Slight tears at paper edges.
Ref: Colin Affichiste,183; PAI-XXV, 279
"Having developed a bad reputation during the Second World War as the seat of the collaborationist government, the city of Vichy, once the war was over, tried to regain its reputation as a pleasant, quiet spa, famous worldwide for its mineral water. Colin's helter-skelter montage evokes all of its pleasures" (Colin Affichiste, p. 130).
**Est: $1,200-$1,500.**

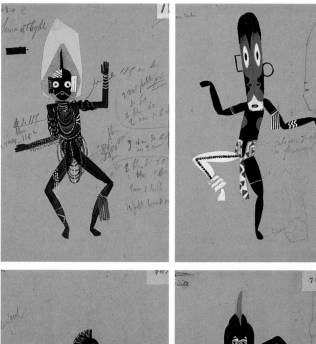

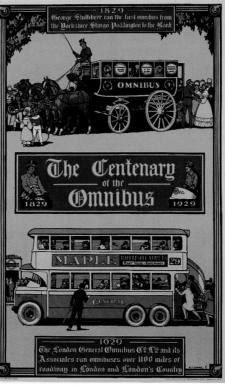

213            214            215

## PAUL COLIN (cont'd)

### 212. Sculpture Nègre: Five Costume Designs and a Backdrop Design. 1929.
Costumes: 11³/₈ x 17¹/₄ in./29 x 43.8 cm
Backdrop: 30 x 22¹/₄ in./76.2 x 65.5 cm
*Gouache, watercolor, crayon and ink artwork; unsigned.* Framed.
Ref: Ballet Suédois, p. 66
*Provenance: Jean-Louis Fivel Collection, France*
Fierce and boldly primitive, Colin's five costume designs for the 1929 Ballet Suédois production of *Sculpture Nègre* bear the names of the five dancers for which they were intended—Mme Imarka, Jean Borlin, Sonia Albright, Mme Zita and one for an unspecified child—as well as annotations concerning colors and accessories, not to mention actual fabric swatches on two of the designs. And the backdrop design is nothing short of brilliant, a cave painting-cum-set decoration. This is an awe-inspiring design for what appears to have been an incredible presentation. Jean Borlin, the firebrand dancer and choreographer of the Swedish Ballet provided the Parisian public with one final compilation program that played from November 30 to December 24 at the Théâtre des Champs-Elysées before he departed the City of Lights. With music by Francis Poulenc, the *Sculpture Nègre* was a part of that presentation, and it was for this portion of the program that Colin created these peerless design concepts. "Since 1919, Jean Borlin was well-acquainted with Negro Art, which at that point was practically unknown; he had performed a dance at the Comédie des Champs-Elysées which he had called *Sculpture Nègre*. From that point on he dreamed of realizing a *ballet nègre*. The research done by all of his collaborators was extremely serious; in museums of ethnography, they poured over documents concerning black civilizations. On the theme of prehistoric monsters slowly extricating themselves from chaos

and evolving towards the light with more and more assured steps, Jean Borlin introduced little known principles: dancers on stilts, animals moving about on all fours. The mise-en-scene signaled very important progress in the manner in which scenery was viewed" (Ballet Suédois, p. 67).
**Est: $40,000-$50,000.** (6)

### 213. Transatlantique/French Line. 1949.
24¹/₂ x 39¹/₂ in./62.3 x 100.3 cm
Imp. Transatlantique, Paris
Cond A−/Slight tears in blue background.
Ref: Colin, 101; Colin Affichiste, 187; PAI-XLI, 240
Threatened by airlines, the French Line countered with this poster that emphasized stability, safety, comfort, style and luxury. Colin indicates all that here by the massive proportions of the ship at close range, the simplified linear treatment, the milling passengers on deck, and, above all, that formidable red-and-black stack.
**Est: $2,000-$2,500.**

## R. T. COOPER

### 214. The Centenary of the Omnibus. 1929.
25¹/₈ x 40 in./63.8 x 101.5 cm
Baynard Press, London
Cond A.
From carriages to double-decker buses and coachmen to conductors, Cooper's design celebrates the 100th anniversary of public transportation in London courtesy of the Omnibus. Though clothing styles may have changed and it's clear that advertising is much more a part of the commuting game in 1929 than it was in 1829, the primary thrust of the poster is to present how affordable mass transit has broadened the horizons of a great number of people. London-native George Shilli-

beer was offered work in Paris where he was commissioned to build some unusually large horse-drawn coaches capable of transporting a whole group of people—perhaps two dozen—at a time. His design worked and he concluded that operating similar vehicles in London—but for the fare-paying public with multiple stops —could be a lucrative enterprise. His first London "Omnibus" took up service on July 4, 1829, on the route along Paddington, the Yorkshire Stingo and the Bank via the newly built "New Road" (now Marylebone Road), Somers Town and City Road. Four services were provided in each direction daily. The success of the omnibus was almost instantaneous. The London General Omnibus Company was founded in 1855 to amalgamate and regulate the horse-drawn omnibus services then operating in London. The company began producing motor omnibuses in 1910. In 1933, the London General Omnibus Company became part of the new London Passenger Transport Board.
**Est: $1,700-$2,000.**

## A. COSNE

### 215. La Charité.
34¹/₈ x 54¹/₈ in./86.7 x 137.5 cm
Imp. Cassan Fils, Toulouse
Cond A−/Unobtrusive tears near edges.
"Beneath the bells of delirium sometimes charity weeps." It's a rather poetic way of placing the focus back on the worthy causes behind the events rather than dwelling on the frivolity that they typically generate. And even with the party in silhouetted full swing in the background, Cosne's literal interpretation of the poster's proverb is refreshing, moving in its earnestness and affecting in its simplicity.
**Est: $1,200-$1,500.**

POUR RÉUSSIR EN PHOTOGRAPHIE
PLAQUES PAPIERS
AS DE TRÊFLE
PLAQUES PAPIERS

216

VOITURETTE "LION"
LES FILS DE PEUGEOT FRÈRES, BEAULIEU (DOUBS)
Agent:
CRAM

217

PAUL HANKAR
ARCHITECTE
RUE DEFACQZ 63

218

CUBA
BRANIFF International AIRWAYS

219

## RAPHAEL COURTOIS

**216. As De Trêfle.** ca. 1909.
$61^{7}/_{8}$ x 47 in./157 x 119.3 cm
B. Chapellier Jeune, Paris
Cond B+/Unobtrusive tears, largely at folds.
Ref: Célébrités, 149; PAI-XXIX, 326
In order to convince the public of the success brought about by the use of their photographic supplies, Ace of Clubs parades out this oddball group of notables to inspire the film-buying public's confidence. "Celebrities have naturally always been associated with the progress of photography and cinematography. We join President Falliès as he sets off to live his life on the path of glory; he's followed by his new Council president Aristide Briand, transformed by circumstances into a reporter and by Uncle Sam loaded down with film. The trio is accompanied by two personages who resemble Sherlock Holmes and Doctor Watson like two peas in a pod, present without a doubt to elucidate the many mysteries of the Third Republic" (Célébrités, p. 94). It's also interesting to note that the printer titled his posters "Les Affiches Humoristiques" and that his trademark indicates that he lived professionally by the admirable axiom "L'Idée c'est tout" ("The Idea is everything").
**Est: $2,000-$2,500.**

## CRAM

**217. Voiturette "Lion".** ca. 1906.
85 x 55 in./215.8 x 139.7 cm
René Rousseau, Paris
Cond B+/Unobtrusive tears at folds and bottom text area.
Ref: Phillips I, 184
The most recognizable landmark in the City of Lights lights-up this little "Lion" as it takes to the cobblestoned streets—with a peddle-powered Peugeot cruising through the background for additional brand-name placement. By 1905, the question raised at any auto race was never who would win the race, but which Peugeot would win it. When a family feud occurred between Armand Peugeot and his young second cousin Robert, Armand split from the company and began manufacturing under the name "Société Anonyme de Peugeot Automobiles." Clearly, he didn't wish to abandon the highly successful family name altogether. Robert, in turn, continued to manufacture under the name "Les Fils de Peugeot Frères" and further distinguished his automobiles from those of Armand by calling them *Voiturettes Lion* or "Lion Peugeots." Within a few years, Armand returned to the family business. The lion was then adopted as the company's logo. As is the case in another Voiturette Lion poster done by Walter Thor (*see* PAI-XX, 79), Michelin tires are here promoted as the pneumatic of choice for this particular automobile.
**Est: $1,500-$1,800.**

## PAUL CRESPIN (1859-1944)

**218. Paul Hankar Architecte.** 1894.
$15^{1}/_{4}$ x 21 in./38.7 x 53.2 cm
Imp. Ad. Mertens, Bruxelles
Cond A. Framed.
Ref: DFP-II, 1019; Weill, 88; Belgische Affiche, 44; Maitres, 91; Word & Image, p. 38; Reims, 1444; Affiches Etrangères, p. 90; Beaumont, p. 48; PAI-XLI, 244
Drafting tools (triangles, rulers, etc.) as well as bees and *their* architecture, the honeycomb, are incorporated into a most effective design for Crespin's colleague, the architect, Paul Hankar. "The poster 'Hankar' is in every way perfect. The principal subject, positioned just right, is interpreted in a very modern style. There are many details, but they are chosen with such pleasure and arranged with such taste, such discretion—in a single word, such tact—that far from removing importance from the principal subject he lends it more value, creating a particular atmosphere, technical if I may say so. The warm and vivid coloring further adds, if that's possible, to the merit of this print which remains one of the best—if not the very best—of Crespin" (Beaumont, p. 48).
**Est: $10,000-$12,000.**

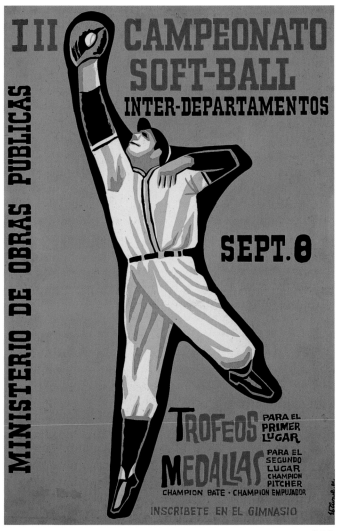

**220**

**221**

**222**

## CUBAN POSTERS

### 219. Braniff International Airways/Cuba.
Artist: **Anonymous**
20 x 25⁷/₈ in./51.2 x 66 cm
Cond A.
Ref: PAI-XL, 95
Braniff International started life in 1930 as Braniff Airways from the former Braniff Airlines that began two years earlier. Its first scheduled service was between Tulsa and Oklahoma City. The airline steadily grew, taking over other small airlines as it went. The new name of Braniff International was taken up in 1948 after new routes were established to Havana and Lima,

Peru. Braniff ceased operations in the late 1980s. However, at the time of this poster's production, the airline was in its heyday. And to that end, an anonymous posterist calls upon the talents of a conga-playing native to drum up a little Braniff business.
**Est: $1,200-$1,500.**

### 220. Campeonato Soft-Ball Inter-Departamentos/ Ministerio de Obras Publicas.
Artist: **Eladio Rivadulla Martinez (1923- )**
19³/₄ x 29³/₄ in./50 x 75.6 cm
Cond B/Mounted on board; slight stains.
Well run, there were trophies and medals on the line in the Third Interdepartmental Ministry of Works Softball Championship, but you have to believe that bragging rights were the real reason people took to the diamond. Rivadulla's silk-screen poster is an unadulterated sports classic in its composition, the stretched-out game saving catch in the clutch that's the stuff of every man or boy's dream whose heart beats for the ball and bat. In the course of an uninterrupted sixty-two-year career, Cuban graphic artist Rivadulla Martinez has remarkably designed more than 3,500 posters, 3,000 books and publications, not to mention postage stamps and logotypes. His film and political posters, as well as his paintings, are collected throughout the United States, Europe, Africa and Asia.
**Est: $1,400-$1,700.**

### L. DAMARÉ (?-1927)

### 221. Parisiana/La Princesse des Flirts.
35¹/₄ x 49¹/₂ in./89.5 x 125.8 cm
Imp. Louis Galice, Paris
Cond B+/Slight tears at folds.

At first, you have to wonder if a poster featuring a decorously nippleless coquette that promotes a "Fantaisie-Operette" titled "The Princess of the Flirts" might not be something of an overstatement. However, once you notice that the theatricality stars Arlette Dorgère, all doubts quickly fade away. The toast of Victorian Paris, Dorgère was an attractive blonde who combined a natural talent for comedy with an avid taste for novelty to create one of the major personalities of the gaslight era. After appearances in several café-concert establishments, she eventually settled at the Scala where, for a time, she became the house *chanteuse*. Her affairs with royalty and tycoons, from Russia to South America, made her a celebrity, and she became a trend setter in fashions and lifestyle. No biographical data for Damaré is available, yet he (or she) worked for the Folies-Bergère, the Olympia and other top music halls for years, always coming up with humorous, attention-getting designs.
**Est: $2,000-$2,500.**

### ANDRE DAUDE (1897-1979)

### 222. Pianos Daudé. 1926.
46⁷/₈ x 62³/₄ in./119 x 159.4 cm
Publicité PAG, Paris
Cond A–/Unobtrusive tears near edges.
Ref: Art Deco, p. 94; PAI-XXXVIII, 309
The creator of this stunning poster for the piano store on Avenue Wagram in Paris (still there today) is none other than the former president of the company. It is an inspired design: the diagonal placement of the piano instantly animates the entire scene, and the overhead view of the baldheaded pianist adds just the right note of humor.
**Est: $2,000-$2,500.**

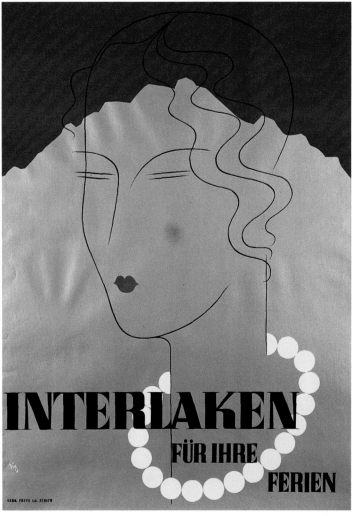

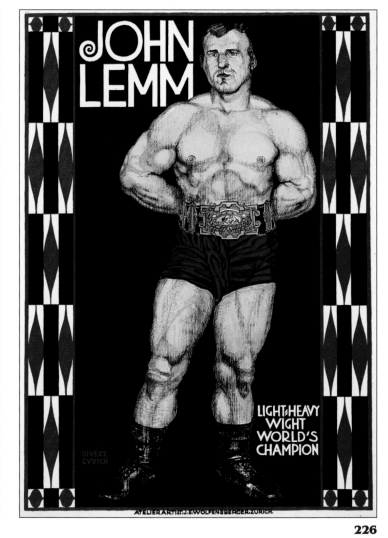

## CHARLES DELAVAT

**223. Bicyclette Liberator.** ca. 1900.
63 x 45$^1$/$_2$ in./160 x 115.6 cm
Affiches Humoristique B. Chapellier-Jeune, Paris
Cond B+/Restored tears in borders.
Ref: Collectionneur, p. 216
"The social and political overseers of the 19th and
20th centuries all had to discuss the mobilizing topic
of weekly rest . . . Some dates deserve to be pointed
out. 1841, weekly rest becomes obligatory for children;
1842, it becomes the same way for women and in
1906, the law applies itself to all commercial and industrial workers. After the Second World War, everyone
who collects a salary benefits from the law. Humorists,
always at the ready to taunt political decisions, push
logic to the extremes. And that's how we find our-
selves at this comical Sunday scene. Economic activity
is totally paralyzed. A panel on a railroad crossing gate
indicates: 'Closed for Weekly Rest' a result, all the
same, of the possible risks of relaxation in the working
population. Bicycles then become unanimously adopted
salutary machines. Groups of people form; proletarians
and tourists find themselves rubbing elbows, a gendarme and an old maid with a cat, a chimney sweep
and a cook, an enterprising and elegant businessman,
a soldier and a domestic, a middle-class man in a top
hat and a facetious civil servant. This poster that evokes
the beginning of a social right goes on to insist on an
economic phenomenon: the increased demands and
consumption of the masses. The manufacturers of Liberator bicycles couldn't be anything but delighted"
(Collectionneur, p. 216).
**Est: $2,000-$2,500.**

## MAURICE DENIS (1870-1943)

**224. L'Art Italien.** 1935.
46$^7$/$_8$ x 62$^3$/$_4$ in./119 x 159.3 cm
Imp. H. Chachoin, Paris
Cond A.
Ref: Phillips III, 403
Combining the sacramental with the classical provides

223*

an overwhelmingly respectful and solemn tone in this
Denis promotion for a three-month Italian art exhibition
at Paris' Petit Palais—except for the red-winged, year-
toting cherub down-right who looks as if he's a little
sick-and-tired of being taken for granted. This rare
poster by the celebrated painter, printmaker and theo-
retician is the only known poster to be created by
Denis after World War I.
**Est: $1,500-$2,000.**

## ALEX W. DIGGELMANN (1902-1987)

**225. Interlaken für Ihre Ferien.** ca. 1935.
35$^1$/$_2$ x 50 in./90 x 127 cm
Gebr. Fretz, Zürich
Cond A–/Slight tears at edges.
Ref: Paradis, p. 193; PAI-XVII, 247
A light line portrait, the lips a warm red dot over the
icy metallic-silver of the background mountains, con-
veys the fashionableness, even sexiness, of the Swiss

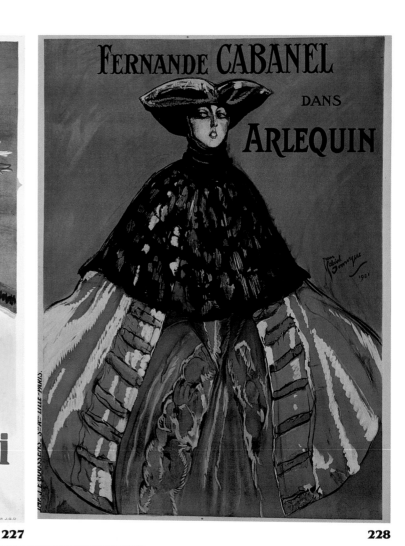

**227**

**228**

**224**

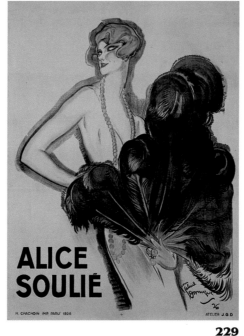

**229**

## JEAN-GABRIEL DOMERGUE (1889-1962)

**227. Emmy Magliani.** 1923.
$41^1/_2$ x $53^7/_8$ in./105.5 x 136.7 cm
Imp. H. Chachoin, Paris
Cond A.
Ref: PAI-VII, 136
Domergue resided in Monte Carlo where he moved in the best circles, organized glittering balls, designed fashion accessories and became something of a local celebrity himself. In his art, women are always long-necked beauties with supple bodies and delicate faces, glowing with rich colors. His poster output is actually his best contribution to the artistic world, with a flair uniquely suited to the high-society pleasures he advertised. Seeing as all of Domergue's women are lithe and graceful, it's to be expected that a ballerina would be especially good at projecting these qualities. The white of her costume gives her the spotlight; her partner, while complementing her perfectly, is modestly tucked away into the background in browns and greys.
**Est: $7,000-$9,000.**

**228. Fernande Cabanel dans Arlequin.** 1921.
$47^1/_4$ x $62^3/_4$ in./120 x 159.3 cm
Imp. J. Goosens, Lille-Paris
Cond B+/Slight tears at folds and edges.
Not even Domergue's knack for glamorizing women could help to make Ms. Cabanel a celebrity despite his spectacular advertisement for "Harlequin," presumably a theatrical production in which she appeared. In fact, Fernande Cabanel appears to have been little more than a blip on show biz radar—nine years after this poster's appearance on the streets of Paris, she had a supporting role in a film titled "L'Etrangére," after which she appears to have faded into the sunset. But, if at the end of the day, someone looked back on their chosen profession and realized that they had been nothing more than an also-ran, could there be a more achingly lush souvenir of the time that they almost made it to the big time than this? Hardly. *Rare!*
**Est: $5,000-$6,000.**

resort of Interlaken. Diggelmann started out as an elementary school teacher then studied art in Leipzig and Paris. He established himself in Zurich as a posterist specializing in travel and sports, and won awards for poster designs for the 1936 Berlin and 1948 London Olympics.
**Est: $3,000-$4,000.**

## JOSEPH DIVÉKY

**226. John Lemm.**
$30^3/_8$ x 42 in./77.1 x 106.7 cm
J. Wolfensberger, Zürich
Cond A.

What a slab of man meat! Seriously, as portrayed by Divéky—and in real life as well—John Lemm was a mountain of a man, a Swiss champion wrestler who plied his testerone-fueled trade during the first two decades of the Twentieth Century. Though the details of his time in the ring are sketchy beyond the fact that he won a lot, lost a lot and injured himself with expected frequency, it can be said that Lemm was one of the athletes that helped to popularize catch wrestling—the progenitor of today's professional wrestling.
**Est: $1,700-$2,000.**

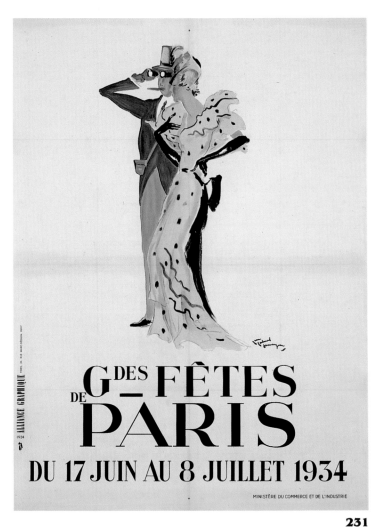

**230**

**231**

**232**

**235**

**DOMERGUE (cont'd)**

**229. Alice Soulié.** 1926.
47 x 62⁷/₈ in./119.5 x 159.7 cm
Imp. H. Chachoin, Paris
Cond B+/Slight tears and creases.
Ref: PAI-XLIII, 307
Blond cabaret performer—and rumored transvestite—
Alice Soulié is no exception to the sleek, elegant and
smart Domergue rule, with her rope of oversized pearls
and sumptuous black feather fan.
**Est: $1,500-$1,800.**

**230. Galeries Lafayette.** 1920.
47 x 62³/₄ in./119.3 x 159.4 cm
Imp. J. Goosens, Lille-Paris
Cond B/Slight tears at folds.
Ref: Affiche Réclame, p. 64; PAI-XXIII, 239
This poster for the Paris department store is actually
meant to encourage the purchase of French savings
bonds. The text indicates that Galeries' customers can
subscribe at their favorite store, and Domergue provides a chic—though, for him, restrained—illustration.
**Est: $3,000-$4,000.**

**231. Gdes Fêtes de Paris.** 1934.
46¹/₂ x 62³/₈ in./118.1 x 161 cm
Alliance Graphique, Paris
Cond B/Unobtrusive tears and slight staining along folds.
Ref: PAI-XLIII, 312
You don't need to show any Paris landmarks in the
background or anything at all for that matter, reasoned
Domergue: the ultrachic couple will amply suffice to
affirm the splendor of the event. And so they do—in
little more than shades of yellow, beige and green.
**Est: $2,500-$3,000.**

**232. Monte-Carlo.** ca. 1937.
26⁷/₈ x 37⁷/₈ in./68.3 x 96.2 cm
Imp. Nationale, Monaco
Cond A–/Slight light-staining.
Ref: PAI-XLIII, 314
Domergue reels us into the sunny world of Monte
Carlo with this temptingly tanned willow wisp, with a
spectacular pyrotechnic display of indigenous flora
thrown in for good measure.
**Est: $1,500-$2,000.**

**233. Reveillon du Corset.** 1922.
46¹/₄ x 62¹/₄ in./117.2 x 158 cm
Imp. Devambez, Paris
Cond B+/Slight tears at folds and edges.
Ref: Karcher, 293; PAI-XXVI, 281
But, of course. Seeing as he was one of the great
fashion illustrators of his day and a lover of the female
form, the New Year's Eve Corset Party was a natural
project for Domergue. A simultaneously revealing and
restrictive affair for the ladies, the *reveillon* must
have been a gentleman's delight, and who better than
Domergue to present it.
**Est: $5,000-$6,000.**

**233**

**234**

**236**

**237**

### JEAN DON (1900-1985)

**234. Maurice Chevalier/Casino de Paris.**
45$^1$/$_2$ x 62$^1$/$_4$ in./115.4 x 158.2 cm
H. Chachoin, Paris
Cond A–/Unobtrusive tears along folds.
Who says that Kiffer had a promotional stranglehold on the appearances of Maurice Chevalier on the walls of Paris? Clearly Don was as capable of placing a straw boater at a rakish angle and recreating the infamous prominent lower lip, so Chevalier's people turned to him to supply the poster for an appearance at the

Casino de Paris. Don was a prolific illustrator whose specialty were portraits and posters of celebrities of stage and film; otherwise, little is known of him.
**Est: $2,000-$2,500.**

### F. FELIX DOUISSET

**235. Fêtes de Charité.** 1899.
37 x 49$^1$/$_8$ in./94 x 124.7 cm
Affiches J. Guillau, Montauban
Cond B–/Restored tears at folds and edges.
Located thirty-one miles to the north of Toulouse, Montauban is beautifully situated on the right bank of

the Tarn River at its confluence with the Tescou, second only to Mont-de-Marsan as the oldest fortified town of southern France. Set out in a geometric pattern, it's built entirely of the same pink brick used in Toulouse and boasts a charming main square (*Place Nationale*) surrounded by quaint shops. Of course, none of this is included in the Douisset poster lest it detract from the five-day charity festival being held there, promoted here with a female harlequin making her way sidesaddle through the floral-strewn festivities atop a stalwart donkey.
**Est: $1,400-$1,700.**

### DRANSY (Jules Isnard, 1883-ca. 1945)

**236. Gitanes.** 1931.
15$^1$/$_4$ x 22$^3$/$_4$ in./38.7 x 57.7 cm
Imp. Vercasson, Paris
Cond A–/Slight stains at edges.
Ref: PAI-XXXVIII, 319 (var)
Although Dransy's fame rests mainly on his immortal wine-delivering Nectar (*see* PAI-XLIII, 318), he is also responsible for creating a reasonable number of enduring advertising icons, such as this enticing gypsy upon whose delectable shoulders firmly rests the duty of seducing the nicotinic public into giving Gitanes a puff. *This is the smaller format.*
**Est: $800-$1,000.**

### H. DRY

**237. Bal des Etudiants.** 1906.
29$^1$/$_2$ x 41 in./74.9 x 104.2 cm
Litho. J. Coubé, Nancy
Cond B+/Tears and stains at fold and paper edges.
From a male perspective, this student ball initially looks like a pretty sweet deal, because if you can believe the Dry promotion, the ladies will literally be jumping right into the arms of any handsome Bohemian that comes their way without much provocation whatsoever. But not so fast there, Skippy: before you dive in headfirst, you better take note of the two words in the upper-right quadrant that indicates that optional cross-dressing is allowed at the event. In short, caveat emptor.
**Est: $1,500-$1,800.**

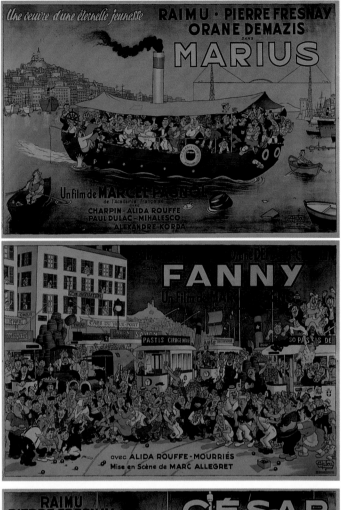

**239**

## ALBERT DUBOUT (1905-1976)

**238. Three Pagnol Film Posters: Marius, Fanny and César.** 1950.
Each: 46³/₄ x 31³/₈ in./118.7 x 79.7 cm
Imp. Monégasque, Monte-Carlo
Cond A–/Unobtrusive folds. Framed.
Ref: Dubout, pp.20 & 21, 44 & 45, 60 & 61; Cinema Français, p. 65 (Fanny & César);
  Phillips IV, 235 (Fanny); PAI-XXV, 295 (Marius) & PAI-XXXI, 429 (César)
The film trilogy—*Marius* (1931), *Fanny* (1932) and *César* (1936)—has been re-released at least five times, and these three posters come to us from the 1950 reissue of the films. An ardent populist, Pagnol lovingly depicted the lives of colorful characters of the Marseilles waterfront. The whole saga is filled with warmth, humor and compassion, plus a true insight into the motivations behind the concept of honor among ordinary citizens. Dubout's famous humorous caricatures—teeming with humanity—are perfectly suited to Pagnol's style; he created posters for the original releases of all three parts, as well as for this 1950 re-release.
**Est: $3,000-$4,000.** (3)

## MARCELLO DUDOVICH (1878-1962)

**239. "Agent Provacateur".** 1913.
12¹/₂ x 15⁷/₈ in./31.5 x 40.3 cm
*Hand-signed oil, gouache and crayon on board.* Framed.
At the age of nineteen, Dudovich arrived in Italy from his native Trieste. After an initial stint at Ricordi, he was hired at Chappuis in Bologna. He was there from

**238**

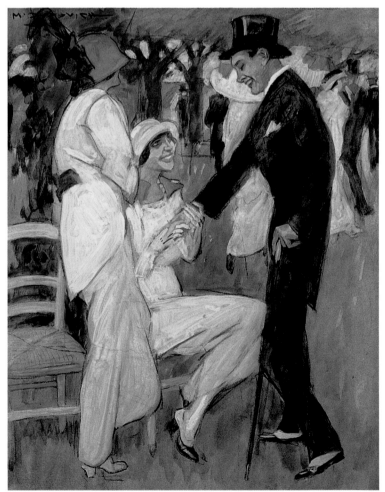

"Thence to Hyde Park, where much good company, and many fine Ladies"

241

1899 to 1905 before rejoining Ricordi, where he established himself as Italy's premier posterist, largely as a result of his refined yet lively posters for Mele, the Naples department store. After many years of successful work, Dudovich accepted an invitation from his friend, Albert Lange, editor of the influential German humor magazine, *Simplicissimus*, and worked on the publication in Munich from 1911 to 1914. This and the following artwork were created expressly for that purpose. The artwork here, entitled "Agent Provocateur" (indicated verso, No. 5240) and intended for the July

1913 issue of *Simplicissimus* is a peculiar little number indeed. Precisely who or what is this gentleman attempting to ally himself with in order to bring about their demise? Maybe it's the lady in white who's the agent provocateur. Or perhaps it's the diminutive orange vendor who may or may not be a statue. But once again, how does it all add up? So few answers, but with such stylish execution one doesn't mind the prospect of pondering over the possibilities for hours.
**Est: $5,000-$6,000.**

**240. Fur Austellungspark.** 1913.
12³/₈ x 17³/₈ in./31.4 x 44 cm
*Hand-signed oil, gouache and crayon drawing on board.* Framed.
Well, hello. Pure Dudovichian charm and elegance grace this artwork for the June 1913 issue of *Simplicissimus*. The title, "Fur Austellungspark" appears verso (No. 5243) and would seem to provide an utterly apt name for the piece. Because this tony crowd is definitely placing themselves on display for the world to see. Or more accurately, for the right type of person to see. In Dudovich's world, fashion for fashion's sake was often occasion enough to convene.
**Est: $5,000-$6,000.**

## JEAN DUPAS (1882-1964)

**241. We Moderns/Saks Fifth Avenue.** ca. 1925.
8 x 9¹/₂ in./20.3 x 24.1 cm
*Gouache artwork on paper.* Framed.
In all of his poster-related work, Dupas presents highly stylized, very fashionable people from the very fringes of our imagination, occupants of the realm that exists in the split second before true wakefulness alchemizes into peaceful slumber, gorgeous quasi-humans with Modigliani necks in idealized and extravagant settings.

His women are statuesque in a nearly literal sense. And to the contemporary eye, they appear, in fact, as monuments to a natural extension of a time and place when all was glitter and sophistication, so many head-turning mannequins in the chic 1920 window of our psyche. In this artwork executed for the chain of upscale department store's perfume counters, we find "We Moderns" perfume—quite possibly a tie-in product with a popular silent film with which it shares an identical name—bending to Dupas' will. Though the presentation of the bottle is concentrated Art Deco sophistication, the label shows a *tête*-heavy maiden bathing in what we have to assume is We Moderns.
**Est: $2,500-$3,000.**

**242. Thence to Hyde Park.** 1930.
48¹/₂ x 39¹/₄ in./123.2 x 99.7 cm
John Riddle, London
Cond B+/Restored tears at top and bottom. Framed.
Ref: Richmond, p. 115; PAI-XLI, 260
A rare and beautiful romantic tableau for the London Underground Railway, with the accompanying quote: "Thence to Hyde Park, where much good company and many fine ladies . . . "Between 1930 and 1933, Dupas created a total of six designs for that client, and all of them are a credit to the talent of this distinguished artist. Dupas worked on both sides of the English Channel: in London, he was best known for several designs for the Transport system, and in Paris he prepared posters for the Palais de la Nouveauté and other stores as well as special events. "Dupas was totally at home with Art Deco stylization . . . Over and over he depicted the same type of elongated, statuesque woman, which to him represented the ideal beauty of the period" (Art Deco. p. 35). His many murals for the *Normandie* were among the artistic treasures of the famed ocean liner.
**Est: $25,000-$30,000.**

## HANS RUDI ERDT (1883-1918)

**243. Fritz Schulze.** 1907.
34 x 47³/₄ in./86.3 x 121.5 cm
Vereinigte Druckereien und Kunstanstalten, München
Cond B/Slight tears at folds.
Ref: PAI-XXXVII, 303
Ostensibly, Erdt's poster for the Munich sporting goods store places its focus on the apparel one might find there. Not to slight the sporty togs on display, but it's the unsettled business playing itself out between this ruggedly natty trio on their getaway to the great outdoors that lends spectacular dramatic impact to the design. Clothes, it seems, may make the man or woman as the case may be, but it's stoically unspoken narrative that makes the poster. Although he only lived to age thirty-five, Erdt amassed an impressive record as a graphic artist and lithographer in the single decade form 1908 to 1918. He depicted upper-class people in their sports and luxuries, and had a keen eye for reducing a scene to a few essential forms and flat colors.
**Est: $4,000-$5,000.**

## ERIC

**244. 49e Salon de l'Auto.** 1962.
45 x 61 in./114.5 x 155 cm
Imp. Bedos, Paris
Cond B/Slight tears at folds.
Cleverly composed and stylishly uncluttered, Eric's poster for the 49th Annual Paris Automotive Show—which also features the latest innovations in bikes and motorcycles—relies on perspective, a bit of speed and a knee-high vantage point to reveal three essential overlapping modes of transport and commerce.
**Est: $1,000-$1,200.**

## RICARD FABREGAS (1906-1947)

**245. Frescuva.**
28³/₄ x 42³/₄ in./73 x 108.5 cm
Affiches Fabregas
Cond A-/Slight tears at paper edges.
Knee-high to an effervescing glass of freshly-dispensed

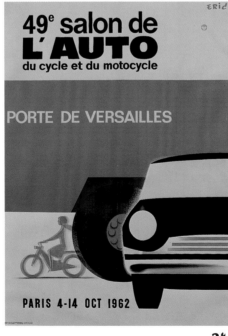

Frescuva, this lithely vivacious redhead puts the squeeze on an oversized bunch of grapes, presumably to procure more of the juice that makes this soda so refreshing. And the bottom text provides a maxim that not only applies to soft drinks, but to all gustatory dabblings as well: "Never Forget Flavor."
**Est: $2,500-$3,000.**

## HANS FALK (1918-2002)

**246. Hier Telephonieren.** 1951.
35³/₈ x 50¹/₄ in./90 x 127.5 cm
J. C. Müller, Zurich

Cond A/P.
Ref (All Var): Swiss 1941-1965, p. B65; Margadant, 471; Swiss Posters, p. 78; PAI-XXIII, 249
Falk was a fine painter who used his easel technique to suit his client's messages in numerous Swiss posters. Muller-Brockmann speaks of him as "a sublime illustrator with graphic means" (p. 41). Here, a sophisticated yet fresh-looking woman encourages us to use public telephones. That is, if you can find one anymore in the era of the cell phone takeover. *This is the German-language version.*
**Est: $1,400-$1,700.**

**248**

**250**

**249**

## GEORGES DE FEURE (1868-1943)

**249. Paris-Almanach.** 1894.
23³/4 x 31¹/8 in./60.3 x 79 cm
Imp. Bourgerie, Paris
Cond B/Slight tears at horizontal fold; slightly light-
    stained. Framed.
Ref: DFP-II, 342; Maindron, p. 64; Abdy, p. 155;
    Timeless Images, 40; De Feure, p. 72; Gold, 79;
    PAI-XLII, 288
"The advertised booklet was a guide to Paris attractions
published by Ed. Sagot, which de Feure shows in the
hand of a woman traveling alone and wishing to sam-
ple the pulse of the city. As always, the artist manages
to suggest hidden depths. Although looking at the
merry throng, the figure remains a bit apart, oddly aloof,
and slightly mysterious" (Gold, p. 58). De Feure, the
consummate designer, created not only this poster,
but the fashionable garb on the arresting viewer.
**Est: $2,000-$2,500.**

**250. Aux copains du diable au corps.** 1893.
12¹/2 x 18¹/4 in./31.8 x 46.5 cm
Imp. G. Bataille, Paris (not shown)
Cond B+/Slight staining. Framed.
Ref: De Feure, p. 56
Once Christianity became the predominant religion in
western Europe, hares and rabbits—who had long been
associated favorably with the Goddess figures in the re-
ligions that Christianity supplanted—came to be seen in
a less laudatory light, viewed suspiciously as the famil-
iars of witches, or as witches themselves in animal form.
Numerous folk tales tell of men led astray by hares who
are really witches in disguise, or of old women revealed
as witches when they are wounded in their animal shape.
Seeing as these ruminants often symbolized fertility
and lust, and naked women have forever been seen as
a threat on some inexplicable level in patriarchal soci-
eties, de Feure created this puritanical panel on the
subject called "The Friends of the Devil in the Flesh."
An intriguing, oddly-bewitching Art Nouveau curio.
**Est: $2,500-$3,000.**

**247**

## CANDIDO ARAGONESE DE FARIA (1849-1911)

**247. The Original Hamilton.**
25¹/2 x 36⁵/8 in./65 x 93 cm
Affiches Faria, Paris
Cond B/Slight tears, largely at folds.
Here's a combination that you don't see too often—physical slapstick comedy and rapidly-fabricated artwork. And
the combination of lion-faced tramp clown and traditional
minstrelsy couldn't have been all that common either.
**Est: $800-$1,000.**

## FERNAND FERNEL (1872-1934)

**248. Compagnie Française des Cycles & Automobiles.**
39 x 55¹/8 in./99 x 140.2 cm
Imp. H. Laas, É. Pécaud, Paris
Cond B+/Slight tears in margins.
Ref: PAI-XLIII, 329
No doubt some day soon, this little wannabe cyclist
will be able to ride away of her own volition, exploring
horizons of which she can only dream today. But seeing as of this moment she can't quite reach the pedals,
her mother helps her to get a taste of what hitting the
open road is all about atop her Compagnie Française
bicycle. A charmingly naive Fernel creation.
**Est: $2,000-$2,500.**

**252**

**251**

**255**

**256**

## PIERRE FIX-MASSEAU (1905-1994)

**251. Le Transport Gratuit.** 1935.
24 x 38¹/₂ in./61 x 97.8 cm
Edita, Paris
Cond A.
To advertise the fact that the French railways will transport your car free of charge if you travel by train, a porter hoists a couple's sedan as if it were just any old piece of luggage. Dynamic and compelling.
**Est: $1,700-$2,000.**

## JEAN-LOUIS FORAIN (1852-1931)

**252. La Vie de Bohême.** ca. 1895.
43 x 17¹/₂ in./109.3 x 44.4 cm
Herold, Paris
Cond A–/Slight tears at folds.
Ref: DFP-II, 363; PAI-XXXIII, 334
Commenting in the August/September, 1898, edition of *The Poster*, critic P. Duverney observed: "At the present moment we think the best posters on the Paris *murailles* are one by E. Grasset and the other by Forain . . . Forain's poster is for Puccini's 'Vie de Bohême.' The artist shows us the finishing scene: the lovely *lorette* Mimi Pinson in her attic, forgotten by her lover, dying as she lived, with a smile on her lips. This page carries

with itself a penetrating charm, and is full of delicacy and grace. The vision—for vision it is—brings many of us back to our youthful days, as Mimi Pinson always whispers, like an echo, the vanishing song of years long gone by" (p. 110).
**Est: $3,000-$4,000.**

## FELIX FOURNERY (1865-1938)

**253. Trouville/Casino Municipal.** 1912.
44³/₄ x 60³/₈ in./113.8 x 153.4 cm
Imp. Via-Decor, Paris
Cond B/Restored tears; margins partially recreated.
Ref: Mer s'Affiche, p. 18; Trouville/Deauville, p. 51
"The promotional subject of this poster is placed in the background in order to allow the grace of an elegant young woman to make the sales pitch. The principle was habitual, it had functioned for 15 years at Trouville and seemed as if (the method) would work as effectively for the casino as it had for the sea bathing . . . The (Fournery) poster . . . transports us back to this . . . period. Trouville's Municipal Casino, built by Alexandre Durville, takes its place on the edge of sea with its grandiloquent silhouette set behind the young women out for a sailboat ride" (Trouville/Deauville, p. 50). Of course, as is the case in a large number of destination posters, the couture that you're seen in during your stay is equally

as important as actually getting where you're going. Fanfreluche, a writer for *L'Illustration*, made these observations regarding seaside attire in 1892. And as you can see from the fashions on display here, not much has changed in the twenty years since she made her remarks: "The most elegant eccentricities are permitted in the array of outfits for the casino and the beach. White dominates; girls, young women, appear stunningly fresh. I see someone adorned in a delicious wardrobe of white muslin, the simple muslin 'communicates', with the transparency of taffeta snow, with sleeves puffing out, with black velvet bracelets and Valencian shoes . . . Muslin is indispensable when it comes to creating pretty outfits with see-through colors" (Mer s'Affiche, p. 18).
**Est: $4,000-$5,000.**

## R. FRANCISI

**254. La Sigaraia del Tabarin.** 1928.
50 x 75¹/₂ in./127.2 x 191.8 cm
Margherita, Napoli
Cond B/Recreated bottom margin; restored tears at
          folds and edges; image and colors excellent.
Trecherously-low flying planes, an errant flock of birds and women who aren't precisely what they appear to

253 254

257

be. And though the action is pretty lightweight, when you add up all of the elements it shouldn't come as that much of a surprise that this Francisi poster promotes the Italian release of an early silent film directed by none other than Alfred Hitchcock. Originally titled *Champagne*, it follows the exploits of the irrepressible madcap daughter of a millionaire who falls in love with a penniless French artist and goes with him to Paris, where she starts spending her ample allowance like water. To teach her a lesson and force her to return home, her father pretends to have lost all his money. But, she simply goes to work as a cigarette girl at the Tabarin nightclub (hence the Italian title) and in the end has her way. You'd think that Dorica Film—apparently an Italian bottom-feeding outfit that acquired foreign films and released them with their own title to make it appear as if they had produced them—would have had Francisi slap Hitchcock's name somewhere on the poster to capitalize on his fame. However, at this point in time, Hitchcock's name didn't mean anything

yet. But the name Betty Balfour did—popular throughout Europe as a cast member of the "Squibs" film series (which focused on women with lively, bubbly personalities), Dorica Film hoped to cash-in on her name recognition to bring in the Italian moviegoers in droves. **Est: $2,500-$3,000.**

## GEO FRANCOIS

**255. Evian les Bains.** 1906.
25 x 39³/₄ in./63.5 x 101 cm
Imp. Lucien Serre, Paris
Cond A.
Ref: Golf, p. 9; PAI-XXXVII, 317
The view of the course at the famous spa resort of Evian is lined up like a good golf stroke in order to show to best advantage the superb site overlooking the town and Lac Leman (also known as Lake Geneva), with Switzerland on the far shore. The designer's rich color scheme of greens, golds and turquoise virtually

causes it to pulsate with an inner glow. Both in coloring and composition, François recalls the far better known Broders.
**Est: $1,400-$1,700.**

## STANLEY WALTER GALLI (1912- )

**256. United Air Lines/Hawaii.**
24⁷/₈ x 40¹/₈ in./63 x 102 cm
Cond A.
A more commonly seen Galli design for United Air Lines service to the Hawaiian islands features a group of people out for a vigorous ride in an outrigger canoe. Here, the artist presents us with the exact opposite side of the tourism coin—a promise of rest and relaxation: tropical flora, fruit and a lovely wahine, far less overtly seductive than many promotional women, yet all the more welcoming. Galli, in addition to creating a number of persuasive images for United, was a founding member of the San Francisco Society of Illustrators and elected into the national Society of Illustrators Hall of Fame in 1981.
**Est: $1,200-$1,500.**

## JOHN GALLUCCI

**257. Lake Placid 1980: Three Posters.** 1979.
Each: 24 x 36 in./61 x 91.3 cm
George Little Press, Burlington, Vermont
Cond A/P.
Ref: PAI-XL, 456
1980 was an amazing Olympic year—from the United States' "Miracle on Ice" (*see* PAI-XXXVIII, 97) to Eric Heiden's five golds to Ingemar Stenmark's victories in the slalom and giant slalom to Leonhard Stock's downhill gold. It also was the second time that Lake Placid played host to the Winter Games, the first being in 1932 (*see* PAI-XLI, 450). Executed by Gallucci in chilling white and delph, this trio of images feature a speeding downhiller and an in-flight Nordic jumper, as well as Whiteface Mountain, a majestic feature of the Games that needed no athletic embellishment.
**Est: $1,700-$2,000.** (3)

**258**

**259**

**260**

MISTINGUETT

*e. gesmar.*

MOULIN ROUGE

**263**

**PIERRE-HENRI GELIS-DIDOT (1853-?) &
LOUIS MALTESTE (1862-1928)**

**258. Absinthe Parisienne.** 1896.
32³/₈ x 46³/₄ in./82.2 x 118.7 cm
Imp. G. De Malherbe, Paris
Cond A–/Unobtrusive tears at folds.
Ref: Reims, 659; Boissons, 287; Absinthe, p. 110;
   Absinthe Affiches, p. 75; PAI-XLIII, 338

Molière's medical fool, Diafoirus, and a young woman
join forces to promote the effects of this brand of
absinthe. "Drink it and see," they urge. The author of
the Reims catalogue terms the deeply decolletaged
dress as being blue, but it seems clear to us that this
young woman with her copper hair swept up in a top-
knot is a fresh-looking version of *la féerie verte*, the

"green fairy" who was the Parisians' personification of
this potent, and eventually outlawed, drink. Reims
describes Gelis-Didot as a freelance art director and
author of many works, including Le *Peinture décorative
en France*; about his partner Malteste, we have discovered nothing.
**Est: $2,500-$3,000.**

261

262

## CHARLES GESMAR (1900-1928)

### 259. Folies-Bergère/Betty Rowe.
9⁵/₈ x 13⁵/₈ in./24.5 x 34.7 cm
*Gouache and pencil drawing.* Framed.
*Provenance: Archives of the Folies-Bergère*
Apart from the single fact that Betty Rowe appeared briefly as a dancer at the Folies-Bergère, nothing is known about the career path of this lithesome, auburn-haired flapper. But in reality, Gesmar's drawing has very little to do with talent and everything to do with glamour—swaddled in mink, adrip with jewels and puffing away discreetly on a pipe, Ms. Rowe becomes the embodiment of all things feminine and desirable in Jazz Age Paris.
**Est: $2,500-$3,000.**

### 260. Playing Chicken.
18³/₄ x 11³/₈ in./47.5 x 29 cm
*Hand-signed gouache and pencil drawing;* slight staining at left paper edge. Framed.
Is it permissible to call this trio of chorines "chicks?" They are dressed like chickens, after all. I'm just sayin'. Gesmar's costume design for the poultry outfits in the "Revue Piquée" is high-spirited and amusing as all get out. And you have to imagine that they were intended to be, because it doesn't matter how gorgeous, how seductive a woman might be, once you put her in a chicken outfit, she immediately goes from hot to hilarious.
**Est: $2,000-$2,500.**

### 261. Mistinguett. 1928.
44³/₄ x 123¹/₄ in./113.7 x 313 cm
Imp. H. Chachoin, Paris
Cond B/Tears and stains at folds.
Ref: Theaterplakate, 155; PAI-XLIII, 88
In this spectacular two-sheet poster, Gesmar showed the two distinct stage personae affected by Mistinguett: the flamboyant showgirl and the Parisian street urchin. She was equally effective and popular in both guises. The poster is usually referred to as "Rags to Riches."
**Est: $4,000-$5,000.**

### 262. Mistinguett/Casino de Paris. 1922.
45¹/₂ x 61¹/₄ in./115 .5 x 155.5 cm
Imp. Karcher, Paris
Cond B/Slight tears at folds, edges and top text area.
Ref: PAI-XLIII, 86

Mistinguett was Gesmar's chief client and close friend from the time he was seventeen years old. This represents one of the simplest, and yet best of his hommages to the diva: He simply places her head—small—in the center and sets it off with an enormous framing headdress of feathers. Striking!
**Est: $5,000-$6,000.**

### 263. Mistinguett/Moulin Rouge. 1926.
31¹/₈ x 47¹/₂ in./79 x 120.5 cm
Imp. H. Chachoin, Paris
Cond B+/Slight tears at folds.
Ref: Folies-Bergère, 63; Hillier, p. 249;
    Theaterplakate, 155; PAI-XLIII, 89
Mistinguett achieved her greatest success at the Moulin Rouge, where this 1926 revue was simply called "Mistinguett." Weill indicates: "It is one of Gesmar's most beautiful posters: without jewels or fancy dress, it's the Miss, child of Paris, which he shows us here. . . alluring, tender, and roguish with the rose between her lips which we would like to pluck." (Folies-Bergère, p. 11).
**Est: $2,000-$2,500.**

**266**

**265**

## FRANZ PAUL GLASS (1886-1964)

**264. Park Casino.**
25$^1/_2$ x 18$^7/_8$ in./64.7 x 48 cm
Kunstanstalt Dr. Kohler, München
Cond A–/Restored top margin.
All the calling cards of a sophisticated establishment—proper decor, legitimate jazz, refined tastes, cheek-to-cheek dancing, beautiful people—are all on hand for Glass's advertisement for the Park Casino restaurant, located in Munich's Ausstellungspark. Franz Glass was a member of "The Six" who executed a great number of distinguished posters.
**Est: $1,400-$1,700.**

## MARY GOLAY (1869-?)

**265. Swans: Two Decorative Panels.** ca. 1905.
Each: 15 x 41 in./38.1 x 104.1 cm
Frey & Fils, Zurich
a: Cond A.
b: Cond A–/Slight tears in left border.
Both framed.
Golay, never one to use her talents in the crude service of traditional commerce, takes us on a pondside stroll into the heart of gracious Art Nouveau placidity. Shrewdly she includes a pair of swans in each panel (the long-necked aquatic birds do mate for life, after all) in order to convey the romantic allegory for Geneva publisher Clément Tournier all the more. As in nature, day precedes night in Golay's panel series, with "Daytime Warmth" sumptuously conveyed with the assistance of wild irises. And as nighttime surely must arrive, so does "Evening Calm," a full moon on hand to make certain the twosome is able to navigate their way through a patch of limpid water lilies without incident.
**Est: $6,000-$8,000.** (2)

## EUGENE GRASSET (1841-1917)

**266. A la Place Clichy.** 1891.
32$^1/_2$ x 50 in./82.7 x 127 cm
Imp. Malherbe, Paris
Cond B+/Slight tears and stains at folds.
Ref (All Var but PAI): DFP-II, 401; Reims, 683;
    Berthon & Grasset, p. 37; Maitres, 18; PAI-XLII, 307
This detailed slice of exotica points out in the text that the Place Clichy department store is the premiere importers of oriental merchandise in the entire world, but Grasset's artistic skill makes the boast seem almost redundant as that notion has already been brightly conveyed in the design that went through several printings and editions, beginning in 1891.
**Est: $2,000-$2,500.**

**267**

**268**

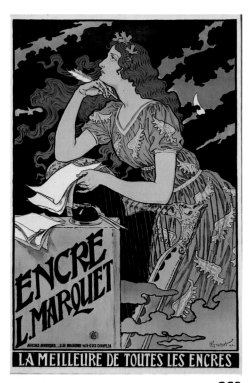

**269**

**270**

Cond A–/Unobtrusive tear at top paper edge.
Ref: Berthon & Grasset, p. 37; Murray-Robertson, p. 107;
DFP-II, 416; Takashimaya, 5; PAI-XXXII, 329
If there's a certain formalism in Grasset's work, there
is also a warm, human touch. That is literally true of
this image of a mother treating her daughter to a cup
of cocoa. Yet it manages not to be too saccharine (as
the copy reads, "Peu sucré," Less sugar), while remaining as rich as cocoa.
**Est: $3,000-$4,000.**

**269. Encre L. Marquet.** 1892.
$31^3/4$ x 47 in./80.6 x 119.4 cm
G. de Malherbe, Paris
Cond B/Slight tears at folds.
Ref: DFP-II, 404; Maitres, 158; Berthon & Grasset, p. 33;
Musée d'Affiche, p. 52; Gold, 3; PAI-XLI, 308
This contemplative young woman looks into the distance, quill poised, as she ponders how best to translate her innermost thoughts to paper. Whatever
her words, the fine ink she is using is sure to make the
most of them. "Grasset adheres to the classic mode of
portraying women as serenely composed and dignified.
Only the fluttering hair and scurrying night clouds suggest any wild untamed thoughts" (Gold, p. 5). *This is
the larger format.*
**Est: $1,700-$2,000.**

**270. Librairie Romantique.** 1887.
$33^7/8$ x $51^1/2$ in./86 x 130.9 cm
Imp. J. Bognard, Paris
Cond B–/Restored tears at folds and edges.
Ref: DFP-II, 398; Maindron, p. 129; Maitres, 42;
Berthon & Grasset, p. 32; Timeless Images, 25;
Gold, 84; PAI-XXX, 196
This poster advertises the publication of "L'Age du
Romantisme," one of the entries in the series titled
"Librairie Romantique" published by Monnier. Comments
Jane Abdy: "Pastiche rarely succeeds, but here Grasset
has made it delightful, and combined all that is graceful
with what is nostalgic . . . This gentle and delightful work
is singled out by Maindron for special praise, as one of
the four best posters of the period . . . In the exhibition
at the Salon des Cent, it was generally considered to
be Grasset's masterpiece" (p. 124). It remains so.
**Est: $1,700-$2,000.**

**267. La Morphinomane.** ca. 1894.
$16^7/8$ x $22^3/8$ in./43 x 56.9 cm
Cond A.
Ref: Berthon & Grasset, p. 67; PAI-XL, 345
Spectacular and remarkable because of—not in spite
of—its uneasy subject matter, this panel throws open
a window into the world of the addicted without attempting to pretty-up or glamorize the situation in the
least. In "La Morphinomane" ("The Morphine Addict"),
"The girl sits forward, injecting herself in the left thigh.
Her tenseness is all: the rigid posture, teeth clenched,
eyes unfocused, brow furrowed, fingers gripping her
thighs like claws. Except for a single upswept lock, her
hair tumbles down like a monstrous octopus, framing

and emphasizing the pale, drawn features. The lithograph, hand-coloured, is Grasset's most expressive
image, eschewing facility to emphasize the absolute
horror which is, somehow, made even more effective
by the decorative touches: the flash of gartered stock-
ing, the richness of the colouring" (Berthon & Grasset,
p. 64). Also, it's important to note that this is one of an
edition of only 101 lithographs hand-colored by Grasset.
**Est: $7,000-$9,000.**

**268. Chocolat Mexicain/Masson.** 1897.
$19^1/2$ x $25^3/8$ in./49.4 x 64.5 cm
Imp. de Vaugirard, Paris

La Musique.

**271**

SALON DES CENT 31, RUE BONAPARTE, PARIS (DU 5 AU 25 AVRIL)
5 FR. LE MARDI — 1 FR. LES AUTRES JOURS.
LIBRE LE DIMANCHE ◆◆◆◆◆◆◆◆◆◆◆◆◆◆◆◆◆◆

EXPOSITION E. GRASSET

**272**

**273**

**NOUVEAU DESSERT**
# EXQUIS GUILLOUT

Exiger la Marque
*Dans toutes les bonnes maisons*

**276**

## GRASSET (cont'd)

### 271. La Musique.
16¹/₄ x 22⁷/₈ in./41 x 58 cm
*Hand-signed gouache and ink drawing.* Framed.
Grasset did much to introduce the concept and practice of Art Nouveau in France. In fact, Grasset "brought Art Nouveau to the aid of the poster: it was to become a worldwide vehicle of the art of advertising. In France, Grasset was the pioneer of an attempt, like that of William Morris in England, to reconcile art and industry . . . Interested as he was in all the applied arts, he came naturally to the poster" (Weill, p. 32). Though there's no record to indicate that this artwork was ever printed as a poster—in fact it's so rare that not even the most

scholarly texts on the artist contain any mention of it— Grasset's allegorical Art Nouveau authority is in full effect. And as is the case with many of his representative works, a touch of madness imbues this harp-plucking embodiment of music, an inconcealable drive that displays an artist's hunger to create with stunning acuity.
**Est: $4,000-$5,000.**

### 272. Salon des Cent/Exposition E. Grasset. 1894.
16¹/₄ x 24 in./41.2 x 61 cm
Imp. G. de Malherbe, Paris
Cond A–/Slight tears at edges.
Ref: Salon des Cent, p. 19;
    Salon des Cent/Neumann, p. 38; DFP-II, 410;
    Reims, 684; Wagner, 54; Berthon & Grasset, p. 6;
    Weill, 39; Gold, 274; PAI-XLI, 512
For his own exhibition at the Salon des Cents, Grasset shows a chestnut-tressed *artiste* soulfully contemplating a tall-stemmed flower—a pose that is almost medieval in its conception—and provides us with a rare glimpse straight into the heart of the moment when observation becomes inspiration.
**Est: $2,500-$3,000.**

### 273. Extravagance. 1897.
16 x 49¹/₈ in./40.7 x 124.7 cm
Cond A.
Ref: Berthon & Grasset, p. 65; PAI-XXXVI, 335
The companion to "Bonne Nouvelle" (*see* PAI-XXVIII, 324) in the *Dix Estampes Décoratives* series. Here, the maiden wandering through the field of cockscomb indulges herself in a bit of extravagance, wielding a fan and lorgnette—two nonessentials where communing with nature is concerned.
**Est: $2,000-$2,500.**

## H. GRAY (Henri Boulanger, 1858-1924)

### 274. Cycles "Brillant". ca. 1900.
23¹/₈ x 30¹/₂ in./58.8 x 77.5 cm
Imp. Lemercier, Paris
Cond B/Restored tears and losses, largely at paper edges.
Ref: PAI-XXI, 209
Winged, ethereal spirits swoon at the radiance of the Brillant bicycle. Gray cleverly works the lines of the

spokes into the pattern of the luminous ray shining from the diamond in the midnight-blue sky. The text boasts of the brand's presence at the 1900 Paris World's Fair and guarantees compensation for any broken-off parts (wings presumably included). Some of Gray's most imaginative, indeed otherworldly works were for bicycles—and this is certainly among the finest.
**Est: $1,400-$1,700.**

### 275. Riz Abadie. 1898.
39 x 55¹/₄ in./99 x 140.4 cm
Imp. Courmont Frères, Paris
Cond A–/Staining at paper edges.
Ref: PAI-XXIII, 278
In the Belle Epoque, it was rare enough for a young woman to smoke, let alone roll her own, which is why cigarette paper companies of the period subtly encouraged women to take up the habit. This is one of Gray's finest posters, with a wealth of decorative detail not usually found in his images. And although the central medallion recalls Mucha, Gray poses his model far more seductively than Mucha's famous poster for Job cigarette papers (*see* PAI-XLIII, 436) done the same year.
**Est: $7,000-$9,000.**

### 276. Exquis Guillout. 1890.
35³/₄ x 50³/₄ in./90.7 x 128.9 cm
Imp. Courmont Frères, Paris
Cond B+/Slight staining in background.
Ref: Alimentaires, 197; PAI-XXXII, 331
When duty calls, it matters very little if you're expected in nursery school the following day. And so, this *petit soldat* calls on his pint-sized lady love with a tin of exquisite Guillout cookies to remember him by, hoping from all appearances to receive a little sugar from her in return. The Guillout cookie factory of Paris was founded in 1841 by Edmé Guillout. At his death in 1893, the Parisian daily, "Le Gaulois," printed the following: "Monsieur Edmé Guillout, the creator of the popular dessert, the Guillout egg cookie, has died at the age of 83 at his property in Mesnil. He leaves behind 3 factories that employ 750 people. It can be said that he broke 12 million eggs during the course of his existence" (Alimentaires).
**Est: $1,700-$2,000.**

## H. GRAY (cont'd)

### 277. Eleven Costume Designs.
Each: 9⁵/₈ x 12¹/₄ in./23.8 x 31.3 cm
Ref: PAI-XXXV, 331
*Hand-signed gouache, ink and pencil artwork on board*; slight staining at edges.
H. Gray provided costume designs for all the major music-halls in Paris. These eleven charming designs are each titled and the actress for which it was intended is indicated verso. The three designs shown (and the actresses who would wear them) are: La Cigarette Espagnole (Mlle Marinette), Volume d'Etrennes (Mlle Darey), and Le Grelot de la Bicyclette (for three performers: Mlles Fred, Marinette and Dranette).
**Est: $1,500-$2,000.** (11)

## GREAT IDEAS OF WESTERN MAN

### 278. Fifty Prints in Two Portfolios. 1950-1954.
Each: 11¹/₈ x 14 in./28.3 x 35.5 cm
Cond A/P.
Published by Container Corporation of America, this was a breakthrough series in corporate advertising. Rather than promoting CCA products directly, this series instead was intended to promote a favorable corporate image to the public. In essence, this was one of the first corporate message campaigns produced in America. These advertisements were commissioned from the top artists of the period, including Ben Shahn, Leonard Lionni, Hans Erni, Paul Rand, Herbert Bayer, Herbert Matter, Richard Lindner, Felix Topolski, Max Bill, McKnight Kauffer, Jan Tschichold and Erik Nitsche. Their art accompanied "ideas" of all of the most profound figures in philosophy, literature and historic forethought, including Socrates, Montesquieu, Thomas Paine, Thomas Jefferson, Abraham Lincoln, Thoreau, James Madison, Charles Darwin, Sigmund Freud, John Locke, Goethe and Spinoza.
**Est: $1,200-$1,500.** (50)

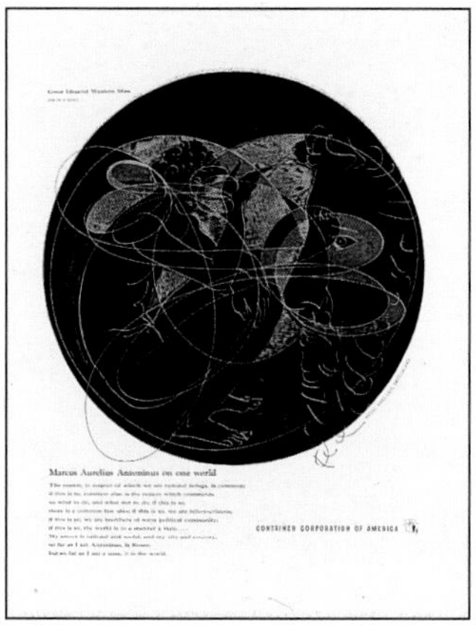

### 279. Ten Posters. 1969-1970.
Each: 30 x 44⁷/₈ in./76.2 x 114 cm
Cond A/P.
The Container Corporation of America went on to produce a poster series based on the previously noted advertisements. Note that one of them, by Wing Fong, was for a shorter companion series titled "Great Ideas of Eastern Man." The notable artists in this series are: Wing Fong, Ben Shahn, James Rosenquist (the three illustrated here), Rene Magritte, Ernest Trova, Jerry N. Uelsmann, Johannes Itten, Hazard Durfee, Hans Erni and John Massey, who was the art director of CCA who commissioned all these works.
**Est: $1,700-$2,000.** (10)

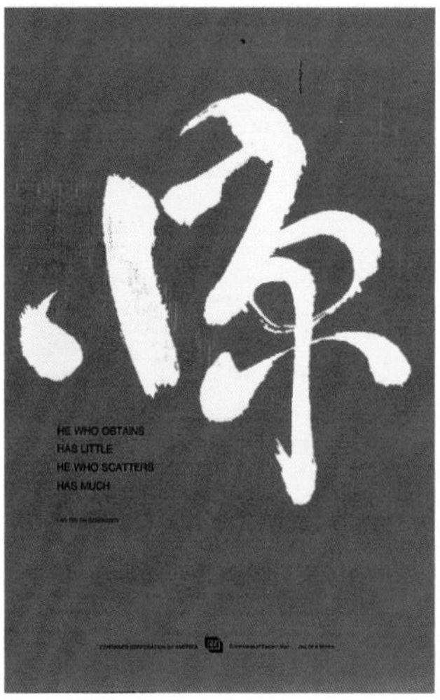

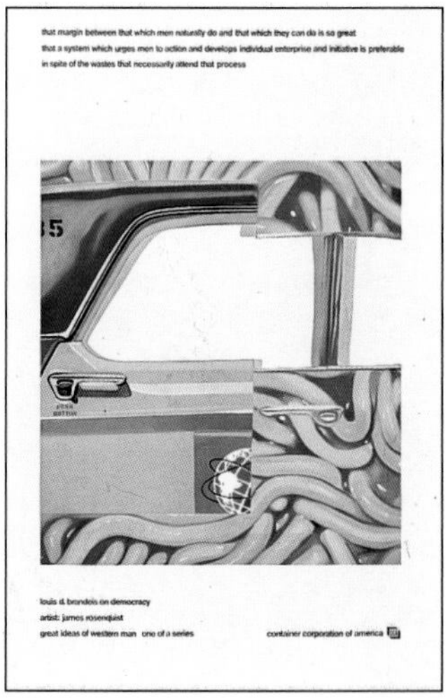

## J. GREENUP (?-1946)

### 280. Harrogate. ca. 1935.
24¹/₂ x 39¹/₂ in./62.2 x 100.5 cm
Waterlow & Sons, London
Cond A.
Ref: Purvis, p. 18; PAI-XII, 236
The bright colors and "smart set" ambiance seen here are utterly in-line with the fine posters produced for the London and North Eastern Railway. Persuasive, isn't it?
**Est: $2,000-$2,500.**

## JULES-ALEXANDRE GRÜN (1868-1938)

### 281. Monaco/Concours de Canots. 1905.
35⁷/₈ x 50 in./91.8 x 127 cm
Imp. F. Daubenbis, Levallois-Paris
Cond A–/Slight staining in margins.
Ref: Grün, p. 127; Image de la Mer, p. 78; PAI-XLII, 312
"Multiple events, renewed and enhanced every year, represented one of the assets of the Principality and a reason to retain the rich clientele after the traditional Winter season and the climax of the Nice carnival. The month of April was therefore chosen for the motorboat competition. The fact that Grün produced two posters tells us that he worked for several years for the principality. Both posters are equally luminous . . . elegant visions retaining . . . their individuality. In one of the pictures, a figure in a red dress on a sailboat looks at the race on an ultramarine sea with grey glints . . . One notices that the typography, generously drawn by hand, is everything but an improvisation by the artist . . . Convenience is not the opposite of precision" (Grün, p. 126).
**Est: $10,000-$12,000.**

**277**

**278**

**279**

### 282. Tournées Ch. Baret/L'Ange de Foyer. 1905.
34³/₄ x 49⁵/₈ in./88.4 x 126 cm
C. Launay, Toulouse
Cond B/Restored tears at folds and edges.
Ref (All Var): Grün, p. 23; DFP-II, 449; PAI-XL, 352
Sometimes you need the whole poster to get the whole picture—most especially in early posters that combined a letterpress text with changing lithographic tip-ons to convey the changing message. That is true, for instance, of Toulouse-Lautrec's "Le Pendu," whose inclusion as one of the master's posters only makes sense in the larger context of its placement in the larger text poster for "La Dépêche" newspaper (*see* PAI-IX, 517). And this method, successfully used in earlier theatrical posters, as seen in this Grün creation, which illustrates the second-half billing of the Baret theatrical tour, "A Serious Client," whose further title, "A Judicial Fantasy in One Act," hints at the mayhem to ensue.
**Est: $1,400-$1,700.**

### 283. Model Assets.
10³/₈ x 13¹/₈ in./26.3 x 33.4 cm
*Hand-signed ink and gouache drawing.* Framed.
There's no doubt that this is a self-portrait of Grün standing next to one of his models. And there can be little doubt regarding another aspect of the drawing: Grün's fixated on her breasts, plain and simple. And you know what else—she's not insulted in the least. In fact, it appears as if she may be actively puffing herself up a bit for his benefit. She knows the score. Humorous, insightful and just a touch self-deprecating, the artist's handiwork speaks volumes as to the nature of commercial imagery that's as valid today as when he first set the image to the page. Because no matter how enlightened we like to believe we've become, one promotional dictum resonates above all the others and for good reason: Sex Sells.
**Est: $2,500-$3,000.**

## HARROGATE
### YORKSHIRE
ON THE
**LONDON AND NORTH EASTERN RAILWAY**
**OF ENGLAND AND SCOTLAND**

280

**AVRIL**
**EXPOSITION**
ET **CONCOURS**
DE **CANOTS**
**AUTOMOBILES**

281

TOURNÉE CH. BARET
## THÉATRE DU HAVRE
### Jeudi 21 Décembre 1905
Une seule Représentation de l'immense Succès
# L'ANGE DU FOYER
Comédie en 3 actes de MM. de FLERS et de CAILLAVET
**M. CH. BARET jouera le rôle de SIGISMOND**
On terminera par le chef-d'œuvre de COURTELINE
# UN CLIENT SÉRIEUX
Fantaisie judiciaire en un acte

**M. CH. BARET** jouera le rôle de **LAGOUPILLE**
Imprimerie spéciale de publicité pour Tournées Artistiques, C. LAUNAY, 10, place Saint-Martin, Vendôme

282

283

**284**

**285**

**286**

**287**

**288**

## GRÜN (cont'd)

**284. La Cigale/Y a du linge.** 1904.
15³/4 x 23¹/8 in./40 x 58.8 cm
Imp. Chaix, Paris
Cond A. Framed.
Ref: Grün, p. 53; Spectacle, 971; Theaterplakate, 43; PAI-XLI, 321
"'Y'a du linge', which is entitled 'Revue Féerie' had to closely adhere to the style chosen by La Cigale. The plot had to be non-existent. Grün, playing with the title, portrays a full-length *Grünette* dancing wildly and displaying her petticoat. Linen—which in slang ('Beau linge') also means a posh public—is ironically represented in the background by its opposite . . . wearing a monocle and who drops his cigar out of sheer rapture" (Grün, p. 53).
**Est: $2,000-$2,500.**

**285. Automobile Club de France.** 1905.
62¹/4 x 46⁷/8 in./158.3 x 119 cm
Imp. Charles Verneau, Paris
Cond B/Restored paper loss along horizontal fold.

Ref: Grün, p. 102; PAI-XXVI, 44
"The Automobile Club de France was created on the initiative of three automobile enthusiasts, the Comte de Dion, Paul Meyran and the Baron de Zuylen who became its president upon its inception on November 2, 1895. It is under his leadership that the competitions and the main salons took place. As proven by this poster, the salon did not only cater to races and tourism but also to the industrial and military vehicles—important markets as well. Beginning with the army maneuvers in 1900, the generalissimo only traveled by automobile. The army is outfitted with Georges Richard and Mors vehicles and Renault enters fully into the military market. In 1905 Grün discovers the world of color. He doesn't fall into the trap of trying to describe —which would have been impossible. He decides to evoke. In the foreground a gendarme, saluting at attention, on the left a joyous crowd and in the background, standing out against the setting sun, as in a shadowgraph, a stream of barely identifiable vehicles" (Grün, p. 102).
**Est: $3,000-$4,000.**

**286. Cocoricol** 1913.
30¹/8 x 45¹/4 in./76.5 x 115 cm
Atelier Grün, Paris
Cond A.
Ref: Grün, p. 88; PAI-XXXII, 340
"The light opera by Ganne bearing the same title (as the well-known magazine) is justly forgotten and the poster by Grün extremely rare. Louis Ganne (1862-1923) who was a conductor at the Cabaret des Incohérents (where Grün designed a bit of the scenery) had a full career as a conductor and composer of unremarkable light operas. If he remains known today it is as the composer of the Marche Loraine—one of the jewels of our military repertory—which bring us to this light opera undoubtedly belonging to the same sphere. The black background as well as the red color dressing the rooster are de rigueur. Obviously, Grün doesn't like to switch palettes and always seems to be radically allergic to the color blue. A few Napoleonic souvenirs and some roses on a feedbox put finishing touches to the picture. The 'Cocorico', itself, is all done in yellow" (Grün, p. 88).
**Est: $1,700-$2,000.**

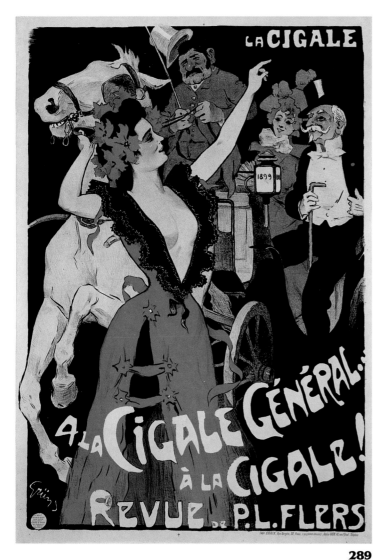

**289**　　　　　　　　　　　　　　　　　　　**290**

**291**

**287. Concert Européen/Veux-tu Grimper?** 1898.
15⁷/₈ x 23³/₈ in./40.2 x 59.4 cm
Cond A. Framed.
Ref: Grün, p. 55; PAI-XL, 354
"The Concert Européen, located on Rue Biot close to the Place Clichy, was primarily known as a realist theatre (which it became after 1905). Although barely mentioned in its time, it staged at least one revue

written by P.L. Flers with Marville, a star in those days, as captain. Wearing a boater and dressed all in red she displays her generous bum presumably suggesting ideas to the passerby—especially given the title of the revue ("Want to Climb up?") (Grün, p. 55). *This is the smaller format before the addition of letters.*
**Est: $1,700-$2,000.**

**288. Heureusement que je suis Assuré!!!**
23¹/₈ x 31 in./59 x 78.8 cm
Imp. Formstecher, Paris
Cond B/Restored tears at folds and edges.
"I'm happy to be insured," says the cyclist as he and his bicycle tumble over a squashed pooch. This essential service for the early cyclist gives us his address, tells us that the policy can be bought at all bicycle dealers and renters, and can be purchased on a daily or weekly basis, but fails to give us the company's name. An important message forcefully and charmingly conveyed. *Rare!*
**Est: $1,400-$1,700.**

**289. A la Cigale Général.** 1899.
34 x 48⁷/₈ in./86.3 x 124.3 cm
Imp. Chaix, Paris
Cond A.
Ref: Grün, p. 50; DFP-II, 433 (var); PAI-XLIII, 359
"On July 27, 1899 P. L. Flers creates a new revue at the Cigale: 'A la Cigale Général, à la Cigale'. Grün, once again in demand, returns to his favorite black background with the heroine dressed in red in the foreground. Behind the horse that she is reining in, stands a coachman, losing his hat and a well-accompanied old dandy. The rosette of the Legion of Honor he is wearing may well indicate that he is a general. As usual, everything is well laid out, funny and done with brio" (Grün, p. 50). *This is the larger format.*
**Est: $1,700-$2,000.**

**290. Scala/Revue à Poivre.** 1903.
16¹/₈ x 23¹/₄ in./41 x 59.2 cm
Imp. Charles Verneau, Paris
Cond A-/Slight stains at edges.
Ref: Grün, p. 63 (var); DFP-II, 436 (var); PAI-XLI, 319
"As far as the 'Revue à Poivre' which opens in 1904 is concerned . . . (a) cheerful and exposed young lady takes up the whole picture. She is wearing the customary low-cut red dress shown against a black background. As usual the show was a major production, led by Suzanne Derval and Miss Dieterle and accompanied by a 30-piece orchestra conducted by Beretta. Appearing in supporting parts were two comedians who would become the talk of the town, Gaby Deslys and Eugénie Fougère" (Grün, p. 63). *This is the smaller format.*
**Est: $2,000-$2,500.**

**291. Un derrière menu et le menu derrière.** 1929.
10³/₄ x 14³/₄ in./27.3 x 37.5 cm
Imp. H. Hachard, Paris
Cond A/P.
There's no shortage of images of naked women in classic poster design. To be sure it's somewhat exploitative, but the one thing that Grün has going for him over practically any other artist is that his creations are always refreshingly playful. Even more so than with Pal, there seems to be a genuine affection for and appreciation of the female form that transcends mere T & A. Perhaps that's a hopelessly XY chromosome interpretation, but I present as evidence this menu cover design for "Le Cornet" dinner of February 28, 1929. In case you don't speak French (although that's barely a requirement for this design), allow me to provide a translation for the single line of text: "A slender fanny and the back of the menu." Which is precisely where this appeared. Granted the wordplay is far more clever in its native tongue, but the bottom line is that it's fun. And that certainly should count for something, shouldn't it?
**Est: $600-$800.**

**292**

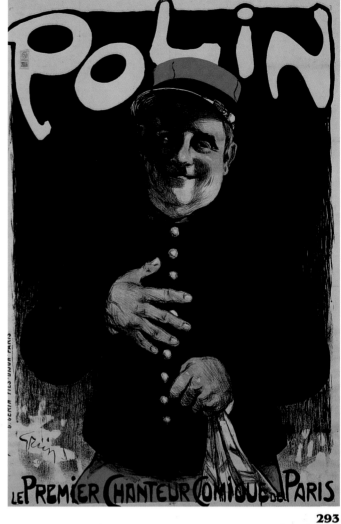

**293**

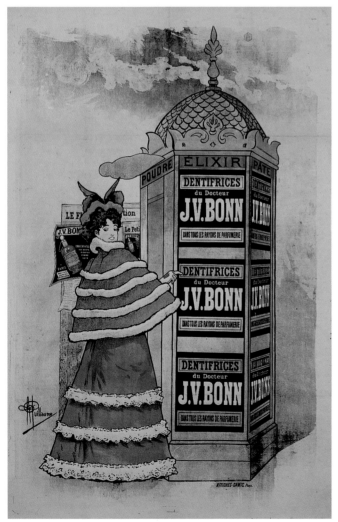

**294**

**296**

OUVERTURE DE NOUVEAUX RAYONS DE CHAPELLERIE
VOIR LES ÉTALAGES

295

297

## GRÜN (cont'd)

**292. Magic City.** ca. 1910.
$11^1/2$ x $15^5/8$ in./29.3 x 39.8 cm
Dauvin, Paris
Cond A.
Ref: Grün, p. 87; PAI-XL, 355 (var)
"Located on the Quai d'Orsay, Magic City was a huge, Luna-Park that survived until the Second World War. The Surrealists loved its entertainment and Brassaï used it for some of his pictures. Grün draws a group of crazy revelers emerging from a heart with a décor of attractions in the background" (Grün, p. 87).
**Est: $1,500-$1,700.**

**293. Polin.** 1900.
$36^1/2$ x 54 in./92.7 x 137 cm
G. Guerin, Dijon
Cond B/Slight tears at folds. Framed.
Ref: Grün, p. 80 (var); PAI-XLII, 311
"In 1877, Ouvard creates the 'comique troupier' genre at the café concert by launching 'L'invalide à la jambe de bois.' At a time when military service was endless, the character of the dim and clumsy peasant draftee delights the public. In 1891, when wearing a uniform is allowed on stage, every concert hall has its own

'comique troupier' act" (Grün, p. 80). For over forty years, café-concert legend Polin (the stage name of singer Pierre-Paul Marsalés (1863-1927) reigned supreme over the musical halls of Montmartre and the Champs-Elysées. Making his debut in 1886 at *Concert de la Pépinière*, he would go on to delight audiences well into the next century with the timid sincerity and naive charm of the character he created. This poster portrait of the performer isn't precisely the fare one has come to expect from the most titillating chronicler of the Montmartre nightlife scene. Grün does an admirable job of capturing the essential Polin, setting down "Paris' Premiere Comic singer" with impish delight, decked out in his trademark ill-fitting uniform, with his beloved security handkerchief clasped firmly in his hand. Though other versions of this poster show Polin in a full-length pose (*see* PAI-XXXI, 65), this particular variant places the focus on the performer and less on the costume he wore. *For Barrère's view of the performer, see No. 86.*
**Est: $1,700-$2,000.**

## ALBERT GUILLAUME (1873-1942)

**294. J. V. Bonn Dentifrices.** 1893.
$49^1/4$ x $74^3/4$ in./125 x 189.8 cm
Affiches Camis, Paris
Cond A–/Unobtrusive folds.
Ref: Gallo, p. 122; PAI-XXXIX, 314
To sell Dr. Bonn's dentifrice, Guillaume gives us a very accurate portrait of a turn-of-the-twentieth-century kiosk—a "Morris column," as it was called, after the Morris printing firm, whose letterpress posters dominated such hoardings. From a small table at the opening to the left, a lady usually sat and sold the day's newspapers and magazines. Guillaume was one of the most prolific illustrators of his day, displaying thirty-two of his posters in the landmark Reims exhibition in 1896 and acting as a regular contributor of numerous illustrations to such journals as *Gil Blas* and *Figaro Illustré*.
**Est: $2,500-$3,000.**

**295. Delion.** ca. 1895.
$73^1/4$ x $48^1/2$ in./186 x 123 cm
Affiches Camis, Paris
Cond B/Slight tears at folds and edges.
Ref: DFP-II, 455; Maindron, p. 73; Timeless Images, 13; Célébrités, 203; PAI-XLII, 318
To announce the opening of a hat department in the Delion store, Guillaume showed a reviewing stand with a broad caricature of contemporary notables, including the critic Sarcey on the far left, possibly Toulouse-Lautrec next to him, Valentin le Desossé, Aristide Bruant and Emile Zola. The fifth figure from the left, with glasses and looking at us, is most probably Guillaume himself. All the assembled gentlemen are wearing hats that they presumably purchased from Delion.
**Est: $2,500-$3,000.**

## RAOUL GUINOT

**296. Goodrich.**
$46^1/4$ x $62^1/4$ in./117.6 x 158.2 cm
Imp. Sirven, Toulouse
Cond B+/Slight tears at folds.
"The road has changed Masters. And so the former master from days gone by bows before today's leader." Thus, this Goodrich tire advertisement plays itself out literally with a coachman subjugating himself before an oversized "Souple Corde" tire. The poster was taken from an original creation by Raoul Guinot (hence, the "d'après" designation), an artist for which no biographical data could be found who nonetheless created a minimum of one design worth interpreting for public consumption.
**Est: $2,000-$2,500.**

## L. GUY

**297. Bal des Etudiants.** 1901.
33 x $97^3/8$ in./83.8 x 247.3 cm
Imp. G. Gounouilhou, Bordeaux
Cond A–/Slight stains at edges.
Ref: PAI-XXXVI, 396
This 2-sheet poster is a mind-blowing tribute to what a Bacchanalia the Students' Ball of February 2, 1901, must have been. As an extravagantly attired female reveler positions herself beneath an ornate archway—unaware that the Devil is lurking beneath her skirt or that one of his impish legion is carefully unlacing her outfit—a tag-team of rogues does their best to ply her with bubbly, one of them distracting her, while the other keeps her glass constantly filled to the rim. A magnificent nod to unbridled merriment, open to any number of lascivious interpretations.
**Est: $2,500-$3,000.**

## EDI HAURI (1911-1988)

**298. Ovignac Senglet.**
$35^1/2$ x $50^1/4$ in./90.3 x 127.7 cm
A. Trüb, Aarau
Cond A/P.
It's true that roosters don't lay eggs, but they certainly can do a fine job promoting egg-infused products. The combination of cognac and eggs hardly seems likely (perhaps it was some form of an eggnog-style product, but this balanced-and-banded barnyard fowl certainly gives off an impression of vitality and well-being, so who's to say? As is the custom with posters produced for the Senglet firm, the text appears in both French and German. Hauri received his training in both his native Basel and Berlin. After Hitler's rise to power, he returned to Switzerland, freelancing for several years before eventually opening his own studio in the early 1940s, specializing in tourist and product posters.
**Est: $800-$1,000.**

## EDWIN HERMANN RICHARD HENEL (1883-1953)

**299. Deutsche Ski-Meisterschaft.** 1927.
23³/₄ x 35 in./60.4 x 89 cm
Kunst in Druck, München
Cond A.
Ref: PAI-XLI, 329
What a rather ingenious creation. From its majestic peaks to its regal violet tonality to its high-flying competitor, one easily makes the assumption that this promotion is intended to draw spectators to the 1927 German ski championship. However, the truth of the matter is that it's an advertisement for a sporting goods store sale featuring deep discounts in conjunction with the winter sports competition. Henel specialized in mountain scenes as a painter; a native of Breslau, he studied there, but most of his adult life was spent in Munich.
**Est: $1,700-$2,000.**

## BERN HILL (1911-1977)

**300. American Airlines/New England.**
30¹/₄ x 39³/₄ in./76.8 x 100.8 cm
Cond A.
Hill was a freelance illustrator and painter. His clean, precise designs are marked by unusual perspectives, panoramic vantage points and striking chiaroscuro. Though he could count General Motors, American Airlines, *Reader's Digest* and *Saturday Evening Post* among his clients, Hill is perhaps best known for his depictions of trains that appeared on model railroad packaging and on the covers of railroad magazines. A native of Toronto, he also had a particular fondness for New England (Hill lived in Connecticut for most of his career), an attitude that comes across loud and clear in his advertisement for American Airlines' service to the region. Most interestingly, Hill manages to underscore the area with one of the craft in American's fleet without intruding into the scene. Or making the airplane a noticeable feature of the design, for that matter.
**Est: $1,000-$1,200.**

## ARMIN HOFMANN (1920- )

**301. Giselle.** 1959.
35¹/₂ x 50¹/₄ in./90.2 x 127.6 cm
Wassermann, Basel
Cond A/P.
Working from a Merkle photograph, Hofmann utilizes little more than balletic simplicity to promote a late-summer open-air presentation of "Giselle" playing in Basel's Rosenfeldpark. One of the few ballets to have survived the Romantic era of the mid-1800s, "Giselle"

tells the story of the title character, a young, innocent village maiden who's in love with a man she knows only as Loys. In reality, the man is Albrecht, a nobleman disguised as a peasant—an already betrothed nobleman. When Giselle discovers the deceit, she is inconsolable and first goes mad, then dies of a broken heart. In the second act, her undying love for Albrecht saves him from the wicked magic of the *wilis*—vampiric ghosts of betrothed girls who died before their wed-

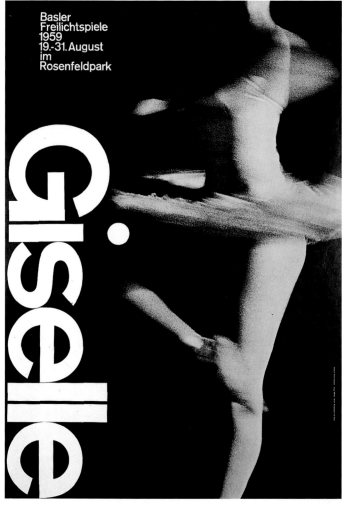

**301**

**304**

**302**

**303. Nivea.** 1953.
46³/₈ x 66 in./117.7 x 167.5 cm
Cond A.
How yummy! With her one-piece looking like a scratch-off applied for more puritanical markets, there's really no question that this bronzed, raven-haired stunner could have achieved her glow with any product other than Nivea. Ironically in terms of this poster, the skin and body-care brand—founded in 1911 in Germany by Oskar Troplowitz—derives its name from the Latin word "nivius," which means "snow-white."
**Est: $1,000-$1,200.**

## LUDWIG HOHLWEIN (1874-1949)

**304. Atlas—Salatoelle.** 1910.
29¹/₂ x 42⁵/₈ in./75 x 108.2 cm
Vereinigte Druckereien & Kunstanstalten, München
Cond B+/Slight tears at folds and paper edges.
Ref: DFP-III, 1383; Hohlwein, p. 81;
    Hohlwein/Stuttgart, 39
Why on earth is this little lady approaching this over-sized bottle of Atlas salad oil with such trepidation? Could it be that she's concerned that even though this particular flavor is delicious, she might be missing out on something by not choosing one of the other four Atlas varieties? Despite her apprehension, she's cute as a button and the advertisement is downright adorable. Hohlwein's "special way of applying colors, letting them dry at different times, and printing one on top of the other, producing modulations of shading, has often been copied, but never equaled. He belonged to no school or group, his art and personality are an unprecedented phenomenon in the history of German poster art" (Rademacher, p. 22). And Weill comments that "Beginning with his first efforts, Hohlwein found his style with disconcerting facility; it would vary little for the next forty years. The drawing was perfect from the start . . . nothing seemed alien to him, and in any case, nothing posed a problem for him" (pp. 107-110).
**Est: $2,500-$3,000.**

## HOFMANN (Atelier)

**302. Ulka.** 1958.
65³/₈ x 47⁷/₈ in./166 x 121.6 cm
F. Adametz, Wien
Cond A.
If you take the lithographic advice of the following poster from this Austrian graphic studio and use Nivea products as a part of a regime to deliver beautiful skin that needs—nay, deserves—to be seen, you might want to get your hands on an Ulka in order to show off in proper style. From one-pieces to bikinis, Ulka can ful-fill your swimsuit dreams. And you simply can't beat their promotional text: "Do it for youth's sake!"
**Est: $1,000-$1,200.**

ding day. Though their leader forces Albrecht to dance again and again, Giselle intervenes long enough to spare his strength and allow him to survive until the dawn, because at sunrise, these ghosts must return to their graves. Giselle, too, must return but not before show-ing Albrecht that she forgives him for his treachery. The two pledge their love to each other and she descends back into her grave. Forever separated from her true love, Giselle becomes a *wili* for the rest of eternity. The revered Swiss graphic artist shows how photography, creatively used, can result in a most effective design.
**Est: $800-$1,000.**

## ROLAND HUGON (1911- )

**305. Superbagnères-Luchon.** 1937.
24¹/₂ x 39 in./62.2 x 99 cm
Ed. Paul Martial, Paris
Cond B+/Slight tears and stains at edges.
Ref: PAI-XL, 83

Hugon's career is closely linked to advertising agent, Paul Martial, "that lover of beautiful printing and of modern typography and layout . . . for whom (Hugon) conceived a whole gamut of advertising material in a style perfectly in accord with the ideas of his employer" (Train à l'Affiche, p. 79). The perfect union of designer to subject is in full effect in Hugon's superbly and cleverly crafted poster for the French National Railways and Superbagnères, a resort to the south of the famous spa of Luchon, deep in the Pyrenees. Located some 3,000 feet higher than Luchon, it offers some of the best mountainscapes around, including a view of the highest point of the range, Pic de Néthou. Who knew that a glove fitted atop a ski pole could be so commanding and persuasive?
**Est: $2,000-$2,500.**

## ROBERT INDIANA (1928- )

**306. New York City Center/25th Anniversary.** 1968.
24³/₄ x 34³/₄ in./63 x 88.2 cm
List Art Poster
Cond A. Framed.
Ref: PAI-XV, 304 (var)

One of the pioneers of pop art, Indiana is perhaps best remembered for his 1973 design with the four letters LOVE arranged in a square. This poster for the twenty-fifth anniversary of the New York City Center comes from the height of his most productive period and shows Indiana's consummate skill in modern graphics, particularly in the use of typography for startling effect. Built in 1923 as a meeting hall for the members of the Ancient Order of the Nobles of the Mystic Shrine, the building with the neo-Moorish facade was saved from destruction by Mayor Fiorello LaGuardia and City Council President Newbold Morris, who created Manhattan's first performing arts center. In the mid-1970s, with the opera and ballet moving to Lincoln Center and the building underused, City Center was again slated for demolition. Under the leadership of chairman Howard M. Squadron, the theater was rededicated as New York's premiere home for dance and was given landmark status.
**Est: $1,200-$1,500.**

## INTOURIST

Established on April 12, 1929, Intourist was responsible for managing the vast majority of foreigners' access to and travel within the Soviet Union. The Russian travel agency had exclusive rights to operate in foreign tourist markets and to open offices abroad, in turn growing into one of the largest tourism organisations in the world, with a network embracing banks, hotels and bureaux de change. And from its inception, its logo has remained the same—a symbolic wing over the globe.

Intourist opened the first door in the "Iron Curtain," allowing visitors to see first-hand—in a, shall we say, controlled manner—what was happening in the USSR. It operated on a very specific two-pronged approach: selling international tours of the Soviet Union to foreigners, while promoting domestic tourism within its vast borders. It is to the first Intourist directive that these three works were intended.

### 307. Intourist/Soviet Armenia.
Artist: **Anonymous**
24³/₄ x 35¹/₄ in./63 x 89.5 cm
Cond B+/Unobtrusive tears, largely at edges.
Though not singled out by name, the unmistakable majesty of the snowcapped, dormant volcanic cone of

Mount Ararat and the smaller Mount Sis—as framed by a towering railroad overpass—clearly identifies the city in the mid-ground as Yerevan. The history of Yerevan dates back to the 8th century BC, but it's "Soviet Armenia" that's being touted here with Colorform prosperity by Intourist. And it was during the Soviet era that Yerevan was metamorphosed from a city of a few thousand residents into a modern metropolis with over a million people, a large industrial, cultural and

USSR HEALTH RESORTS

**308**

THE SOVIET UKRAINE

**309**

**310**

LES PRODUITS
Joseph Milliat
sont vendus
CHEZ VOTRE BOULANGER
et chez les Patissiers

FARINE
PATES ALIMENTAIRES
RIZ, SEMOULE, LEVURE
ETC.

**311**

SOUTH WALES
SEE BRITAIN BY TRAIN · WESTERN REGION

**312**

scientific center, and capital of the newly formed Armenian Soviet Socialist Republic.
**Est: $1,200-$1,500.**

**308. Intourist/USSR Health Resorts.**
Artist: **Maria Aleksandrovna Nesterova (1897-1965)**
24$^1$/4 x 39$^1$/8 in./61.5 x 99.5 cm
Vneshtorg Publishing
Cond B/Restored paper loss at top edge; tears at paper edges.
Of course, not everyone wanted to combine work and play on their visit to the Soviet Union. Some folks just needed to get away from it all and where better to do that than the "USSR Health Resorts" of the Russian Riviera. Though we can't say with complete surety, it seems rather likely that we're being treated to a vertiginous view of Yalta—the dramatically handsome resort on the southern tip of Crimea—in this tropical Nesterov design. The designer is probably the wife of Mikhail Nesterov (1862-1942), a noted Russian poster designer.
**Est: $1,200-$1,500.**

**309. Intourist/The Soviet Ukraine.**
Artist: **Anonymous**
27$^1$/4 x 39$^1$/2 in./69.4 x 100.4 cm

Vneshtorg Publishing
Cond B/Restored paper loss at bottom right corner.
Come for the plums, stay for the wheat. Clearly the Intourist lure for "The Soviet Ukraine" is its agricultural superiority. Granted, that may be Kiev lurking greyly in the background, but this uncredited design isn't about urban attraction—it's about the joy of the harvest, the prosperity of golden fields of wheat being thrashed on the banks of the Dnieper River and the indigenous pride one can feel when one commits to the Greater Good.
**Est: $1,200-$1,500.**

**JAN**

**310. Bowden.** 1910.
25$^1$/8 x 38$^1$/2 in./63.7 x 97.5 cm
Affiches Etienne Faure, Marseille
Cond B-/Tears and stains at folds and edges.
Loaded down with an array of unicycles and bicycles—to say nothing of a lantern to light his way—that borders on the absurd, Bowden makes his way through the streets of France, always at the ready to demonstrate his vehicular skills. A classic tramp-style clown, it's safe to assume that Bowden plied his trade regionally, yet for whatever reason wasn't lucky enough to

cross over into the Big Time. Also supporting this conclusion is the fact that the stock poster displays no specific dates or theater—merely a "music hall" flanked by two further line-drawn posters-within-the poster. The moon, however, approves, as do we—though Bowden may never have become a legend, Jan infuses his design with a playfulness no doubt inspired by the performer himself.
**Est: $1,000-$1,200.**

**PAUL JANIN**

**311. Joseph Milliat.** ca. 1940.
47$^1$/4 x 62$^3$/4 in./120 x 159.3 cm
P.A.L.
Cond B+/Slight tears at paper edges.
Ref: PAI-XXXVIII, 385
Janin, a Lyonese artist best known for his engravings and woodblock designs, lends that artistic bent to this creation—most especially in his use of marked outlines—for the Joseph Milliat line of foodstuffs (pasta, rice, yeast, semolina, flour, etc). This technique also helps to make the genial familial narrative crystal clear, solidifying the fact that everyone involved couldn't be happier that Milliat pasta was on its way to the table.
**Est: $1,200-$1,500.**

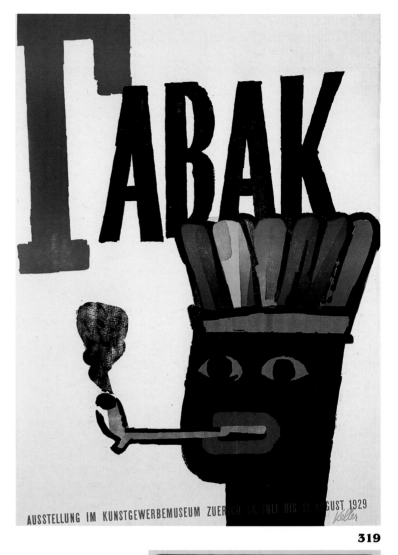

**313**

**319**

## JOHNSTON

### 312. South Wales/See Britain By Train.
49³/₄ x 40 in./126.2 x 101.7 cm
Jordison, London & Middlesborough
Cond B/Tears at folds and edges.
Wales is often called the "Land of Castles" and rightly so, as it's home to some of Europe's finest surviving examples of medieval castle construction. It's tempting to say that Johnston was reproducing Dinefwr Castle —overlooking the Tywi Valley and Gwendaeth River— as a lure to get folks to "See Britain By Train," but the artist's treatment is so impressionistically soft that it's difficult to assign specific identification, especially when it comes to determining architectural ruins as seen from a distance. All conjecture aside, Johnston's pro-motion is simply lovely—assuaging and inviting, the ideal landscape to experience during a roll on the rails.
**Est: $1,400-$1,700.**

## PAUL KAMMÜLLER (1885-1946)

### 313. Schweizerische Nationale Flugspende. 1913.
27 x 39¹/₂ in./68.4 x 100.4 cm
W. Wassermann, Basel
Cond A-/Restored borders.
In 1913, the Swiss government initiated a campaign that they called "Flugspende." Literally translated, these "flight donations" were intended to raise the public's consciousness of the need for military aviation, as well as to raise money earmarked for that purpose. The campaign included fifteen special mail carrying flights, all with unique postmarks furnished by the Swiss postal authority. To promote the event, Kammüller created this minimalist vision whose primary allusion to the funds that the powers-that-be hoped to raise is con-veyed by the design's overwhelmingly golden tone. And with a sunburst fairly erupting over the Matterhorn, an

aircraft bathed in the glow of a prosperous dawn soars up and over the prospective patron, instilling both awe and confidence in the process. When World War I broke out, Kammüller moved from Baden-Baden to Basel, Switzerland, and accepted a teaching post; he thereafter became a Swiss citizen. *Rare!*
**Est: $3,000-$3,500.**

## E. MCKNIGHT KAUFFER (1890-1954)

### 314. American Airlines/Holland. 1948.
30¹/₈ x 39³/₄ in./76.6 x 101 cm
Cond A.
Ref: Kauffer, 299
Kauffer designed some thirty posters for American Air-lines in a period from 1948 to 1953. In his poster for their service to Holland—one of the finest and rarest of his entire body of work for AA—a ubiquitous tulip-and-windmill motif serves to attract the attention of the passersby. As always, the simple design and strong colors reveal Kauffer's expert craftsmanship with sim-ple, powerful travel posters.
**Est: $1,200-$1,500.**

### 315. Civil Aeronautics Administration. 1943.
28⁵/₈ x 39⁵/₈ in./72.7 x 100.6 cm
U. S. Government printing Office, Washington D.C.
Cond A-/Slight tears at edges.
Ref: Livre de l'Affiche, 175; PAI-XXVII, 88
A very striking World War II poster, with the three words in red, white and blue hitting just the right patriotic chord. Although these posters were printed by the Government in large quantities, this is today one of the rarest Kauffer designs.
**Est: $1,500-$1,800.**

**314**

### 316. Pan American/Germany. 1948.
28¹/₄ x 41³/₄ in./71.8 x 106 cm
Cond A.
Ref: Kauffer, checklist, p. 124
Although he was a native of the United States, born in Montana, McKnight Kauffer spent most of his creative years in England. Returning home for the last fifteen years of his life, he designed posters in a New York studio, where his biggest clients were book publishers —Random House, Hartcourt Brace, Alfred A. Knopf, Doubleday, Pantheon and Modern Library—and Ameri-

315

316

317

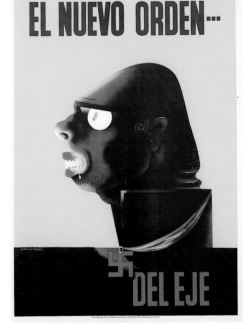

318

320

can Airlines. "His color harmonies, his arrangements of pattern, his sensitivity in the development of an appropriate image or symbol . . . and his mastery of execution have seldom been equaled" (Catalogue of McKnight Kauffer exhibition, Cooper-Hewitt Museum, 1989-1990). In his poster for Pan Am's service to Germany, he dispenses with the mode of transportation altogether, opting instead for a *tal und schloss* approach to promote the loveliness of the destination.
**Est: $1,200-$1,500.**

**317. Pan American/Ireland.** 1953.
28¹/₄ x 41³/₄ in./71.7 x 106 cm
Cond A.
Ref: Kauffer, checklist, p. 124
As was the case in the previous poster, Kauffer utilizes trees and a castle to promote a Pan American destination. However, in the hands of a skilled artist such as this, a tree isn't just a tree and a fortress isn't just a structure—they're nationalistic markers for a specific locale. And once again, no airplane is required to promote air travel—however the bird fluttering about the forest is a nice touch.
**Est: $1,200-$1,500.**

**318. El Nuevo Orden . . .** 1942.
28³/₈ x 40 in./72 x 101.5 cm
Publicado par El Coordinator de Asuntas Interamericanos, Washington, EUA
Cond B/Tears at folds and paper edges.
Ref: Kauffer, checklist, p. 123
Intended for distribution in South America, this grotesque subhuman puts a face to "The New Order of the Axis"—a drooling monster, a monocled orc, ravenous and destructive. In short, an affront to humanity. Regardless of who is executing the propaganda, one aspect remains consistent—it's never difficult to determine which group the artist intends to coalesce his intended audience against. Subtlety takes an immediate back seat, and the same can be said for Kauffer, a posterist typically admired for his gentle persuasion who here, through ogreish distortion (or perhaps simply an outer manifestation of inner decrepitude), expands the boundaries of his creative output towards unanticipated horizons.
**Est: $1,500-$1,800.**

## ERNST KELLER (1891-1968)

**319. Tabak.** 1929.
36⁵/₈ x 49³/₈ in./93 x 125.4 cm
Cond A-/Slight creasing and stains at paper edges.
Ref: Margadant, 484; Müller-Brockmann, 82;
    Keller, p. 81; PAI-XXIX, 428
In a brilliant poster for a tobacco exhibition at the Applied Arts Museum of Zurich, Keller gives us a stark and simple design of a tribal bust. It was at the Applied Art School of this museum that Keller taught graphic arts for many years and became a great influence on a whole generation of Swiss posterists and designers. Weill calls this his best poster, the "perfect simplification and harmonization of text and image" (p. 249).
**Est: $2,500-$3,000.**

## DAVID KLEIN (1918-2005)

**320. Fly TWA/New York.**
24⁷/₈ x 40⁵/₈ in./63 x 103 cm
Cond A.
Klein was an American artist, best known for his influential work in advertising. Born in El Paso, Texas, he moved to California where he attended the Art Center School in Los Angeles, became a member of the California Watercolor Society and displayed his work at various exhibits, most notably the Golden Gate International Exhibition of 1939-40. However, Klein is best remembered for the dozens of destination advertisements he created for Trans World Airlines during the 1950s and '60s. Most of this poster output depicts famous landmarks in the abstract, a style that is widely attributed to his early work in watercolor. For Destination New York, Klein creates a stacked perspective of some of the city's best known sights, piling landmark upon landmark—St. Patrick's Cathedral, Rockefeller Plaza's Prometheus et al.—then crowning them with a bust of Lady Liberty.
**Est: $800-$1,000.**

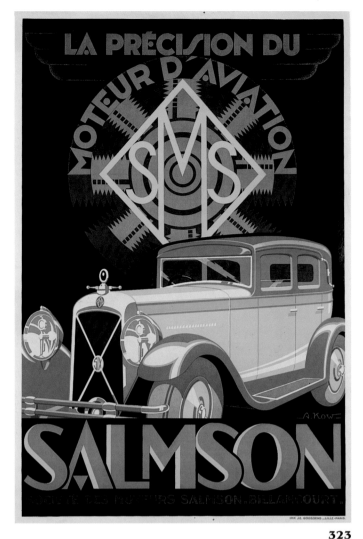

**321**

**323**

*Bien-être en*
# AUTRICHE

**322**

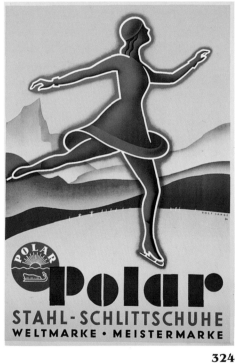

**324**

**326**

## RICHARD KNAB & HANS HEINRICH KOCH

**321. Xaverl als Millionär/Märzenkeller.** 1921.
33⅝ x 45¼ in./85.5 x 115 cm
Kunst in Druck, München
Cond A-/Slight stains at paper edges.
This luggage-leaning swell couldn't be any other than the title character of "Xaverl as a Millionaire." Clearly a rube-out-of-water tale, the show playing itself out at

Munich's Märzenkeller cabaret had to have been popular at least on a local level—the poster indicates that this is "Part 6" in the Xaverl saga. This would seem to indicate that each episodic presentation placed Xaverl into different situations, all of which exploited the character in a different, yet equally side-splitting fashion. Here he's rich; perhaps in a former—or future—installment audiences were treated to "Xaverl as a Dairy Farmer" and another week they could see "Xaverl as an Archeologist." The possibilities seem limitless—

as long as the audience continued to find the character hilarious. Knab and Koch's lithographic partnership was formed in the 1920s.
**Est: $1,400-$1,700.**

## HUGO KOSZLER (1899-?)

**322. Autriche.**
25¼ x 37½ in./64 x 95.2 cm
Gistel, Vienna
Cond A-/Unobtrusive tears and stains near folds and edges.
Mittens hung to dry, shoes leaning lazily against the fireplace, watching the snowy world go by. Could there

be any question that this is the very picture of "Well-Being in Austria"? The Koszler poster tempts the French-speaking wanderer to the landlocked republic with a promise of rest and relaxation, but physical activity isn't that far out of the picture. In fact, it's right there in the picture, just on the other side of the lodge's window—skiing, sleighing and everything that the Alps has to offer.
**Est: $800-$1,000.**

## ALEXIS KOW
## (Alexei Kogeynikov, 1901-1978)

**323. Salmson.**
42 x 61³/4 in./106.5 x 156.9 cm
Imp. J.E. Goosens, Lille-Paris
Cond B+/Unobtrusive tears in bottom text area and paper edges.
Ref: PAI-II, 50
Salmson was originally a manufacturer of water-cooled radial airplane engines—and the poster boasts that the car has the precision of these airplane motors. Their first automobiles appeared in 1921, and graduated from flimsy cyclecars to sports cars to elegant luxury sedans. During the 1920s the Salmson, like the Amilcar (see Lot 68), was known as a fine, sporty machine. In 1925, Salmson won seventy-six races and set fourteen speed records for its class. It continued to be a competitive and winning car throughout the 1920s, but the fun-spirited Salmson ended with the stock market crash of 1929; from then on the company concentrated on practical and long-lasting sedans. In 1957, the firm was bought out by Renault, home-based in the same town of Billencourt/Seine. For forty years, Russian-born Kow created smart and sleek automobile print advertisements and posters. Here, he makes effective use of strong, flat colors, setting a black and yellow auto-

mobile with orange and green headlights against a black background, the Salmon insignia flashed above.
**Est: $7,000-$9,000.**

## ROLF LANGE

**324. Polar.** 1934.
22¹/2 x 32 in./57.2 x 81.5 cm
Cond A-/Unobtrusive tears at bottom edge.
A previously seen poster for Polar ice skates (see PAI-VII, 463) took a more traditional point-of-the-blade, skirt-aswirl approach to affixing the eye to the desired product. However, Lange's advertisement is a bit more abstract and less to the point. Though the Alpine environment is self-explanatory, the burnt sienna silhouette of the skater is somewhat more interpretive. As the text states in no uncertain terms that Polar blades are made of steel, perhaps her tone is meant to convey a certain earthiness, a direct connection to the originating ore. And yet her bold white outline creates a neon-esque effect, though neon fixtures are typically more garish in color. Very curious, but unquestionably magnetic—ultimately, a glyph of ice skating superiority.
**Est: $1,200-$1,500.**

## MIKHAIL FEDOROVICH LARIONOV
## (1881-1964)

**325. Grand Bal des Artistes.** 1923.
11 x 8⁵/8 in./28 x 21.8 cm
Cond A/P. Framed.
Painter, stage designer and graphic artist, Larionov studied in Moscow before moving to Paris in 1914 with his wife—and fellow artist—Natalia Gontcharova. He would become one of the major figures of the Twentieth-Century avant-garde movement, in part because of his relationship to Sergei Diaghilev, with whom he worked

with for years at the Ballet Russes. He was involved with Fauvism and founded the Rayonist movement—a name derived from the practitioners' use of dynamic rays of contrasting color to represent lines of light reflected off various objects. Larionov's work helped to pave the way for the Futurist movement and artists such as Filippo Marinetti (see No. 366) and Man Ray. After moving to Paris, Larionov continued to be involved with the Russian art movements, so it's rather fitting that he designed this poster for one of the first artists' balls of the Union of Russian Artists, the "Travesti Transmental." Using only yellow and black, as well as hand-cut letters, the image suggests smaller yet recognizable versions of Cubist figures and works of art. The overall flavor of the poster is definitely in-synch with the Paris avant-garde of the 1920s. Rare!
**Est: $3,000-$4,000.**

## JULES LARTIGNE

**326. Fete de Charité.** 1907.
43¹/4 x 56³/8 in./110 x 143.2 cm
Moullot Fils Aîné, Marseille
Cond B+/Slight tears at folds.
Here's a scene that you don't come across with any frequency: two revelers, one has to assume, on their way to the Toulouse student ball being held for charitable purposes, stop to give a little extra something to one of the unfortunates for which the event is undoubtedly being held. There's no condescension on display in the Lartigne design, merely a sense that it's not a bad idea to look out for one another. Back that sentiment with stirring sunset hues and the poster's intent becomes a fait accompli.
**Est: $2,000-$2,500.**

![Soirée de Paris poster showing a woman riding sidesaddle on a horse, with text "SOIRÉE DE PARIS" and "SPECTACLES CHORÉGRAPHIQUES ET DRAMATIQUES"]

SOIRÉE DE PARIS

*Organisée par*

*Monsieur le Comte Etienne de Beaumont*

AU THÉÂTRE DE LA CIGALE
120, Boulevard Rochechouart.
DU 17 MAI AU 30 JUIN 1924.

au profit de
l'ŒUVRE d'ASSISTANCE
D'AIDE AUX VEUVES DE LA GUERRE
(RECONNUE D'UTILITÉ PUBLIQUE)
et du COMITÉ de SECOURS
aux RÉFUGIÉS RUSSES

SPECTACLES
CHORÉGRAPHIQUES ET DRAMATIQUES

**327**

**329**

### MARIE LAURENCIN (1885-1956)

**327. Soirée de Paris.** 1924.
23$^1$/$_2$ x 32 in./59.8 x 81.3 cm
Imp. Kaplan, Paris
Cond A.
Ref: PAI-XXXIX, 336
Executed in Laurencin's typically wispy watercolor style, this sidesaddle rider gallops into our consciousness to make us aware of a series of charity galas taking place over the course of 1924's late spring and early summer at La Cigale. With promises of dramatic and choreographed spectacles, the money raised will be doled out to several worthy causes, including war veterans and Russian refugees. While pursuing her career as a painter, Laurencin designed a few posters, worked on stage design and created illustrations for literary works.
**Est: $2,500-$3,000.**

### CHARLES LÉANDRE (1862-1930)

**328. Bagnoles de l'Orne.** 1922.
29 x 41 in./73.6 x 104.3 cm
Imp. H. Chachoin, Paris
Cond A.
Léandre was a painter whose sweet, uncloying portraits of mothers and children made him the darling of Paris. A fine draftsman with a wicked wit who was one of the earliest contributors of drawings to *Le Rire*, as well as *Le Chat Noir* and *La Vie Moderne*, the artist was also known for his landscapes. In his poster for the spa located northwest of Alençon in Normandy, we get to see the artist using all the facets of his talent to arrive at a noteworthy destination. Bagnoles de l'Orne is known for its lush green parks, lake and castle, all of which are shown here. But it's the inclusion of the powerful stallion that makes the design work on several levels. First off, seeing as the commune is famous for its healing hydrotherapeutic baths, a visit here will make you feel healthy as a horse. Secondly, Normandy is a horse-breeding region and Bagnoles de l'Orne plays host to

many equestrian events at both its splendid belle epoque racecourse and in the castle's park. Lastly, legend has it that an over-the-hill medieval lord—not to mention his aging steed—became revitalized and rejuvenated after drinking deep from the waters of Bagnoles. Thus, a spa was born.
**Est: $1,000-$1,200.**

### VLADIMIR VASILIEVICH LEBEDEV (1891-1967)

**329. Rosta Window.** ca. 1920.
6 x 9$^3$/$_4$ in./15 x 24.7 cm
Cond A/P. Framed.
A form of poster art that emerged during the Russian civil war (1919-1922) was called Rosta Windows. Rosta was the acronym for the Russian Telegraph Agency. As the receiver and disseminator of foreign and domestic news, it became the first Soviet news agency. In 1919 it began to issue its "windows," so called because they were hung in shop and office windows. Combining the functions of newspaper, magazine and bulletin, they included text, drawings, cartoons and caricatures. Between 1919 and 1922, some 950 windows were produced in a numbered series, plus over 600 more unnumbered ones and reissues. Painter, graphic artist and illustrator Lebedev "was quick to respond to the requirements of the resolution moved by Meyerhold in 1920 stressing the need for an art of propaganda and was invited to make posters for the Rosta Agency . . . . His designs for posters . . . focused upon images of Foche, Denikin and others in a bold and assertive form of caricature with an easily comprehended political purpose. He was a dramatic graphic artist employing a technique which resembled cut paper in the sharpness and economy of the image. With Vladimir Mayakovsky he designed posters for Rosta windows 1920-1" (Russian and Soviet Artists, p. 254). This Lebedev panel (the Rosta Windows traditionally consisted of four to twelve different frames that told a story)—one part jigsaw puzzle, one part

**328**

Cubist character study—appears to depict a secret agent of some sort, perhaps a double agent as the design's colors are evenly divided between black and brown. It would be helpful to see the other panels with which this one appeared in order to flesh out the story, but on its own it remains a provocative piece of craftsmanship all the same. *A printed map appears verso!*
**Est: $4,000-$5,000.**

**330**

**331**

**332**

**333**

## 330. Rosta Window. ca. 1920.

5¹/₂ x 8¹/₂ in./14 x 21.6 cm

Cond A/P. Framed.

Lebedev's works are fascinating—finely stenciled, thinking-man's graffiti, Cubist character studies that hint at a larger, meticulously-woven narrative without providing any details as to which strand of the story they belong, what overall piece of the puzzle they actively provide. The disassembled sailor on display here definitely gives the impression that he has places

to go and people to see, but whether or not he was paired with the fedora-wearing character of the previous lot is altogether uncertain. However, whether assembled en masse or, as here, seen separately, it's impossible to overlook Lebedev's innate feel for the style in which he was working, the effortless mastery with which he commanded the page. *As is the case with the previous lot, a printed map appears verso.*
**Est: $4,000-$5,000.**

## LEFÈVRE-UTILE

**331. Lefèvre-Utile/Jane Harding.** 1905.

Artist: **Paul Chabas (1869-1937)**

20 x 27¹/₄ in./50.7 x 69.2 cm

Imp. F. Champenois, Paris

Cond A–/Slight tears top and bottom paper edges.

Ref: Art & Biscuits, 19

Fairly adrip with reflective sentimentality, this Chabas portrait of actress Jane Harding not only provides some lovely Art Nouveau eye-candy, it also delivers a testimonial in which Harding declares that there can never be a life without love because with LU cookies readily available there's always something to love.
**Est: $1,400-$1,700.**

**332. Lefèvre-Utile 1893 Calender.** 1892.

Artist: **Anonymous**

17¹/₄ x 24¹/₂ in./43.8 x 62 cm

Imp. F. Champenois, Paris

Cond A.

How sweet it is. Continuing with their tradition of using tempting Art Nouveau darlings to promote their prepackaged treats, Lefèvre-Utile calls upon the abundant talents of an uncredited artist to provide this lovely cameo, executed in soft, sensuous tones, in order to greet the new year of 1893 with the fairest regard possible.
**Est: $1,200-$1,500.**

**333. Lefèvre-Utile.** 1901.

Artist: **Jean Sala**

18⁵/₈ x 25¹/₈ in./47.2 x 63.7 cm

Cond B+/Slight wear at edges; mounted on original display board.

Whispering to her grandmother as if she's sharing a precious secret, this beautiful little girl breathlessly passes along "What good luck, grandma. We're going to have Gaufrette LU this evening." As if grandma didn't already know! What an honestly charming design, as expertly-executed as it is heartwarming.
**Est: $1,200-$1,500.**

334

337

## RENÉ LELONG (1860-?)

**334. "Kodak".**
39¹/₄ x 59 in./99.7 x 149.7 cm
Hachard, Paris
Cond B+/Unobtrusive tears along folds; printer's
    creases in green background.
The wholesome, family and outdoor-life loving "Kodak
Girl" was born in England in 1910, and was soon grac-
ing Kodak posters and ads around the world. Lelong
was chosen to redesign and adapt her in 1923. In all
of these images, the breezy shutterbug is placed in the
foreground, decked-out in her trademark blue-and-
white striped dress and holding a camera. Though frequently she looks smilingly into framed "family pictures"
that include people either taking snapshots or in the
process of posing for them, here she's flying solo, a
totally liberated creature out to explore the Technicolor
beauty of the world. And doesn't she appear to be
having the time of her life. Crisp, fresh and Kodak-
errific! *This is a rare, larger format in this series.*
**Est: $3,500-$4,000.**

## AUGUSTE-LOUIS LEPÈRE (1849-1918)

**335. 2e Exposition des Peintres Lithographes.**
1899.
24¹/₈ x 17¹/₄ in./61 x 43.7 cm
Imp. Lemercier, Paris
Cond A–/Slight tear at vertical fold.
This intense, brooding vision of an artist at work—no
doubt Lepère himself, engraving on a woodblock, with
Notre Dame as his subject in the background—promotes
the second exposition for lithographers at the Salle
du Figaro. It's a bit unusual to promote a lithographic
exhibition with someone working on a woodblock—as
opposed to someone drawing on a stone—but seeing
as this was a preferred method of working for the well-
known printmaker and contributor to *L'Estampe Originale*, it would be appropriate for him to place the focus
on an area of personal expertise.
**Est: $1,700-$2,000.**

335

## HERBERT LEUPIN (1916-1999)

**336. Coca-Cola.** 1954.
35¹/₂ x 50¹/₄ in./90.2 x 127.6 cm
Hug & Söhne, Zürich
Cond A/P.
Ref: Leupin, p. 143; PAI-XXIX, 448
Leupin was simply the most prolific, influential and
award-winning of the postwar Swiss graphic designers.
A combination of all that's best in his French colleagues
Savignac and Villemot, he has created long-running
campaigns for his country's favorite products—textbook
classics filled with endless variety and delicious humor.

In this execution from the second year of the campaign
he created for the soft drink giant, the photographed bot-
tles and "pause" sign accompany a tuxedoed waiter on
his slaloming delivery. This is the rarest of Leupin's Coca-
Cola designs and one of the rarest of *any* Leupin work.
**Est: $1,400-$1,700.**

**337. Coca-Cola/Pause.** 1957.
35¹/₂ x 50¹/₄ in./90.4 x 127.7 cm
Hug & Sohne, Zürich
Cond A/P.
Ref: Leupin, p. 155

336

338

339

340

A NEW GENERATION OF LEADERSHIP

341

According to this charming Leupin warning sign, motorists are supposed to be on the lookout for road workers enjoying Coca-Cola on presumably non-sanctioned breaks. Perhaps the best way for them to avoid the situation altogether is to leave the roadway and get their hands on a Coke of their own.
**Est: $1,400-$1,700.**

**338. Coca-Cola.** 1953.
34¹/₂ x 50¹/₄ in./90.3 x 127.7 cm
Hug & Söhne, Zürich
Cond A.
Ref: Leupin, p. 141; Margadant, 377;
    Swiss Posters, p. 98; Plakat Schweiz, p. 52;
    PAI-XXXV, 362
This design ranks among Leupin's best (and best known), from a Coca-Cola series that ran between 1953 and 1957. It's a collage of photography and Leupin's sprightly linework, communicating the soft drink's famous slogan: "The pause that refreshes."
**Est: $1,400-$1,700.**

**339. Majola Pneu.** 1952.
35¹/₂ x 50¹/₄ in./90.1 x 127.6 cm
Cond A–/Slight creasing at edges/P.
Ref: Leupin, p. 125
The Maloja Pass is a high mountain road in the Swiss

Alps that links the Engadin with the Val Bregaglia and Chiavenna in Italy. You'd think that a tire named after this demanding roadway would be enough to imply that these particular pneumatics were plenty tough. But apparently the manufacturers wanted something a little more. And what better allusion of impenetrability than good-old rhinoceros hide. Never one to miss an opportunity to inject a bit of levity into an inference, Leupin creates a sporty rhino/tire hybrid and declares it to be "hard-wearing!"
**Est: $1,000-$1,200.**

**340. Pepita.** 1958.
35¹/₂ x 50¹/₄ in./90.2 x 127.7 cm
Hug & Söhne, Zürich
Cond A/P.
Ref: Leupin, p. 158
Even the Pepita parrot enjoys the Swiss grapefruit pop when it gets some time away from its label. The placard-bearing bicycle looks more ornamental than practical, but as is the case with the vast majority of Leupin soft drink ads, it supplies the viewer with a naive interpretation of an object that calls to mind kindergarten drawings, which in turn serves as a reminder that maybe not every moment of life need be filled with serious "adult" endeavors.
**Est: $1,000-$1,200.**

## ROY LICHTENSTEIN (1923-1997)

**341. A New Generation of Leadership.** 1992.
38 x 34 in./96.5 x 86.4 cm
Cond A–/Slight creasing/P.
Fresh. If I was allowed no more than a single word to describe this poster, that would be it. After twelve years of Republican presidents, it's no surprise whatsoever that the Democratic National Committee commissioned Lichtenstein to present a version of "The Oval Office" that presented "A New Generation of Leadership." His vision is full of promise, free from clutter and hopeful to a fault, which is both accurate—during the Clinton administration, the United States experienced the longest period of economic expansion in its history— and ironic—as a result of the Lewinsky scandal, Clinton became the second president to be impeached by the House of Representatives, though he was subsequently acquitted by the Senate. Lichtenstein studied at the Art Students League in New York and received degrees in Fine Arts from Ohio State; he taught art at SUNY Oswego and at Rutgers University. His paintings are part of the permanent collections of the Whitney, the Guggenheim and MOMA. As one of the foremost graphic designers of the 1960s, he helped to define the emerging pop art with its whole array of visual effects.
**Est: $1,700-$2,000.**

**342**

**343**

**344**

## HANS LINDENSTAEDT (1874-1928)

**342. Protos.**
$36^3/_4$ x $26^3/_4$ in./93.4 x 67.8 cm
Reklamekunst Lindenstaedt, Berlin
Cond A.

With a look that can best be described as intense, this driving homunculus holds forth a Protos convertible as if it were nothing more than a toy. Were it not for the intensity of his expression we might overlook the serious driving experience offered by Protos. And make no mistake—this was a very serious car. In 1905, Alfred Sternberg began producing Protos automobiles, developing a new motor, known as "kompensmotor", or compensated motor, that resulted in a smooth, fast ride. The six-cylinder vehicle quickly garnered many fans, including Kaiser Wilhelm II. The Protos' greatest fame came from its participation in the New York to Paris Great Race of 1908—the six competitor endurance test that covered a total distance of approximately 23,000 miles, over 13,000 of which was on land. In 1913, the Protos became the first car to ever utilize an electrical starter, but in 1926, due to the severe economic crisis being suffered in Germany at the time, Protos ceased operations after having produced 25,000 vehicles.
**Est: $2,500-$3,000.**

345

347

346

### PRIVAT LIVEMONT (1861-1936)

**343. Cherubs: Two Panels.** 1903.
Each: 38¹/₈ x 14¹/₄ in./96.8 x 36.2 cm
Cond A.
Ref: PAI-XLII, 353
Eight adorable toddlers per panel romp merrily in a sylvan dell. A maximum amount of charm with a limited use of color, consisting of an olive green background, infantile flesh tones and a smattering of pink.
**Est: $2,000-$2,500.** (2)

**344. Manufacture Royale de Corsets: Ceramic Plate.**
Diameter: 19³/₈ in./49.2 cm
Depth: 2 in./5.1 cm
Previously only seen in lithographic form, the Livemont woman on this decorative plate epitomizes the subject of all his works: the long filigree tresses, the luxurious gown, the delicate bearing, the ornamentation that nearly engulfs her, the exquisite sense of self-involvement. An exceptional design with an aura of elegance in every detail. The one major difference between the ceramic manifestation and the previously-seen poster incarnation (see PAI-XXVIII, 378) is that the corset used to achieve this slender look is hidden from view beneath her clothing; in the poster version, it's on public display. It may well be that that the design of the plate preceded the poster. What is certain is that this is a most rare work; we know of no other work in this medium that has survived. Livemont did a good deal of work for tile and glass companies at this time, but no other specimen of any of his ceramic work has survived. As with all of his work in these fields, they were unsigned.
**Est: $4,000-$5,000.**

**345. Bols'.** 1901.
11 x 16¹/₂ in./28 x 41.8 cm
Van Leer, Amsterdam
Cond A. Framed.
Ref: PAI-XXIV, 364
One of Livemont's least known designs shows a well-coiffed matron pouring after-dinner liqueurs. The pattern of grape leaves behind her adds a fitting decorative touch to this delicate composition. *Rare proof before letters.*
**Est: $4,000-$5,000.**

**346. Michiels Frères.** 1902.
19³/₄ x 33³/₄ in./50.2 x 85.7 cm
Van Leer & Co., Amsterdam (not shown)
Cond A.
Ref: Belle Epoque 1980, 103 (var); Gold, 38; PAI-XL, 386
"The woman and her child admire the beauty of a garden, shown behind them in subtle earthy colors, landscaped by the nursery company named on the completed version of this poster with letters . . . (The poster is) a prime example of one of (Art Nouveau's) precepts: a reverence for women, always shown in the best possible light" (Gold, p. 26). Note the thin, halo-like white outline around the ladies' profiles, one of Livemont's special touches. *Proof before letters.*
**Est: $2,500-$3,000.**

### FABIUS LORENZI

**347. Nice.** 1926.
29³/₄ x 44¹/₂ in./75.5 x 113 cm
L'Eclaireur, Nice
Cond B/Unobtrusive restorations near edges.
Ref: Affiches Riviera, 80; PAI-XIII, 291
A lively scene on the beach promenade invites us to take a vacation on the Riviera. It's obvious that we'll meet the cream of the youthful crop, all togged out in the latest flapper fashions from America. Lorenzi was primarily a humorous illustrator whose work appeared in various journals, including *Le Rire* and *La Baionette*.
**Est: $3,000-$4,000.**

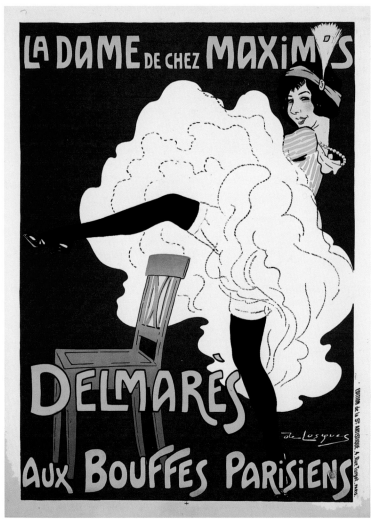

348

349

## DANIEL DE LOSQUES (David Thoroude, 1880-1915)

**348. La Dame de Chez Maxim's.** ca. 1910.
46 x 61³/₄ in./116.7 x 157 cm
Edition de la Ste Artistique, Paris
Cond A–/Slight tears.
Though the only apparent link between "The Lady of Chez Maxim's" and
"The Doorman of Chez Maxim's" (see PAI-XXXIII, 411) is that their promis-
cuities played themselves out at the Parisian night life landmark, it would
seem as if this lighthearted evening of indiscretions at the Bouffes Parisiens
rotated around the high-kicking exploits of the title's popular gal—a proto-
typical unflappable flapper, if you will. De Losques was the pseudonym of
David Thoroude, who studied law and started out as a law firm employee
before switching to art. This is one of the many theatrical posters he
created, along with magazine illustrations and caricatures during the period
1904-1914. His career was cut tragically short by his death in aerial com-
bat during World War I.
**Est: $2,500-$3,000.**

## LOTTI

**349. Bossard-Bonnel/Rennes.**
42¹/₄ x 62³/₄ in./107.1 x 159.4 cm
Imp. Vercasson, Paris
Cond A.
Ref: Pierrot, p. 75
This Lotti poster for a Rennes music store gives us the impression that his
Pierrot is a master musician capable of playing practically every instrument.
It also appears as if the artist may have rendered him at an inopportune
moment, seeing as the look on his face seems to imply that the clown may
have been trying to make an exit without paying. A droll promotion that also
manages to display an impressive array of the store's merchandise. Nothing
is known of the artist other than the fact that Vercasson deposited about
fifteen of his posters at the Bibliothèque Nationale between 1925 and 1931.
**Est: $2,500-$3,000.**

350

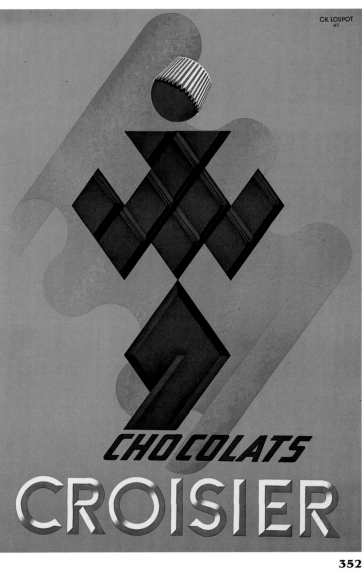

351

352

353

## CHARLES LOUPOT (1892-1962)

**350. La Biere/La Plus Economique.** 1927.
$23^5/8$ x $31^5/8$ in./60 x 80.4 cm
Les Belles Affiches, Paris
Cond A.
Ref: Loupot/Zagrodzki, 67; PAI-XLIII, 409
Loupot studied art at Lyon, but produced his first posters in Switzerland where he stayed for seven years, between 1916 and 1923. He then returned to Paris at the invita-

tion of the printer Devambez, and became one of the top designers of his time. Between 1925 and 1930, most of his work was executed for the agency Les Belles Affiches, founded by two brothers named Damour. He was also Cassandre's partner in the Alliance Graphique. This is an institutional ad for the beer industry, providing sound advice—through straightforward graphic shorthand—about the economic and health benefits of the delectable amber liquid.
**Est: $2,500-$3,000.**

**351. Voisin Automobiles.** 1923.
$31^3/8$ x $47^3/8$ in./79.8 x 120.4 cm
Imp. Devambez, Paris
Cond B+/Unobtrusive tears at folds.
Ref: Loupot, 22; Loupot/Zagrodzki, 50;
　　Modern Poster, 172; PAI-XLII, 19
After WWI, Gabriel Voisin, who with his brother Charles were the pioneers of the French aviation industry, took over a prototype from Citröen to develop his own luxurious model. Loupot created spectacular posters in Switzerland, before moving his studios to Paris the year of this Voisin promotion's production. In fact, it was one of two he designed that year for this automaker (for a very different approach, see PAI-XL, 390). "His qualities as a lithographer, his intransigence and his purity of style make Loupot an example for many disciples" (Weill, p. 209). Here, with surprisingly few scenic elements and sparse use of color, he neatly places a Voison automobile at its rightful place on top of the world.
**Est: $20,000-$25,000.**

**352. Chocolats Croisier.** 1947.
$35^3/8$ x $50^1/2$ in./90 x 128.2 cm
Sauberlin & Pfeiffer, Vevey
Cond A.
Ref: Loupot/Zagrodzki, 110; Chocolate Posters, p. 125;
　　PAI-XXXI, 518
"The first postwar poster published by Loupot reveals

his geometric preoccupation directly linked to his quest for the St. Raphaël mark. One may measure the marked difference in the fashion with which he addresses the difficult subject by comparing it with his image for *Dauphinet* in 1926 (*see* PAI-XXI, 281). It's also another return to his past, as it strikes up an association with one of his printers from the Swiss period" (Loupot/Zagrodzki, p. 94).
**Est: $10,000-$12,000.**

**353. Fourrures Canton/20 rue de Bourg.** 1949.
$35^3/4$ x $50^3/8$ in./90.8 x 128 cm
R. Marsens, Lausanne
Cond A.
Ref: Loupot ,13; Loupot/Zagrodzki, 54D;
　　Margadant, 335 (var); PAI-XLI, 375
This design, one of three that Loupot created for Canton Furriers in Lausanne, first appeared in 1924 with the aloof, slightly sad woman against a black background (*see* PAI-XXI. 274). A second edition, which dates to the early 1930s, is the first of several in which the background is blue. In one version the address is 29 Rue Léopold-Robert in La Chaux-de-Fonds; in another its 20 Rue de Bourg in Lausanne. Here we have the third edition, printed in 1949 from the same lithographic stones, also with the blue background and the Rue de Bourg address. There is now a change in printer: After World War II, master-printer Auguste Marsens turned his plant over to his son Roger. All editions with a blue background contain the notation "d'après" (meaning "from a design by") Loupot. Asked why the original black background was replaced by blue, the current chief of operations, Richard Canton, revealed that the change came about because blue provided better visibility during the winter months. Regardless of which edition one is looking at, the poster retains the enveloping warmth of Canton furs and the exquisite design that Loupot created for the establishment.
**Est: $2,500-$3,000.**

354

355

## CHARLES LOUPOT (1892-1962) & JEAN CARLU (1900-1997)

**354. Monsavon.** 1936.
49³/₄ x 77⁵/₈ in./126.3 x 197.2 cm
Imp. Courbet, Paris
Cond A–/Tears and stains, largely at far bottom.
Ref (All Var but PAI): Loupot/Zagrodzki, 97A;
    Loupot, 47; Affiche Réclame, 11; Cosmetiques, 15;
    PAI-XLII, 362
In 1925, Carlu designed a poster for this soap in which a male figure peeks out from behind a shower curtain holding a bar of Monsavon in his hand (*see* PAI-XLIII, 219). When asked to do another one for the company eleven years later, Loupot evidently felt that he could do no better than use virtually the same pose, this time with a female torso, and accordingly gave Carlu co-credit. *Publicité* magazine had the following comments to make about his reinterpretation in their thirty-seventh issue: "With a great deal of ingenuity and talent, Loupot has subjected this creation to a total metamorphosis, that in the meantime, has not forgotten the original. At the same time, the new poster underlines the transformation brought to the soap itself, that of an everyday hand soap becoming a milk soap, extremely gentle, especially recommended for female skin" (Loupot/Zagrodzki, p. 88). *This is the larger format.*
**Est: $10,000-$12,000.**

## JEAN LUC

**355. Monaco Aquarium.** 1939.
24⁵/₈ x 39³/₈ in./62.6 x 100 cm
Imp. Monégasque, Monte Carlo
Cond A.

Ref: Affiche Riviera, 475; PAI-XXXIV, 429
As opposed to Carlu's melange of fishy delights for the Monaco Aquarium (*see* PAI-XXXI, 364), Luc takes a very straightforward approach that allows the fanciful nature and alien attraction to these aquatic creatures to speak for themselves. And by placing the viewer inside an underwater cave lined with luminescent coral, we're given a nearly predatorial view of this trio of denizens from the deep—an angel fish pair and a single parrot fish—who frolic about in their watery surroundings utterly unaware that they have become the center of our attention.
**Est: $2,500-$3,000.**

## JEAN-DENIS MALCLE (1912- )

**356. la Baule.**
31 x 45³/₈ in./78.8 x 115.3 cm
De Plas, Paris
Cond A.
La Baule, a commune situated in France's Loire-Atlantique *département*, can accurately boast of having the longest beach of France, which runs eight kilometers in length. With all this space, it's no surprise that there's room for twenty health clubs. And with the smart way every single foreground Breton entity appears to be model-thin and ready-to-be-seen, we'd have to imagine that these twenty operations aren't hurting for business. In Malcle's crystal-clear world, sport, fashion and frolic coexist in high style, all set against a bay that is regarded to be one of the most beautiful in all of Europe.
**Est: $1,000-$1,200.**

356

**357**

**ROBERT MALLET-STEVENS (1886-1945)**

**357. Grand Meeting Aeronautique/Buc.** 1920.
46³/₄ x 62³/₄ in./118.7 x 159.2 cm
Imp. Courmont Frères, Paris
Cond A.
*Provenance: Famille Charles Dollfus*
*With black-and-white photograph of the event.*
*Only known copy of a previously unknown poster!*
First and foremost, the greatest reason for the Grand
Aeronautic Meeting being convened at the Aérodrome
Louis Blériot was as a grand manifestation of propa-
ganda—it's important to remember that the Allied
American, English and French forces were the winners

in the First World War's "Air War"—and the Mallet-
Stevens poster for the event reflects this ebullient,
victorious air with its playful, animated abandon. Plus,
it was the most diverse group of aircraft to be put on
display up to this point—dirigibles, planes, spherical
balloons and more—that demonstrated that aviation was
on the verge of becoming an integral part of modern
life. The world-record for speed was set at the October
8 fly-in by Joseph Sadi-Lecointe in a Nieuport-Delage
29v monoplane, while the world-record for altitude was
set by a pilot named Thierry who achieved a height of
more then 7,000 meters in his Breguet biplane. Also,
it was at the Buc meet that air transport was offered to

passengers from the public for the first time, who could
choose five-hour flights to either London or Brussels and
back to Buc. *Two points of interest: the organizers
of the Buc event—French President Raymond Poincaré,
Secretary of State for Aeronautics P. E. Flandin and
A.C.F. president Comte Henri de la Vaulx—can be seen
on the balcony of the black-and-white photo that
accompanies this poster. Also, Charles Dollfus, the
famous aviator and historian—from whose family's
collection this poster originates—participated in the
Buc air show, executing a parachute jump from a
balloon at a height of 480 meters.*
**Est: $30,000-$40,000.**

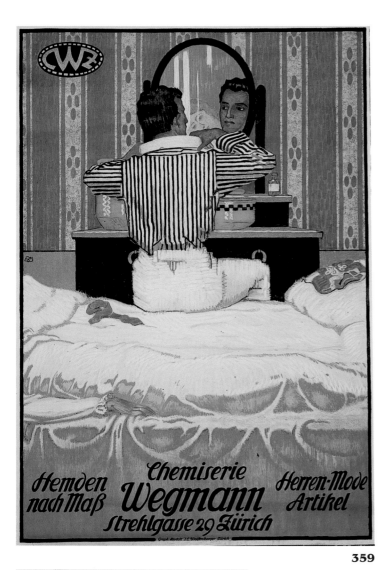

359

360

361

## ROBERT MALLET-STEVENS (cont'd)

**358. St. Jean De-Luz.** 1928.
46¹/₈ x 62 in./117.2 x 157.5 cm
Imp. H. Chachoin, Paris
Cond A
Ref: PAI-XVII, 356
This is one of the most spectacular designs by Mallet-Stevens, France's most influential modernist architect and designer of the 1920s and '30s (after Le Corbusier, who was Swiss). Mallet-Stevens was in the forefront of

those who first explored the functionalism of Le Corbusier and Loos, and from it developed Art Deco. (He can truly be said to have been present at the birth, having designed the Tourism Pavillion at the 1925 *Exposition des Arts Décoratifs et Industriels*—whence "Art Deco.") He was "undoubtedly the most successful of these rationalists, as they were called . . . Prolific and eclectic, he produced a series of sophisticated designs for private homes, apartments, offices, public buildings, shops, factories and exhibition pavilions, as well as for film sets and furniture" (Eva Weber, Art Deco, 1989). Here he illustrates his design for La Pergola, a complex in this Côte Basque resort that he completed in 1924. It included elegant stores on the ground floor, a casino above, a movie theater and a hotel, the Atlantic. The structure still exists, but as an apartment building. Typical of early Modernism, ocean liner shapes influenced the design. The poster, with its elegantly simplified forms and colors, is as sleek as the architecture.

**NOTE:** *Because of some questions regarding the authenticity of this poster when discovered about fifteen years ago, we have had this specimen, unlined, examined by top laboratories. It was tested both for age of paper and age of ink, and in both cases, it was confirmed to have been a poster printed on or about the year indicated above. The laboratories' examination reports will be made available on request.*
**Est: $20,000-$25,000.**

## BURKHARD MANGOLD (1873-1950)

**359. Chemiserie Wegmann/Zürich.** 1915.
35¹/₄ x 50¹/₄ in./89.7 x 127.3 cm
J. E. Wolfensberger, Zürich
Cond A–/Slight staining in margins.
Ref: Mangold, 106
Mangold isn't known for his saucy lithographic narratives, but what's going on here exactly? Has someone been caught sneaking out by a blurry-eyed paramour

from last night's revelry before an appropriate good-bye could be given? Maybe it's not that salacious. Maybe this gentleman was trying to quietly ready himself for a day at the office without rousing an under-the-weather wife (her reflection shows eyes that are clearly on the rheumy side). In either scenario, one thing remains consistent: the man looks fantastic, thanks in large part to the striped shirt he surely procured at Wegmann's.
**Est: $5,000-$6,000.**

**360. Rollschuhbahn.** 1910.
28¹/₈ x 39⁵/₈ in./71.4 x 100.7 cm
J. Wolfensberger, Zürich
Cond A.
Ref: Mangold, 103; PAI-XXXII, 404
The interesting way the colors are applied—like small splashes or mosaic tiles—distinguishes this design for a roller rink in Zurich. Mangold, born in Basel, spent seven years in Munich (1894-1900) where he received grounding in the principles of the popular *Jugendstil* movement. He became involved with every facet of decorative arts, and after returning to Switzerland in 1900, he practiced many of them, including glassblowing, woodblock printing, illustration, painting and lithography. He produced some 150 posters, choosing his graphic style very carefully for each assigned message.
**Est: $5,000-$6,000.**

**361. Café Tearoom Singer.** 1914.
27³/₄ x 39¹/₄ in./70.6 x 99.7 cm
W. Wassermann, Basel
Cond A.
Ref: Mangold, checklist #71; PAI-XVII, 359
For the chichi Singer Café and Tearoom in Basel, Mangold shows us the pre-World War I ancestors of today's "ladies who lunch." The rendering has the delicacy and rich grainy texture characteristic of Mangold in this period. *Rare!*
**Est: $2,000-$2,500.**

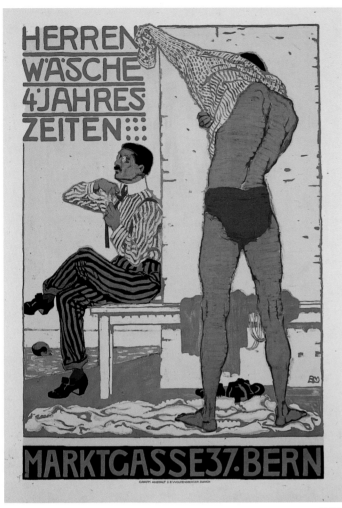

**362**

**363**

**364**

**366**

## MANGOLD (cont'd)

**362. Herrenwäsche/4 Jahreszeiten.** 1912.
29¹/₂ x 41¹/₄ in./75 x 104.9 cm
Wolfensberger, Zürich
Cond A.
Ref: Mangold, 105; Margadant, 319; PAI-VIII, 441
Overwhelmingly metrosexual in tone—though designed
nearly a century before anyone even conceived of the
term—this advertisement for the 4 Season's public
bathhouse for men amply displays that no matter how
natty the fellow, at his core he's something of a slob—
I mean, take a look at the number of towels scattered
about the floor. The manner in which the poster is executed reflects Mangold's respect and admiration for
the up-and-coming German artist of the era—Ludwig
Hohlwein. One of Mangold's finest designs. *Rare!*
**Est: $3,000-$4,000.**

**363. Seidengrieder.** 1913.
36⁷/₈ x 48⁷/₈ in./93.7 x 124 cm
J. E. Wolfensberger, Zürich

Cond B+/Slight tears and creases at paper edges.
Ref: Mangold, 63; PAI-XXIII, 354
To announce the Zurich silk goods store Seidengrieder's
move to new headquarters, Mangold created a fanciful,
grand processional—and the copywriter rose to the
challenge in rhyme, roughly as follows: "Where do all
these people race? Why this surge to the Parade Place?
What do these wagons signify? These people toting
packages—why, why, why? Why, it's Seidengrieder,
heading off to its new location in the Peterhof!"
**Est: $3,500-$4,000.**

## CATHLEEN S. MANN (1869-1959)

**364. Film Stars Use Shell.** 1938.
44¹/₄ x 29³/₄ in./112.4 x 75.7 cm
The Baynard Press, London
Cond A.
Ref: Shell, 78; PAI-XVIII, 27
Filmdom's glamour is evoked in a star-studded design
that features an array of multicolored spotlights with-
out which celebrities would wither and die. Mann was

a painter who created works for Shell-Mex and British
petroleum as well as the London Underground. She
came from a family of artists, including both parents
and various aunts, uncles and cousins. She also bore
the title of Marchioness of Queensbury. Her grandfa-
ther-in-law—decidedly not the artistic type—was the
Marquess of Queensbury who established the modern
rules of boxing and hounded Oscar Wilde all the way
to jail for seducing his son.
**Est: $2,000-$2,500.**

## G. MARCHAND

**365. Paris-Saint-Lazare à Londres Victoria.**
29 x 41 in./73.6 x 104 cm
Hachard, Paris
Cond A–/Unobtrusive tears in upper left margin.
Ref: PAI-XXVIII, 397
A shipboard view of the port of Dieppe is called upon
to advertise a joint venture between the French State
Railways and England's Southern Railways for travel
between Paris and London. Eschewing the rail portion

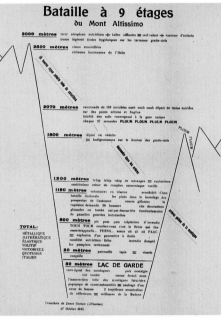

367

365

of the equation, Marchand focuses on the two companies' mail boat service, boasting here to be the fastest on the Channel.
**Est: $1,000-$1,200.**

## GERHARD MARGGRAFF (1892-?)

**366. Christian Mendel.** 1914.
$36^5/8$ x $28^3/4$ in./93.2 x 73 cm
Geschäftkunst, Berlin-Friedenau
Cond A–/Unobtrusive tear and stain at edges.
This pair of fashion plates is sitting pretty in the latest springtime styles being offered by the Christian Mendel boutique. And from the way they're perusing the catalogue of the other togs being offered by the elegant retailer, it's hard to imagine that they'll be stationary for much longer before the need for additional apparel moves them Mendel-way.
**Est: $1,700-$2,000.**

## FILIPPO TOMMASO MARINETTI (1876-1944)

**367. Les Mots en Liberté Futuristes: Four Plates and Book.** 1919.
Each: $10^1/4$ x 13 in./26 x 33 cm
Cond A/Usual folds. Framed.
Ref: Modern Poster, p. 21; Futurismo e Publicità, p. 104
Filippo Marinetti was an Italian ideologue, poet, editor and founder of the Futurist movement of the early-twentieth century. Marinetti, most noted for his author-

ship of the "Futurist Manifesto"—first published in the Paris newspaper *Le Figaro*—also published this important Futurist touchstone, "Les Mots en Liberté Futuristes," into which these four plates—displaying the typographic method fervently espoused by that particular movement—were inserted, folded several times in order to make them fit into the small book. "The postwar years gave new impetus to the spread of modernist aesthetics to the more popular artistic mediums . . . Marinetti sought to give visual expression to the anarchic energy of war, the big city, and the rioting crowd . . . Setting out to destroy all literary and typographic rules, Marinetti called for the abolition of punctuation, the adverb, and the adjective to break down completely the traditional continuity and order of writing. His poems also offend all traditional criteria for good taste and clarity in layout and design . . . The Futurists also had a particular interest in the medium of print, not just as a vehicle for their poetry but for the purpose of proselytizing their ideas on subjects touching all aspects of life —from sculpture to lust. Although they produced almost no typographically advanced posters, the revolution the Futurists initiated in typography proved fundamental. Through their influence on Dada and the Russian avant-garde they contributed to the development of the new typography in the 1920s . . . The Futurist typographic poem was usually orchestrated to provide a sense of simultaneity of sounds and events and a physical jostling of one element by another" (Modern Poster, p. 20-21).
**Est: $8,000-$10,000.** (5)

## PIERRE MARRAST

**368. Cherry Kobler/Columbia.** 1937.
$31^3/4$ x $47^3/8$ in./80.6 x 120.4 cm
Cond A.
Ref: PAI-XLI, 380
Evidently, Cherry Kobler was a woman who composed songs and sang them while accompanying herself on the piano. Why she chose a fruity dessert as a stage name is anyone's guess. According to the French files of Columbia Records, she recorded four songs during June and July of 1937, but other specifics of the recording session go unmentioned. Marrast enlivens this portrait of the blonde ivory-tickler with shining eyes, cherry-red fingernails and a wide-open regard cast directly at her potential audience.
**Est: $1,000-$1,200.**

## JOAQUIM MARTRA-BALLBÉ (1898-?)

**369. Smoking/papel de fumar.**
$13^7/8$ x $19^3/4$ in./35.3 x 50.1 cm
Marti. Mari, Barcelona
Cond A.
Whoooooo needs cigarette rolling papers? The wise choice would appear to be Smoking, the brand that's mechanically manufactured without the taint of the human touch with a name that makes it impossible to mistake what it's used for. A very satisfying Martra-Ballbé design, from the bird-of-prey ashtray to the purse-lipped animus of addiction hovering over the scene.
**Est: $1,200-$1,500.**

## ALFRED MARXER (1876-1945)

**370. Wintersport/Zürcher-Oberland.** ca. 1920.
$30^3/8$ x $42^1/8$ in./77.1 x 107 cm
J. E. Wolfensberger, Zürich
Cond A/P.
Ref: Plakat Schweiz, p. 230; Paradis, 15;
Swiss Winter Sport, 78; PAI-XXIX, 478
Advertising the winter fun to be enjoyed in the Zurich

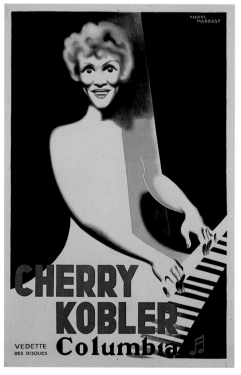

Highlands are two tourists in matching outfits, the gentleman ready to take on the slopes, while his companion opts for the gentler sledding life. The unusual color treatment in bold brushstrokes lends interest and impact to this rare poster. Marxer learned decorative painting from his father and the Applied Arts Department of the Technical School in Wintherthur. After fur-

ther studies in Munich and traveling throughout Europe, he settled in Kilchberg to begin his artistic career. He created a body of painterly works, mostly in oils, but also worked in graphics, especially woodcuts and book illustrations, plus murals for public buildings.
**Est: $2,500-$3,000.**

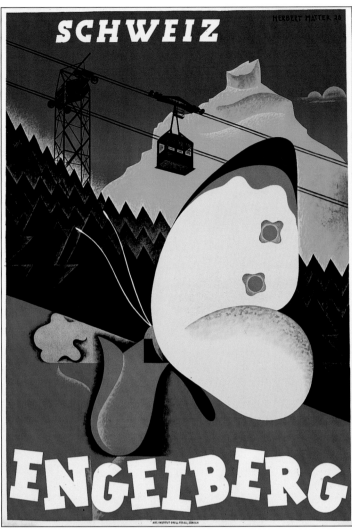

**373**

**374**

**372**

## J. MATAGNE

**371. Fort-Mahon.** 1908.
29³/₄ x 45¹/₄ in./75.6 x 115 cm
Cond A–/Unobtrusive folds.
The sense of well-being is so prevalent, the childhood calm so unaffected that the quietude speaks simply and directly to the harried and overburdened in this Matagne poster for Fort-Mahon, the pleasant French seaside resort just down the coast from Boulogne, with a long sandy beach and air so pure that you can't even

feel it gently embracing your skin. And what better way to make your journey than with the Northern Railway? So, what are you waiting for?
**Est: $2,000-$2,500.**

## MATSUDA

**372. Port Festival/Otaru.**
20⁷/₈ x 29¹/₂ in./53 x 74.9 cm
Cond A.
The seagulls certainly seem to be enjoying the fireworks and streamers from their funnel-top perch and chances are that you'll lose yourself in the mirthful atmosphere as well once you make your way to Otaru's Port Festival. Otaru is a small port city with a population of 141,000 on the northern island of Hokkaido, facing Ishikari Bay on the Sea of Japan. Located thirty kilometers to the west of Sapporo, tourism plays a major role in the local economy. With its many classic buildings still standing from the Meiji era, Otaru's been promoted as a "romantic city," and there's both beaches for the summer and mountains for skiing in the winter. At the seaport, one can find fresh squid, crab and other seafood, as well as plenty of the local brew, Otaru Beer, to wash it down. The city is well-known for its charming canal district adorned with Victorian-style street lamps and the now-defunct "herring houses," where the herring trade was once plied.
**Est: $1,200-$1,500.**

## HERBERT MATTER (1907-1984)

**373. Schweiz/Engelberg.** 1928.
35¹/₄ x 50¹/₈ in./89.5 x 127.3 cm
Orell Füssli, Zürich
Cond A.
Ref: Wobmann. 149; Matter, p. 21; PAI-XXXIV, 446
Matter created a number of travel posters for his native Engelberg, a quiet, unspoiled village popular year

'round. In this early graphic poster from the Swiss designer who would become one of the pioneers of photomontage we get a giant butterfly sipping from a cheery red tulip—a playful image of spring in this meadow-strewn valley. Sunlit in the distance is the town's major attraction: the permanently snow-covered peak of Mount Titlis. Matter studied in Geneva and Paris, created a number of posters in Zurich between 1928 and 1936, then emigrated to the U.S. where he worked as a photographer for fashion magazines. In 1952, he started teaching photography at Yale. He died in New York in 1984.
**Est: $2,000-$2,500.**

## CARLO MATTIOLI (1911-?)

**374. Parma.** 1937.
27 x 39¹/₈ x 68⁷/₈ in./68.7 x 99.4 cm
Grafiche I.G.A.P., Roma-Milano
Cond A–/Unobtrusive tears at edges.
The Duomo is one of the main examples of 12th century Romanesque architecture in northern Italy. The cathedral's facade features three orders of loggias and is flanked by a tall gothic tower that contains brickwork from the 1294 post-earthquake reconstruction. It's also home to magnificent works of art by Antelami and Correggio. And it just happens to be situated in Parma, a city in the Italian region of Emilia-Romagna, famous for its architecture and the fine countryside around it. Mattioli's destination design focuses on—and condenses—the art and architecture, transferring the terra rosa typically seen on buildings throughout the city directly onto the normally grey exterior of the cathedral. It's interesting to note that the poster identifies both the typically accepted Gregorian year for the poster's production and the Fascist era "XV" notation —not once, but twice—to indicate that it was the fifteenth year of Mussolini's reign.
**Est: $1,000-$1,200.**

375

376

## LUCIANO ACHILLE MAUZAN (1883-1952)

**375. Bertozzi.** 1930.
38⁷/₈ x 54¹/₄ in./98.7 x 137.7 cm
Mauzan-Morzenti, Cernusco-Lombardone
Cond A–/Unobtrusive folds.
Ref: Mauzan/Treviso, p. 76; Mauzan, A033 (var);
    Mauzan Affiches, p. 99; PAI XXXVIII, 430
Mauzan goes for a touch of the grotesque in publicizing Bertozzi cheese, but does it with such chutzpah that the overall effect is pleasing—so much so that this represents the fourth edition of this particular design. And with three judges putting their olfactory reputations on the line, it can be safely assumed that although justice may be blind, it is quite keen in the other senses. Mauzan produced well over 2,000 posters during the course of his long, prodigious career. Born in France, Mauzan would begin his life as an illustrator in Italy in 1909, working for Ricordi and other topnotch printing firms. He remained there until 1927, when he and his wife were invited to Buenos Aires. There he continued a frantic pace of poster production until 1933, when the Mauzans returned to France, where he would continue his work for the rest of his days.
**Est: $2,500-$3,000.**

## ALBRECHT MAYER (1875-1952)

**376. Basler Elektrizitäts Ausstellung.** 1913.
27¹/₂ x 39¹/₂ in./69.7 x 100.4 cm
W. Wassermann, Basel
Cond A–/Unobtrusive folds.
Sometimes it's so startlingly obvious why artistically-conceived posters were crucial to promotion in the pre-electronic media age. Take this Mayer poster for example. What if one read an all-text notice in a local Basel newspaper that there was to be an Electrical Exhibition that showcased both household and industrial use? Well, seeing as it's 1913, it's a fairly interesting concept, so one might consider attending briefly before moving onto the society section. However, if during the course of one's daily travels about town one came across this Mayer poster with its naked jade

embodiment of the expo holding an aura-casting ring of purest energy that lights up the night and appears as a portal into the future, chances are good that one would be stopped in one's tracks and take immediate notice of when the event was transpiring. Behold the power of the poster! *Rare!*
**Est: $2,000-$2,500.**

## LEOPOLDO METLICOVITZ (1868-1944)

**377. Impermeabili Moretti.** 1921.
38¹/₄ x 55¹/₈ in./97 x 140 cm
G. Ricordi, Milano
Cond A.
In a previously seen advertisement for Moretti products (see PAI-XXXV, 381), we saw an elephant using a large tarpaulin as a rain coat while his handler huddled beneath an inferior-looking umbrella. Here, with the pachyderm out of the promotional equation, Metlicovitz pulls something of a reversal: the umbrella now serves as a platform from which an unflappable puffer can best be seen braving the elements—and emphysema—in his Moretti overcoat. Metlicovitz was born in the Adriatic port city of Trieste, and appears to have become a painter and portraitist without any formal training. In 1891, he showed up in Milan at Ricordi's print shop as a lithography trainee, proving to be such a quick study he was promoted to technical director within a year.
**Est: $1,400-$1,700.**

## MICH (Michel Liebeaux, 1881-1923)

**378. Westinghouse.**
45¹/₂ x 61³/₈ in./115.6 x 155.8 cm
Publicité Wall, Paris
Cond B/Slight tears at folds.
Mich gives us a "Sacred Feminine" for the Industrial Age, an electrified Westinghouse goddess who without question is "The Most Elegant, The Least Fragile." And though it's not typically considered polite to ask a woman to show us what she has going on in her nether regions, this radiant beauty clearly wants us to see.

377

Perhaps most surprisingly, this fusion betwixt bulb and woman actually comes across as elegant, Empire-waisted and perfectly composed. An advertisement that's brilliance personified from master humorist Mich. The artist's main clients were the bicycle and auto industries at the beginning of the Twentieth Century, and in the 1912 Salon des Humoristes, he exhibited fifty sporting designs. His drawings also filled the pages of *La Vie Parisienne, L'Auto* and *L'Echo de Paris. Rare!*
**Est: $2,000-$2,500.**

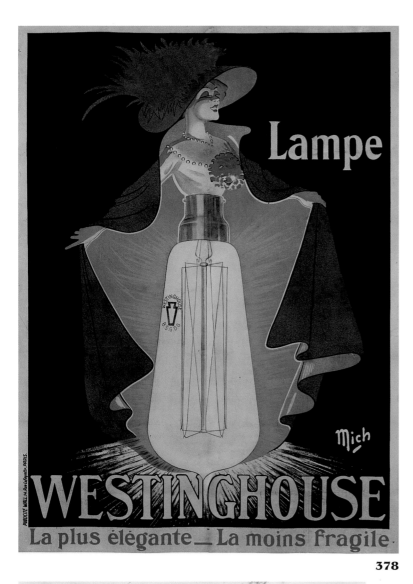

**378**

**379**

**380**

## MISTI (Ferdinand Mifliez, 1865-1923)

**379. Grand Magasins.**
53³/₄ x 86¹/₈ in./136.6 x 218.8 cm
Cond B/Slight tears at folds.
Misti was a busy poster artist who, between 1894 and 1914, designed more than 100 images—many for bicycles, as well as department stores, railroads, publishing clients and the Neuilly fair. In this text-free poster (whose left-hand decorative border seems to indicate that this may have been the image half of a larger billboard with text to the right, quite possibly for the Pygmalion department store) everyone appears to be rather pleased with their trip to the store, to a person loaded down with freshly-wrapped boxes. And though the murk of evening may dwell in the design's background, it's clearly been relegated there by the sunny disposition of the foreground family.
**Est: $3,000-$4,000.**

**380. Paris-Mode.**
46³/₄ x 63¹/₂ in./118.8 x 161.3 cm
Affiches Kossuth, Paris
Cond A-/Slight tears and stains at edges.
Misti announces the opening of a new showroom at the Paris-Mode emporium with this very clever design: by leaving the right side of the poster-within-the-poster blank, the parasol-toting woman checking out the text becomes fashionable artwork, the finishing touch needed to lure others to the boutique. And the shadow that she casts adds interesting texture and depth.
**Est: $2,000-$2,500.**

## MISTI (cont'd)

### 381. Humber/Beeston.
53 x 36³/₄ in./134.6 x 93.4 cm
Imp. B. Sirven, Toulouse-Paris
Cond A–/Slight staining in margins.
Ref: Collectionneur, p. 212; PAI-XLI, 22
Positively one of Misti's best designs, whose sepia color
scheme adds surprising warmth and instant nostalgia
to a design for Humber bicycles that serves-up infor-
mation and charm in equal portions.
**Est: $2,000-$2,500.**

## EDOUARD MONGE

### 382. Cycles Strock.
34 x 23³/₄ in./86.4 x 60.3 cm
Pomeon et ses fils, St. Chamond
Cond A.
Maybe she should have worn a different hat. Because
clearly, as a result of her white riding outfit and the
smooth rapidity afforded this woman by her Strock bicycle, this flock of doves has mistaken her chapeau for
the real deal, making her the point bird in their flocking
activities. Monge then goes on to frame the scene with
a series of gear wheels, contrasting the natural and
technical worlds one off another. A somewhat naive
treatment, but very effective, clever and pleasing. *Rare!*
**Est: $1,700-$2,000.**

## CARL MOOS (1878-1959)

### 383. Gordon Bennet Wettfliegen/Metzger Brau. 1909.
29³/₄ x 45¹/₈ in./75.5 x 114.6 cm
Wolfensberger, Zürich
Cond A–/Unobtrusive folds.
Ref: Litfass-Bier, 215
"Beer is poured at all sorts of places and drunk at the
most different occasions . . . the true beer festivals . . .
are celebrated elsewhere . . . before the Tuborg-portico
or at the Swiss balloon race" (Litfass-Bier, p. 204).
Beer and ballooning. Together at last. You'd be hard
pressed to say that the Fourth Gordon Bennett Balloon
Race was a temperate event—just take a look at the
steins literally littering the field. But it's clear that the
"largest brewery in Switzerland" knew how to sponsor
a party, even if the foreground keg-leaner appears to
need just one more beer to top things off in style. A
wonderful design that celebrates both beer and ballooning. By the way, the winners of the event were
Edgar W. Mix and Andre Roussel for the United States.
Carl Moos was the son of Swiss painter, Franz Moos.
Carl was trained and raised in Munich; he had a successful span of seven years of poster design there
before returning for good to his more peaceful father-
land at the start of World War I.
**Est: $2,500-$3,000.**

### 384. Bazar/Gottfried Keller-Haus. 1912.
35¹/₂ x 48¹/₂ in./90.1 x 123.3 cm
Gebr. Fretz, Zürich
Cond A.
Surely a fair for the sale of useful and ornamental
articles for charitable ends—specifically in this case to
benefit the Gottfried Keller-Haus building fund—taking
place during Old Zurich's fall festival had any number
of spectacular items to choose from. Fut Moos' design
makes it clear that the best thing one can ever hope
to find is a meaningful relationship. So, even though
October isn't generally considered to be the most
romantic month of the year, that nip in the air might
not just be an autumnal chill—it might be love.
**Est: $2,000-$2,500.**

### 385. Gebr. Fretz. 1912.
35³/₄ x 49¹/₄ in./90.8 x 125 cm
Gebr. Fretz, Zürich
Cond A–/Staining, largely at paper edges.
For those of you who've been reading every single
word to every single PAI description (which I have to
imagine is the majority of you), the Fretz Brothers name
should be a familiar one seeing as that particular firm
is responsible for printing a number of quality Swiss
posters that have come through our auctions, past
and present. The full array of their services are spelled
out below, but you may not take immediate notice of
them since Moos' noble, allegorical artwork should
garner the lion's share of your attention.
**Est: $1,700-$2,000.**

### 386. Kemm & Cie.
36³/₈ x 48⁷/₈ in./92.4 x 124.2 cm
Fretz Frères, Zürich
Cond B+/Unobtrusive tears, largely at paper edges.
How they love the sporting life! Even if you're not
actively participating in any equestrian activities at the
moment, it's always a good idea to look your best.
And clearly the men's clothier of choice in Neuchatel
is Kemm & Company, the best possible option for the
discriminating gentlemen.
**Est: $6,000-$8,000.**

**383**

**384**

**385**

**386**

387

388

## ALPHONSE MUCHA (1860-1939)

**387. Zodiac.** 1896.
18³/₄ x 25³/₈ in./47.7 x 64 cm
Imp. F. Champenois, Paris
Cond B/Slight tears and creases. Framed.
Ref: Rennert/Weill, 19, Var. 5; Lendl/Paris, 43 (var); Mucha/Art Nouveau, 46;
     DFP-II, 629 (var); Wagner, 72 (var); Gold, 97 (var); PAI-XLII, 393
"This is one of Mucha's most frequently used designs. Originally it was produced for the publisher Champenois for an 1897 calendar (*see* PAI-XLI, 417) and almost immediately it was chosen as well by the editor of *La Plume* for a calendar for the same year (*see* PAI-XXXV, 410). After that the lithograph appeared without text as a decorative panel and again as calendars
. . . The great success of this composition is due to several factors. First is the beauty of the central figure. Mucha's contemporaries perceived her to be an oriental princess, desirable and at the same time unreachable. Next is the remarkable connection between the stylization of the figure . . . and the naturalistic drawing of the foliage in the upper part of the lithograph. This is one way that Mucha created subtle tension . . . Last but not least is the harmony of the composition and the colors as a whole. It is obvious from the lithograph that it was produced when Mucha could fully afford to concentrate on every detail of this time-consuming composition. After 1897, the year of his exhibitions in Paris and his celebrity in artistic circles, he had much less time for such details, and the naturalistic elements seem to disappear from his work" (Mucha/Art Nouveau, p. 189).
**Est: $12,000-$15,000.**

**388. Lefèvre-Utile/Sarah Bernhardt.** 1903.
20⁷/₈ x 28¹/₈ in./52.8 x 71.6 cm
Imp. F. Champemois, Paris (not shown)
Cond A. Framed.
Ref: Rennert/Weill, 86, Var. 1; Lendl/Paris, 19 (var); PAI-XLII, 64 (var)
*Rare proof before the addition of Bernhardt's hand-written testimonial!*
In the full-text version of this design, this "sensitive portrait of Sarah Bernhardt in a wistful pose from one of her major stage successes, *La Princesse Lointaine*, is used here to promote Lefèvre-Utile's biscuits, with Sarah's own hand-written testimonial: 'I haven't found anything better than a little LU—oh, yes, two little LU'" (Lendl/Paris, p. 51). One of the earliest examples of a celebrity endorsement, proving that Sarah was not only a great actress, but a sharp business woman as well. "Bernhardt's instinct for publicity led

389

**391**

**392**

her beyond the unique object to the realm of the mass-produced. Her savvy recognition of how a designer of exceptional talent could advance her career was groundbreaking" (Bernhardt/Drama, p. 13).
**Est: $7,000-$9,000.**

**389. Paris 1900/Austria at the World's Fair.** 1899.
27¹/₂ x 39¹/₂ in./70 x 100.2 cm
Kunstanstalt Czeiger, Wien
Cond A.
Ref: Rennet/Weill, 66; Lendl/Paris, 41; DFP-II, 649;
 PAI-XLIII, 445
"Mucha's design shows a handsome youth lifting a veil off the standing lady—'Paris revealing Austria to the world,' according to contemporary publicity. The heraldic symbol of Austria-Hungary, a two-headed eagle, may be seen behind the girl's head on both sides" (Rennert/Weill, p. 248).
**Est: $5,000-$6,000.**

**390. Lygie.** 1901.
23 x 69¹/₂ in/58.5 x 176.5 cm
Imp. F. Champenois, Paris
Cond A–/Restored tears in top text area.
Ref: Rennert/Weill, 77; Lendl/Paris, 10; PAI-XLII, 396

"Lygie was the stage name of a young Parisian dancer who took up an unusual sideline: creating special presentations on stage of the Folies-Bergère in which she would appear in poses taken from Mucha's most celebrated posters. These tableaux were done with Mucha's approval and he helped with the staging; apparently, he also gave the girl the name under which she did it, Lygie being one of his favorite characters from literature—she is the heroine of Henrik Sinkiewicz's epic novel, *Quo Vadis*" (Lendl/Paris, p. 23). A smaller version of the poster without text was probably used by the dancer for personal publicity. The design features Mucha's signature circular elements and decorative borders, with stylized irises serving as hair decoration and background color inspiration. *This is the larger format.*
**Est: $17,000-$20,000.**

**391. Lorenzaccio.** 1896.
13⁷/₈ x 41¹/₂ in./37.5 x 105.4 cm
Imp. F. Champenois, Paris
Cond A.
Ref: Rennert/Weill, 20, Var. 2; Lendl/Paris, 4; DFP-II, 626;
 Maitres, 144; Mucha/Art Nouveau, 28; PAI-XLII, 56
"The character of Lorenzaccio, in the play by Alfred de Musset, is based on Lorenzo the Magnificent (1449-1492), the most powerful of the Medicis, who ruled the city state of Florence. In the play, Lorenzaccio struggles desperately to save Florence, which had

grown rich during his reign, from the grip of a power-hungry conqueror. Mucha represents this tyranny by a dragon menacing the city coat of arms and portrays Lorenzaccio pondering the course of his action. Sarah Bernhardt adapted the play, first written in 1863, for herself, and the new version, for which this poster was produced, opened December 3, 1896. Never afraid to tackle a male role, Bernhardt made Lorenzaccio into one of the classic roles of her repertoire" (Lendl/Paris, p. 18). *This is the smaller format.*
**Est: $6,000-$7,000.**

**392. Moët & Chandon/Grand Crémant Impérial.**
 1899.
8³/₄ x 23³/₄ in./22.2 x 60.2 cm
Imp. F. Champenois, Paris
Cond B/Restored tears in dress and lower-left margin.
 Framed.
Ref: Rennert/Weill, 65; Lendl/Paris, 32;
 Wine Spectator, 68; Mucha/Art Nouveau, 28;
 PAI-XLII, 401
"In their relentless pursuit of excellence, Moët and Chandon was among the first business concerns to recognize the genius of Mucha . . . The Imperial came in three grades, 'Dry', 'Crémant' and 'Grand Crémant,' and all of them have been advertised by the same design, with the lettering adjusted as needed. Note the Byzantine ornamentation and elaborate jewelry on the dark-haired girl: Mucha was as an imaginative jewelry designer with highly original ideas" (Wine Spectator, 68).
**Est: $8,000-$10,000.**

393

394

## ALPHONSE MUCHA (cont'd)

**393. Cycles Perfecta.** 1902.
40$^1$/$_2$ x 58 in./103 x 147.2 cm
Imp. F. Champenois, Paris
Cond A.
Ref: Rennert/Weill, 81; Lendl/Paris, 51; Weil, 57; Mucha/Art Nouveau, 29;
    PAI-XL, 46
"It is clear that Mucha understood well the principle of selling not the object itself, but the feeling that is associated with it. Here, he is barely showing a piece of the bicycle—not enough to tell one brand from another, anyway —but as to the pleasure of riding, this sylph has it all over any dreary mechanical details. Airily she caresses the machine, her windblown hair embodying motion and a restless spirit, a vision of idle loveliness and a perfect Mucha maiden. Her gaze at us is straight and direct, not flirtatious but inviting and challenging, daring us to take her on in a race. The face is still in repose, but the unruly tresses have already anticipated her wished and commenced to gyrate wildly in the breeze. Mucha finally had a perfect subject that justified hair in motion, and he took full advantage of it, giving her the most dizzying configurations of his famous 'macaroni' to be found in his works. The Perfecta was an English brand bicycle, which makes this one of the very few Mucha posters for an English client. It was also sold in France, and many posters may be found with a sticker or a stamp identifying a local bicycle dealer carrying this brand" (Rennert/Weill, p. 294).
**Est: $20,000-$25,000.**

**394. La Primevère.** 1899.
12$^1$/$_2$ x 30 in./31.8 x 76.2 cm
Imp. F. Champenois, Paris (not shown)
Cond A.
Ref: Rennert/Weill, 64b; Lendl/Paris, 73 (var); Much/Art Nouveau, 51b;
    PAI-XLI, 434 (var)
One half of "Mucha's "The Quill and the Primrose" decorative panel set, specifically the "Primrose" half. "This series of decorative panels sold for 12 francs in the paper version, and on satin, for 40 francs. It represents two pensive young girls, a blonde and a brunette, the one holding a primrose, the other a goose quill and some foliage. Typically Art Nouveau ornamentation predominates in the background motifs and on the jewelry. As was the case with all the decorative panels, conceived from the start as decorative works, Champenois ended up selling the art to clients to use as calendars, posters or advertising material." (Lendl/Paris, p. 93). Particularly outstanding is the manner in which Mucha has constructed the floral ornamental halo that backs *Primevère*'s moment of natural indulgence.
**Est: $8,000-$10,000.**

**395. Revue pour les Jeunes Filles.** 1895.
19$^3$/$_4$ x 49$^3$/$_8$ in./50 x 125.4 cm
Cond B/Unobtrusive tears, largely at folds.
Rennert/Weill, 4; Lendl/Paris, 35; PAI-XXVII, 526
One of Mucha's very earliest posters, a monochromatic drawing proclaim-

395

396

ing the publication of a new magazine for young ladies by Armand Colin & Cie., with whom Mucha had been involved as an illustrator since 1891. The initial issue appeared on June 5, 1895. Since the publisher had a printing press, we assume the printing is by him, although this is not expressly stated on the poster.
**Est: $4,000-$5,000.**

**396. Salon des Cent/XXme Exposition.** 1896.
17 x 24¹/₂ in./43.2 x 62 cm
Cond A. Framed.
Ref: Rennert/Weill, 12, Var.1; Lendl/Paris, 100; DFP-II, 634 (var);
    Modern Poster, 9 (var); Wine Spectator, 74 (var); Salon des Cent/Neumann, Cover & 19; Mucha/Art Nouveau, 18 (var);
    Gold, 192 (var); PAI-XV, 405
*The rare, signed-and-numbered edition of the poster (#16 of 50) before the addition of bottom text.*
"This poster is one of the artist's first works to follow his standard archetype. It advertises the twentieth exhibition of the group of artists who exhibited at the premises of the art journal *La Plume*. The members were famous Parisian artists: Toulouse-Lautrec, Bonnard, Steinlen, Ensor, Grasset, Rassenfosse, and the American Louis Rhead. Mucha's ambition was to become a member of the group, and he succeeded with this poster, which attracted the attention of the gallery owner, Léon Deschamps. (He) visited Mucha in his studio while he was designing the poster. Fascinated by what

he saw, he persuaded Mucha to print it in this unfinished version, according to the artist. Mucha agreed, and the publisher's feeling, that this lightly outlined, impressive poster would make Mucha famous, proved to be correct" (Mucha/Art Nouveau, p. 156).
**Est: $20,000-$25,000.**

**397. The Seasons.** 1896.
25³/₄ x 18¹/₂ in./65.5 x 47 cm
Imp. F. Champenois, Paris (not shown)
Cond A. Framed.
Ref: Rennert/Weill, 18, Var. 3; PAI-XLI, 420
"One of Mucha's most endearing and enduring sets . . . Spring is a blonde sylph who seems to be fashioning a makeshift lyre out of a bent green branch and her own hair, with some birds as interested spectators. Summer . . . sits dreamily on the bank of a pond, cooling her feet in the water and resting her head against a bush. Autumn is an auburn lady, making ready to partake of the ripe grape. Winter, her brown hair barely visible as she huddles in a long green cloak, snuggles by the snow-covered tree trying to warm a shivering bird with her breath . . . All four panels were printed in smaller format and placed in an ornamental frame, with the names of the seasons on a decorated background underneath. Each panel is surmounted by a cameo-like ornamental motif. For unknown reasons, Summer comes first, then Spring, Fall and Winter" (Rennert/ Weill, pp. 90 & 96).
**Est: $20,000-$25,000.**

397

## ALPHONSE MUCHA (cont'd)

**398. The Seasons/Winter.** 1896.
$22^5/8$ x $42^3/8$ in./57.5 x 107.6 cm
Imp. F. Champenois, Paris (not shown)
Cond A. Framed.
Ref: Rennert/Weill, 18, Var. 1; Lendl/Paris, 62;
    Mucha/Art Nouveau, 44d (var); PAI-XXXIII, 462
"The idea of personifying the four seasons was nothing
new—the printer Champenois had done it before with
other artists—but Mucha breathed so much more life
into it that this became one of the best-selling sets of
decorative panels, and he was asked to repeat this
theme at least twice more, in 1897 and 1900, and he
also did another panel with only three of the seasons
. . . Winter, her brown hair barely visible as she is
huddled in a long green cloak, snuggles by a snow-
covered tree trying to warm a shivering bird with her
breath" (Rennert/Weill, p. 90).
**Est: $15,000-$20,000.**

**399. The Seasons.** 1897.
$25^3/8$ x $18^5/8$ in./64.3 x 47.2 cm
Imp. F. Champenois, Paris (not shown)
Cond A. Framed.
Ref: Rennert/Weill, 37; Lendl/Paris, 63; PAI-XXIV, 447
A set of beguiling women symbolizing the seasons—
the second such by Mucha in as many years. Other
than Winter, who is cozily hooded against the cold,
they all sport Mucha's trademark flowing cascades of
hair and assume languid poses of sensual allure. A big
marketing success for the printer Champenois, this set
was used in a number of ways—with calendars for various years or without them, with the names of each
season imprinted or not, sometimes with commercial
clients' names, sometimes entirely blank. *This is the
smaller format, printed entirely on a single sheet—
and the finest specimen ever seen of these images.*
**Est: $15,000-$20,000.**

398

401

**400. Biscuits Lefèvre-Utile.** 1896.
17³/8 x 24 in./44.2 x 61 cm
Imp. F. Champenois, Paris
Cond A–/Slight stains at edges. Framed.
Ref: Rennert/Weill, 22; Lendl/Paris, 17; Weill, p. 42; Gold, 59 (var);
    PAI-XLIII, 451
"One of Mucha's most personable young ladies, her hair cascading irre-
pressibly in fine style, is offering a dish of wafers in this exquisite design.
The calendar for 1897 is imprinted on a semi-circular base. Note the initials
LU in that part of the golden ornamental border that protrudes into the
picture at right. The design of the girl's dress incorporates sickle and
wheat emblems . . . appropriate to the subject" (Rennert/Weill, p. 113).
**Est: $10,000-$12,000.**

**401. Restaurant du Pavillion Bosniaque.** 1899.
10¹/4 x 25 in./26 x 63.5 cm
Imp. F. Champenois, Paris
Cond A. Framed.
Ref: Rennert/Weill, 67, Var. 1; Lendl/Paris, 42 (var);
    Mucha/Art Nouveau, 27 (var); PAI-XXXVIII, 465
"Previously known to us only as a menu cover . . . this design with a Bosnian
maiden bringing a coffee service was also used as an advertisement for
the restaurant in the Bosnian Pavilion at the Paris Exposition of 1900. The
Bosnian Pavilion was a major assignment for Mucha from the Austrian
government; he designed the entire interior including wall decorations . . .
Bosnia . . . at the time was simply one of the many provinces of the Austro-
Hungarian Empire. Its colorful native costumes and diverse crafts provided
enough products to warrant having its own pavilion, which also had a
restaurant" (Rennert/Weill, p. 250).
**Est: $3,000-$4,000.**

407

## ALPHONSE MUCHA (cont'd)

**402. Sarah Bernhardt/American Tour.** 1896.
29 x 77³/₄ in./73.7 x 197.5 cm
Strobridge Litho., Cincinnati & New York
Cond A/Usual overlapping creases. Framed.
Ref: Rennert/Weill, 3, Var. 2; Lendl/Paris, 13; Masters 1900, p. 24 (var);
    PAI-XLII, 38
Sarah Bernhardt made one of her periodical tours of the United States from January through June of 1896. In the process, not only did she introduce American audiences to her luminescent acting style, but also to her personal posterist, Alphonse Mucha. She had the "Gismonda" design (see PAI-XXXIX, 388) recreated at Strobridge and used it throughout her American tour.
**Est: $8,000-$10,000.**

## JOSEF MÜLLER-BROCKMANN (1914-1996)

**403. Argenta/Backhaus.** 1956.
35¹/₂ x 50³/₈ in./90.2 x 127.8 cm
City-Druck, Zürich
Cond A–/Unobtrusive stain at right paper edge.
Ref: Müller-Brockmann, 451 (var)
Müller-Brockmann is one of the most influential graphic artists of the post-World War II period. His style ranges from geometric abstraction to photo-montage and typographic treatments. Among his influences was Ernst Keller, who taught at the Zurich Applied Arts School, as well as the 1939 Swiss Expo held in Zurich, which convinced the twenty-five-year old artist to align himself with the best new trends in graphic design exhibited there. He soon became an innovator and trend setter in Swiss poster circles, and his designs won him much admiration, not to mention a number of prizes. For a program of Vivaldi, Mozart, Debussy and de Falla being presented as a part of a June Festival Week in Zurich—led by famous Spanish conductor, Ataulfo Argenta Maza (1913-1958), accompanied by virtuoso German pianist, Wilhelm Backhaus (1884-1969)—he presents us with an overlapping geometric

402

**403**

**404**

**405**

**406**

**408**

creation that appears to both deconstruct a keyboard and represent the subtle intricacies of the music being presented.
**Est: $1,000-$1,200.**

**404. Musica Viva.** 1955.
35³/₄ x 50¹/₈ in./90.6 x 127.3 cm
lithographie & cartonnage ag
Cond A.
Hans Rosbaud (1895-1962)—the Austrian conductor who would become the Chief Conductor of the Zurich Tonhalle Orchestra the year after this particular concert, a position he would hold until shortly before his death —specialized in the classical music of the Twentieth Century. Müller-Brockmann specialized in graphically contemporizing classical concepts. To that end, maestro and posterist were perfectly suited to be associated with this evening of "Living Music," a musical extrapolation that the posterist expresses promotionally with a series of mutely-toned arciforms intersected with sudden peaks and towering vertical outcroppings.
**Est: $1,000-$1,200.**

**405. Beethoven.** 1955.
35³/₈ x 50 in./90 x 127 cm
lithographie & cartonnage ag, Zürich
Cond A–/Slight creasing and tears at paper edges.
Gdansk-native Carl Adolph Schuricht (1880-1967) may have conducted the country while violinist Wolfgang Eduard Schneiderhan (1915-2002) provided the inspirational solo work, but you have to believe that Müller-Brockmann was equally responsible for getting Beethoven lovers' attention focused on this February concert evening, his black-and-white arcs creating a hypnotic vortex that alludes to the complexities and clear-cut passions of one of the greatest composers in the history of music.
**Est: $1,400-$1,700.**

## JACQUES NATHAN-GARAMOND (1910-2001)

**406. Air France/Chili.** 1962.
24¹/₈ x 38³/₄ in./61.2 x 98.5 cm
Imp. S. A. Courbet, Paris
Cond A–/Slight tears and stains at paper edges.
Ref: Air France, Index, p. 134
The South America country—officially known as the Republic of Chile—occupying a long and narrow coastal strip wedged between the Andes mountains and the Pacific Ocean is the destination of choice in this richly-hued Nathan-Garamond promotion for Air France. Dis-

pensing with urban centers and indigenous citizenry altogether—not to mention the airline's famous winged sea horse logo—the artist generates a Chilean pastiche, a purposeful combination of culturo-artistic touchstones intended to generate atmosphere rather than landmark specificity. Nathan-Garamond was an interior designer and posterist of the Constructivist school and is best known for the many posters he created for *L'Habitation*, the Paris home show.
**Est: $800-$1,000.**

## MAURICE LOUIS HENRI NEUMONT (1868-1930)

**407. Yvette Guilbert.** 1905.
36 x 55⁵/₈ in./91.3 x 141.3 cm
Imp. Minot, Paris
Cond B+/Unobtrusive tears at folds and paper edges.
A great Neumont promotional portrait for Guilbert, the greatest *chanteuse* and monologist of the period with a vast repertoire of roles at her disposal. Gone are her trademark black gloves, replaced with a sheer-and-speckled fingerless version ideally suited to the haughty, Marie Antoinette-ish character seen here. A lifelong Parisian, Neumont was a painter, lithographer and posterist best-known for his somber, moving political posters during World War I. Towards the end of his life, however, his form lightened considerably and he became president of the Salon des Humoristes.
**Est: $1,700-$2,000.**

## WILLIAM M. NICHOLSON (1872-1949)

**408. The New Review.** 1897.
9³/₄ x 12¹/₂ in./24.8 x 31.7 cm
Cond A–/Slight stains at edges. Framed.
Nicholson was an accomplished painter, portrait artist and stage designer. In 1894, he and his brother-in-law James Pryde (1869-1941) established a graphic studio under the pseudonym The Beggarstaff Brothers and pioneered the simple lines and cut-out flat colors that became their unique poster style. *The New Review* would feature a number of Nicholson portraits in supplements for various issues throughout their publishing history, but this announcement for the June 1897 issue of the magazine marks the first printing of the iconic image of Queen Victoria out for a stroll in the company of a steadfast Yorkie. Some two years later, *The New Review* issued a portfolio of the artist's work under the title "Twelve Portraits."
**Est: $1,200-$1,500.**

**409**

**411**

**410**

## RAFAEL DE OCHOA Y MADRAZO

**409. Calais-Lucerne-Interlaken-Engadine Express.**
1899.
30 x 41¹/₂ in./76.3 x 105.4 cm
A. Gallice Litho
Cond A–/Slight tears at paper edges.
Ref: Wagons-Lits, 56 (var)
The name of the summer service being offered by the
Wagons-Lits rail company is almost as long as the deluxe
train ride being advertised in this Ochoa promotion.
Granted, it's nice to know how—and how stylishly—one
is going to arrive at one's intended destination. However, all the textual specificity in the world doesn't
really hold a candle to Ochoa's painterly, balustrade
view of Lake Lucerne, which truly convinces the viewer
that some quiet time away might just be the best idea
in the world.
**Est: $1,700-$2,000.**

## JEAN OLIVIER

**410. Air Union Lignes d'Orient.** ca. 1929.
15³/₈ x 23¹/₂ in./39.2 x 59.7 cm
Imp. Reunies, Paris
Cond A.
Ref: PAI-XLII, 415 (var)
Olivier calls upon an Art Deco shorthand to create a
design that is simple, direct and effective, putting a
redux spin on the classical use of perspective and
vanishing point to effortlessly convey the expanses that
the Air Union Line is willing to traverse in order to deliver your mail to Eastern extremes. This particular
version of the poster includes a map of the route that
one's letters would travel, as well as all fee and delivery
specifics. Air Union was founded in 1927 and in 1933
it, along with French airlines, was folded into the new
national Air France amalgamation. As stylish as it is
arresting, the sight of the silhouetted three-engined
Short Calcutta, stripped to its barest essentials and miles

from land, evokes a cinematic association that in turn
bolsters the image of solitary reliability. A perfect
example of a minimalist imperative.
**Est: $1,500-$2,000.**

## ORSI (1889-1947)

**411. La Revue Nègre.** 1925.
15¹/₂ x 23³/₄ in./39.4 x 60.3 cm
Phogor, Paris
Cond B/Stains and tears, largely in top and bottom
text area. Framed.
Ref: Takashimaya, 145; PAI-XXXIII, 483
The posterist known only as Orsi produced hundreds
of posters, many of them for the theater, and all with
strong, eye-catching designs. "In the history of this art,
his name must occupy an important place because of
the innovative character of his esthetic . . . and the
importance of his work" (Benezit). And though Colin's
poster for La Revue Nègre may be the most famous
(see PAI-XXXV, 267), this Orsi design for the career-
establishing music hall event is far-and-away the most
rare. It marks a watershed in the spectacular career of
Josephine Baker, who substituted as the headliner
at the last moment. It's true that even back home,
Josephine, in the chorus line of a big Broadway nightclub show, was already very far indeed from her humble
background as daughter of a poor St. Louis laundress,
but even in her wildest dreams, she couldn't have anticipated what would happen to her in Paris: she became
virtually the toast of the town within a few weeks of
the show's opening. "Ten glorious weeks La Revue
Nègre played at the Music Hall of the Champs-Elysées.
Booked for a fortnight, it was extended and extended.
Early in November, Josephine and company were still
dancing there while the great Pavlova waited impatiently
for the theater she had been promised . . . At the end
of the month, La Revue Nègre was finally forced to

move to the Théâtre de l'Etoile, where Josephine added
insult to injury by performing a wicked parody of Pavlova
as the Black Swan" (Josephine, p. 121). The lively
angular design shows a nearly nude Baker in a lively
Charleston step with a male partner in full-tilt boogie
close behind.
**Est: $7,000-$9,000.**

412

413

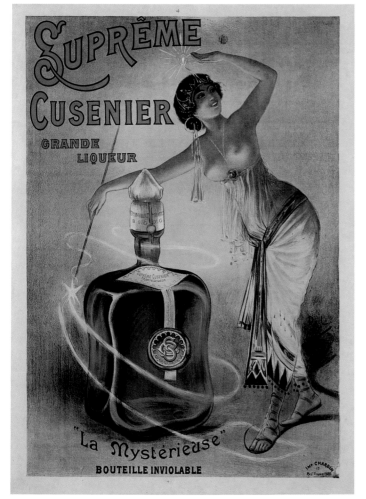

414

## PAL (Jean de Paléologue, 1860-1942)

**412. Whitworth Cycles.** ca. 1894.
56 x 84¹/₂ in./142 x 214.6 cm
Imp. Paul Dupont, Paris
Cond A/Linebacked in two sheets.
Ref: Maindron, p. 120; Reims, 958; V & A, 242; PAI-XXV, 446
Pal executed a minimum of three designs for Whitworth Cycles, all of them featuring a gentleman cyclist showing his bike off to a group of six women either seen peering down from atop a wall—as seen here in this two-sheet format—or at a midway point in the poster narrative, with the women divided equally between wall and ground (*see* PAI-XXXIX, 426) or with the ladies having completely descended from their perch (*see* PAI-XXX, 289). Exactly what they are more enraptured with—bike or roguish rider—is left for the viewer to decide. A bit of a departure for Pal, leaving the women's no-doubt fine figures concealed behind a wall. Quick, fetch a stepladder.
**Est: $2,500-$3,000.**

**413. La Vache Enragée.** 1896.
43¹/₂ x 57 in./110.5 x 144.8 cm
Imp. Paul Dupont, Paris
Cond B+/Slight tears at folds.
Ref: Reims, 956; Affichomanie, 90; PAI-XXIX, 569
Trying to write an article for "La Vache Enragée" (*The Angry Cow*), which he envisions graphically as a ghostly cow charging up Montmartre, a writer burning the midnight oil finally gets his inspiration—a heavenly vision of an exuberant Muse brought to him on the wings of imagination. The satirical periodical, founded by Willette, lasted only about a year.
**Est: $2,000-$2,500.**

**414. Suprême Cusenier.**
45¹/₂ x 61³/₄ in./115.6 x 159.4 cm
Imp. Chardin, Paris
Cond B+/Slight tears, largely in borders.
Ref: PAI-II, 202
Supreme Cusenier liqueur is specially marketed in a mysterious "bouteille inviolable," a feature obviously intended to lend value and mystery to the product. Pal's design enhances the image of voluptuous—to say nothing of magical—oriental splendor that the advertiser wanted to convey—uncommon, cabalistic and, without question, intoxicating. *Rare!*
**Est: $2,000-$2,500.**

**415**

**416**

## PAL (cont'd)

**415. Folies-Bergère/La Loïe Fuller.** 1897.
36 x 51¹/₂ in./91.5 x 131 cm
Imp. F. Hermet, Paris
Cond A.
Ref: Loie Fuller, 69; Spectacle, 1140; PAI-XVI, 398
Pal created a total of five posters for Fuller's appearances at the Folies-Bergère. Here, the billowing folds of her diaphanous dress are rendered in flaming orange, adding considerably to the light-and-motion image with which we are presented. "Loïe Fuller's meteoric rise to fame is one of the oddest success stories of the 1890s. Coming from a small Midwestern town in the United States . . . she studied singing, dancing and acting . . . In one play, she noticed how the spotlights, with various color filters, created a rainbow effect on the material of her dress. Fascinated, she experimented with the effect, eventually working up a specialty dance wearing diaphanous materials on which the colored lights played with dazzling results" (Gold, p. 116). In a recent and quite revealing biography of the dancer, we read that "the French had always taken Loie more seriously than the Americans had, and they did so again after she reappeared at the Folies-Bergère on October 21, 1897 . . . She had maintained her fame by constantly adding something new to her work . . . but with her latest creations, especially the fire dance and the lily dance, she was again enthralling the Paris public" (Fuller/Goddess of Light, p. 111).
**Est: $7,000-$9,000.**

**416. Phébus.** ca. 1898.
43¹/₄ x 58¹/₂ in./109.8 x 148.6 cm
Imp. Paul Dupont, Paris
Cond B+/Unobtrusive tears at folds and edges.
Ref: Petite Reine, 28; Collectionneur, p. 232;
    Pierrot, 69; PAI-XLIII, 478
A poignant scene on a deserted country road: the female biker—from her get up one can only guess that she's a circus trouper—has grown weary and dismounted, so that the clown, who has presumably been racing her in a motorized three-wheeler, was able to overtake her. Far from sympathizing with her, he's

**417**

thumbing his nose at her in the flush of victory. A peculiar, yet strangely appealing narrative for a brand of bicycles—one in which Pal simply had to include one of his charming women somehow!
**Est: $7,000-$9,000.**

**417. Arista.**
23⁵/₈ x 32¹/₂ in./60 x 82.6 cm
Imp. F. Levée, Paris
Cond B+/Slight tears at paper edges.
Ref: XL, 458 (var)
Seen in the full-text version, this alabaster nymph personifies the salutary properties of Arista mineral water, as the water itself rushes forth from the seal-faced

**418**

fountain to the clamoring throng below. This version of the poster was actually executed by another artist working from Pal's design and bears an appropriate "d'après" designation. Though virtually identical, some slight differences do exist here, primarily in the face of the goddess figure, the bottle's label and the lettering. *This is the smaller format.*
**Est: $1,700-$2,000.**

**418. Eyquem.** ca. 1898.
39⁵/₈ x 54⁷/₈ in./100.7 x 139.4 cm
Caby & Chardin, Paris
Cond A–/Unobtrusive tears at folds.

**419**

**420**

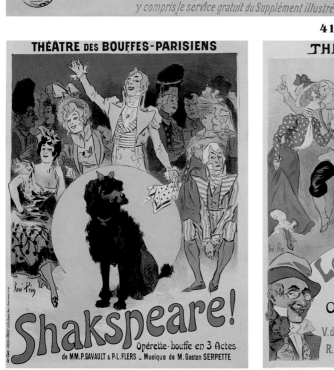

**421**

It's a bit curious as to why Liberator bicycles would hire the services of a capable designer to create a poster for their product and then have another simply redraw an image from a successful earlier campaign (*see PAI-XXXI, 579*). But that would definitely be the case with this Clouet work for the company, which leaves the central image virtually untouched—hence the "d'après Pal" credit—while removing all of the background. *This is the smaller format.*
**Est: $1,500-$2,000.**

## RENÉ PEAN (1875-1940)

**421. Two Operetta Posters.** 1899 & 1900.
Each Approx: 23⁵/8 x 31¹/8 in./60 x 79 cm
Imp. Chaix, Paris
Cond A.
Ref: Spectacles, 126 (a) & 259 (b);
French Opera, 51 (b only);
PAI-XXXVI, 495 (a) & PAI-XXXVII, 464 (b)
Two delightful Pean designs perfectly suited to the musical theater confections they promoted. To bark or not to bark, that is the question that arises upon seeing the first of the two posters. Taking namesake inspiration from The Bard on Avon, this classy little pup is placed in the spotlight as the title character in "Shakespeare!," the comic-operetta that opened at the Bouffes-Parisiens on November 23, 1899. In the second, "The scene is Stockholm. Thylda's fiancé is Otto, and her father is the same Baron von Gondremarck who appeared as a young man in Offenbach's *La Vie Parisienne* . . . The baron decides that before the wedding his future son-in-law should have the same opportunity for adventures in Paris that he had. He sends him off but Thylda makes him miss his train. He goes anyway . . . in a dream. On awakening, he finds that the dream has sufficed and is content to confine his travels to a honeymoon trip" (French Opera, p. xxiv). Pean was a pupil of Chéret, working under him at the Chaix printing firm. He specialized in theater and cabaret posters from around 1890 to 1905. After being among the first to produce posters for the fledgling movie industry, he faded into obscurity.
**Est: $1,700-$2,000.** (2)

Ref: Gold, 17; PAI-XXXIX, 427
"Secretarial work was one of the first non-menial employment opportunities for women in the labor market created by the Industrial Revolution, and countless thousands of girls began to acquire office skills as a normal part of their education. This poster is for an early copying machine, showing that the clerk can handle it with ease while keeping her white cuffs spotless" (Gold, p. 12).
**Est: $1,700-$2,000.**

**419. L'Echo de Paris.** ca. 1899.
43⁷/8 x 61¹/2 in./111.5 x 156.2 cm
Imp. Caby & Chardin, Paris
Cond B–/Restored tears, largely at folds.

Ref: Fit to Print, 107; PAI-XLIII, 485
One of Pal's flimsily-dressed divine creatures takes plume in hand to transcribe the morning's literary, artistic and political news for this Paris newspaper. But one does have to wonder from which cloud her information comes from.
**Est: $2,500-$3,000.**

## PAL & EMILE CLOUET

**420. Liberator Cycles & Motocycles.**
40³/4 x 57³/8 in./103.4 x 145.6 cm
Imp. Jules Simon, Paris
Cond B/Unobtrusive tears near paper edges.
Ref (All Var): DFP-II, 696; Bicycle Posters, 48;
Petite Reine, 33; PAI-XXXI, 580

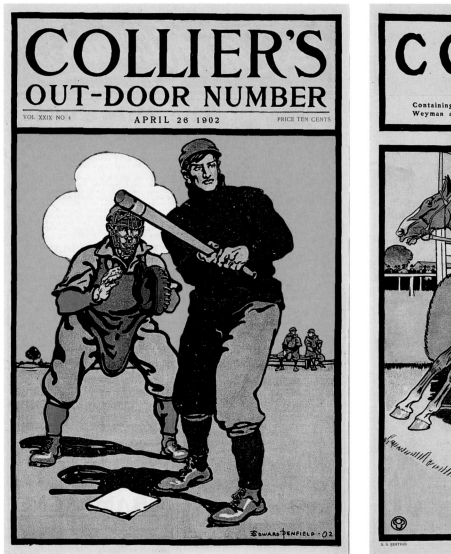

**423**

**424**

# EDWARD PENFIELD (1866-1925)

**422. Collier's/Sporting Number.** 1901.
$10^1/4$ x $14^3/4$ in./26 x 37.4 cm
Cond A–/Unobtrusive folds.
Ref: PAI-XLI, 478
For the October 12th edition of *Collier's*, Penfield presents us with a Harvard football player making a determined run to glory. The expressive design, though fairly simple in its approach, is the perfect choice to invoke autumnal athletic prowess. The artist's vision of all-American virility is nothing short of magnificent.
**Est: $1,200-$1,500.**

**423. Collier's/Out-Door Number.** 1902.
$9^5/8$ x $14^3/4$ in./24.5 x 37.5 cm
Cond A–/Slight tears at paper edges.
Ref: PAI-XVIII, 406b
In this cover for the April 26th "Out-Door Number," Penfield takes us to the heart of spring training with an at-the-ready batter and an ever-alert catcher. This vision of the "National Pastime," decades before any-one ever conceived of something called the "Steroids Era," is one of the artist's most expressive designs.
**Est: $1,200-$1,500.**

**424. Collier's/May 16, 1903.**
$9^7/8$ x $14^1/2$ in./25 x 37 cm
Cond B+/Slight tears and stains at edges.
Founded by Peter Fenelon Collier (1849-1909) and pub-lished from 1888 to 1957, *Collier's* was a pioneering force in investigative journalism with a well-established reputation as a proponent of social reform. But seeing as activism doesn't appeal to every reader, the maga-zine astutely candy-coated their causes with promotional material that put forth more popular diversions. Such as the steeplechase featured in this Penfield cover for the May 16, 1903, edition of the weekly, who handles the race with typical equestrian enthusiasm and mastery.
**Est: $1,200-$1,500.**

**422**

**425. Collier's/July 11, 1903.**
$9^3/4$ x $14^3/4$ in./24.7 x 37.5 cm
Cond A–/Slight tears and stains at paper edges.
Ref: PAI-XXXIV, 93 (var)
Athleticism beat out unionism for the cover of this week's edition of *Collier's*, featuring a brawny oarsman —doubtlessly one of the competitors from the "Inter-

**425**

collegiate Boat Races" being covered in this issue. Pre-viously seen in textless print form (*see* PAI-XXXIV, 93), this paradigm of competitive youth potentially may also have been used in a sport-themed calendar.
**Est: $1,200-$1,500.**

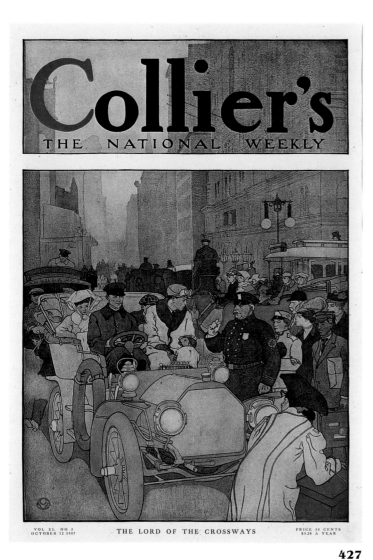

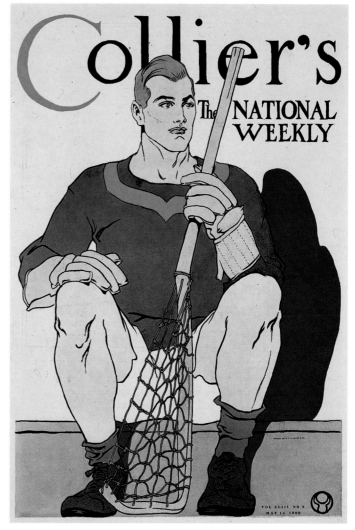

**427**

**428**

**426**

coaches and streetcars all jockeying for position on the crowded thoroughfares of this metropolis. If it looks like chaos now, just imagine what a melee it would be without the titular traffic controller.
**Est: $1,400-$1,700.**

**428. Collier's/The National Weekly.** 1909.
10$^1$/8 x 14$^3$/4 in./25.6 x 37.5 cm
Cond B+/Slight tears and stains at edges.
Not a single one of the athletes set to the page by Penfield show an iota of quit—they're an ever-ready bunch that wear their "Put me in coach" attitude like a badge of honor. Case in point, this vigilant lacrosse player featured on the May 15, 1909, edition of *Collier's*, focused on the unseen action and ready to jump in as soon as he gets the go-ahead. Unlike his work for *Harper's*, all of the *Collier's* designs seen here were executed to be covers for the magazine.
**Est: $1,200-$1,500.**

**429. Harper's/August/Tom Sawyer Detective.** 1896.
13$^1$/2 x 18$^3$/4 in./34.3 x 47.5 cm
Cond A-/Slight tears and stains at edges.
Ref: DFP-I, 359; Reims, 1276; Lauder, 183;
   PAI-XXXV, 443
At the beach, a fashionably overdressed young woman waits impatiently for the barely more daringly attired smoking swimmer to muster his conversational courage. A wonderfully succinct graphic narrative.
**Est: $1,200-$1,500.**

**429**

**426. Collier's/August 8, 1903.**
9$^3$/4 x 14$^1$/4 in./25 x 36 cm
Cond A-/Slight tears at edges.
Not to take anything away from her game, but the woman used as the sporty lure on the cover of *Collier's* August 8, 1903, issue would appear to be in place more as an examplar of appropriate attire rather than for her incomparable club selection. And it works to perfection, thanks to Penfield's impeccable display of fashion sense: functional, streamlined and altogether feminine.
**Est: $1,200-$1,500.**

**427. Collier's/October 12, 1907.**
10$^1$/8 x 14$^1$/4 in./25.7 x 36 cm
Cond A.
*Entire issue of the magazine.*
It looks like a thankless, hectic job, being "The Lord of the Crossways." But it certainly appears as if it's an undertaking that the officer in question performs with pride and well-worn authority. And the cover design executed by Penfield for this edition of "The National Weekly" is a stupendous recreation of the zoo known as the daily commute, with pedestrians, cars, buggies,

**431**

**432**

**430**

**433**

## EDWARD PENFIELD (cont'd)

**430. Ladies' Home Journal/August.** 1908.
$10^5/8$ x $15^1/2$ in./27 x 39.5 cm
Cond A–/Slight tears at paper edges.
This may be the "Summer-Porch Number" of the *Ladies' Home Journal*, but Penfield's cover art doesn't exactly encourage lemonade-and-rocking-chair afternoons. Instead, it appears to be prompting the magazine's readership to stop watching the world go by and to hit the open road to find out what lies beyond their verandas. *Ladies' Home Journal* first appeared on February

16, 1883, as a women's supplement to the *Tribune* and *Farmer*, published by Cyrus H. Curtis. Arising from a popular "women's column" written by his wife, Louisa Knapp, it became an independent publication the following year. Its original name was *Ladies' Home Journal* and *Practical Housekeeper*, but the last three words of the title were dropped in short order. It rapidly became the leading magazine of its type, reaching a circulation of more than one-million copies in ten years.
**Est: $1,200-$1,500.**

## ROGER PEROT (1908-1976)

**431. Delahaye.** 1932.
$45^1/2$ x $62^5/8$ in./115.5 x 159 cm
Les Ateliers A.B.C., Paris
Cond B+/Slight tears and printer's creases at edges.
Ref: Auto Show I, 72; Deco Affiches, p. 71; PAI-XLIII, 25
The Delahaye coming over the horizon makes for one of the most perfect automobile posters ever created. The positioning of the type parallel with the horizon line is especially effective. Although the public most fondly remembers Delahaye as a fast French sporting

**435**

**434**

**436**

### HANS PFAFF (1875-?)

**434. Pianos Kaps.** 1897.
$38^{1}/_{4}$ x $26^{1}/_{4}$ in./97.2 x 66.7 cm
C.C. Meinhold & Sons, Dresden
Cond A. Framed.
Ref: DFP-III, 2537 (var); PAI-XL, 469
Pfaff, born of German parents in Shanghai, was an illustrator and contributor to *Jugend* magazine. In 1896 he began to design book covers for the Dresden publisher Hirth & Pierson and that became his permanent job. This, regrettably, is his only known poster. It won him third prize in a poster competition sponsored by Dresden piano maker Ernest Kaps. His vivid colors and fine design epitomize some of the best and most interesting aspects of the Art Nouveau period. Two other versions of the poster show either a Dresden or Paris address below the image.
**Est: $5,000-$6,000.**

### PHILI (Pierre Grach, 1898-1987)

**435. Le Parisien.** 1944.
$45^{5}/_{8}$ x $62^{3}/_{4}$ in./115.8 x 159.2 cm
Office de Publicité Generale, Paris
Cond A–/Slight tears and stains at paper edges.
Ref: Livre d'Affiche, 140; Fit to Print, 128; PAI-XX, 380
When the Allies ended the German occupation of France, freedom of the press was a welcome aspect of the liberation. New newspapers appeared and established ones were reborn. Here, *Le Parisien* announces its return with the proud addition of "libéré" (freed) in its name. "Workers, businessmen, ladies in fancy hats, even youth are decidedly together on what paper to read. In the newly-liberated city, it seems, 'Everyone reads *Le Parisien*'" (Fit to Print, p. 100).
**Est: $1,200-$1,500.**

### P. PIN

**436. Anis Candela.**
21 x $15^{3}/_{8}$ in./53.5 x 39 cm
Cond B+/Unobtrusive tears.
The Monforte del Cid distillery has been producing various liqueurs since 1895, which makes it one of the oldest manufacturers operating in Spain. This Pin promotion for their Anis Candela couldn't be much more civil, decorous or breezy if it tried. The message conveyed by the seaside scene is crystal clear—if you're looking to get pie-eyed, look elsewhere, because Anis Candela is for sophisticates with refined palates and a working knowledge of moderation. The house of Monforte del Cid is still very much in operation, having recently introduced a new absinthe to the market.
**Est: $1,200-$1,500.**

and racing car of the late 1930s, the marque actually had a sixty-year span beginning in 1894. It was dropped only in 1954 when the company was taken over by Hotchkiss, a truck maker. Little is known of Pérot, an architect who, regrettably, produced only a few posters.
**Est: $6,000-$8,000.**

**432. Delahaye.** 1935.
$45^{1}/_{2}$ x $61^{5}/_{8}$ in./115.6 x 156.6 cm
Les Ateliers A.B.C., Paris
Cond B/Slight tears, largely at folds and edges.
Ref: PAI-XXXV, 76
Due to the popularity of the previous poster, Perot's design was reprinted three years later with very few changes—as seen here, the color of the sky and road has gone from blue to yellow and the car's grille has been updated to more accurately reflect that year's model.
**Est: $5,000-$7,000.**

### JEAN M. PESKE (1870-1949)

**433. L'Estampe et L'Affiche.** 1898.
$51^{1}/_{4}$ x $36^{3}/_{8}$ in./130.2 x 92.3 cm
Cond A.
Ref (All Var): DFP-II, 710; Affichomanie, 52; Color Revolution, 70; Weill, 81; Wine Spectator, 66; PAI-XXXVII, 468
*One of approximately 50 numbered copies (#6) before letters; full margins.*
*L'Estampe et l'Affiche* was probably the most influential publication in the field of color lithography in France at the turn of the twentieth century and, under the editorship of André Mellerio, it did much to encourage poster art in the brief period of its existence. In an article in the magazine announcing the publication of this poster, the critic Crauzat is full of praise for it, indicating that its clear tones and design show the artist to be a master of decorative effect. As far away as London, *The Poster* magazine also lauded the work: "On the green summit of a cliff, two women—one laying down and the other sitting—giving a back view of themselves, look far away into the dying perspective of the ocean. Their dresses, respectively red and blue, give two beautiful contrasting notes to the ambient tonalities. Mountains encircle the bay, the calmness of which is disturbed only by the modulated swing of a smack. The colours are cleverly harmonised, and the light line of water produces a very good effect" (June 1898, p. 28).
**Est: $10,000-$12,000.**

**437**

**440**

**443**

## G. PODUIE

**437. Rhum des Incas.** 1928.
$46^3/8$ x $63^1/8$ in./117.8 x 160.3 cm
Imp. Marcel Picard, Paris
Cond A-/Slight tears at folds.
Ref: PAI-XVI, 426
Certainly a novel idea for a Native American headdress from an artist
whose signature isn't altogether legible. Though not exactly the most
politically-correct concept, it's an image that's difficult to ignore.
**Est: $3,000-$4,000.**

## TOM PURVIS (1888-1959)

**438. Continent via Harwich.**
25 x $39^1/2$ in./63.5 x 100.3 cm
Dangerfield, London
Cond A-/Slight tears at edges.
Ref: PAI-XII, 373
The stylized nightclub scene is rendered in startlingly vivid hues, which
adds to its unusual, almost surrealist appeal. A bold statement, as well as
something of a departure for Purvis who rarely strays this far off the beaten
path. Best known for his British railway posters, the artist ranks among the
best of all posterists working between the Wars, making dramatic impact
with his use of flat colors and simplified design.
**Est: $1,400-$1,700.**

## MAURICE REALIER-DUMAS (1860-1928)

**439. Incandescence par le Gaz.** 1892.
$24^3/8$ x 68 in./62 x 172.8 cm
Imp. Chaix, Paris
Cond B/Unobtrusive tears, largely at folds and paper edges.
Ref: DFP-II, 731; Reims, 980; Maitres, 23
Mason Williams may have made "Classical Gas" an instrumental radio hit
in 1968, but Realier-Dumas beat him to the conceptual punch by more than
seventy-five years with another artistic expression intended for public consumption. His gaslight poster gives us the dealer's address without revealing a name. However, one has to imagine that anyone interested in this
type of illumination beat a path to that address thanks to Realier-Dumas'
statuesque Art Nouveau conception, a breath-catching combination of old-
meets-new, with a meandering side-text that allows the eye of the viewer

**438**

**442**

to freely wander the full length of the central woman's slender figure.
**Est: $1,500-$2,000.**

## GEORGES REDON (1869-1943)

**440. Boulogne S. Mer.** 1905.
$28^7/8$ x $41^5/8$ in./73.3 x 105.7 cm
Imp. E. Marx, Paris
Cond B+/Unobtrusive folds.

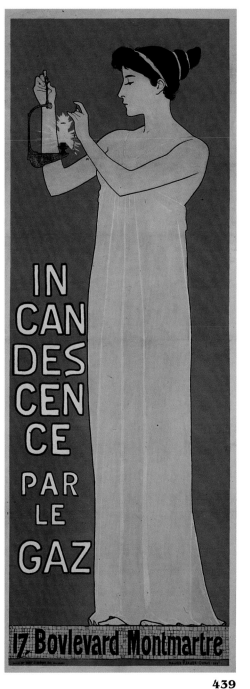

**439**

Ref: Gold, 138; PAI-XXXVI, 83
Unless you choose to bury your head in the sand and naively believe that the posters of the Belle Epoque were created for purely artistic reasons, this design revels in an advertising axiom that has firmly been in place from Day One: Sex Sells. It could hardly matter that the only thing exposed on this fulsome bathing beauty is her arms—her blissful expression as she luxuriates in the lapping waves pounds the message home with about as much subtlety as being thwacked with a sack full of door-knobs. And even if you weren't a woman praying that a trip to this seaside resort would have the same orgasmic effect on you, Redon's design doubtlessly caught the eye of many pedestrians, who once caught, could move onto the text and the familial cameo of non-carnal recreational activities. As effective a design as it is blatant.
**Est: $2,000-$2,500.**

## F. REILS

**441. Deutsche Fachausstellung.** 1897.
$20^3/8$ x $28^7/8$ in./51.7 x 73.3 cm
St?hle & Friedel, Stuttgart
Cond B+/Slight tears at folds.
This Reils poster for a Stuttgart hospitality trade show would seem to imply that the combination of a coy hostess, a bottle of bubbly and a succulent crustacean are all the ingredients necessary to secure the patronage of the masses. And you know what—it's certainly not a bad jumping off point. The poster's obvious elements initiate the attraction, but it's the subtler inclusions—

**441**

the upper cookie-and-pretzel border, the wooden spoon with a saucy taste still clinging to its tip—that gives the predominantly sepia design a more substantive charm.
**Est: $1,400-$1,700.**

## ALEJANDRO DE RIQUER (1856-1920)

**442. The Seasons/Spring.** 1900.
$21^3/4$ x $45^7/8$ in./55.2 x 116.5 cm
Cond A.
Ref: PAI-XLIII, 511
Writing specifically about this 1900 seasonal panel series, Rogers states that "In Spain, de Riquer has executed some charming decorative panels, which are worthy to rank with the best efforts of Mucha. The set representing the four seasons, of which 'Spring' is undoubtedly the best, are single-figure studies in the open air, and treat the subjects from an original and unconventional point of view" (p. 127). And here is that "best" panel, a dreamy, thought-provoking composition done with such ease that not only is the redhead experiencing the rebirth of the world around her, she is irrefutably an essential part of it. Beginning in 1879, the artist traveled widely, from Rome to Paris to London. He became associated with the Arts & Crafts Movement, inspired by William Morris, becoming a protégé of Walter Crane, who admired his attempts to enhance the esthetic value of industrial design, such as window displays, textiles and books. He worked as an illustrator, art director of publications and graphic designer, becoming one of the foremost graphic art stylists and innovators of the Art Nouveau movement upon his return to Spain.
**Est: $1,700-$2,000.**

## A. RITSCHER

**443. U.S. Lines/Bremen-New York.** ca. 1914.
29 x $39^1/8$ in./73.5 x 99.5 cm
Hauschild, Bremen
Cond A–/Slight tears in bottom text area.
When it comes to advertising an ocean-going vessel, it's fairly important that the name of a ship is prominently placed on public display. Unless, of course, the ship is so well known that naming it becomes an extraneous detail. Such would be the case in this Ritscher promotion for the U.S. Lines, which has the newly-acquired *Kaiser Wilhelm II*—hence the appearance of both the U.S. Lines and the Norddeutscher Lloyd Bremen firm on the design —emerging from an Art Deco sunburst like the promise of a dawning new era. At the time of her maiden voyage on April 14, 1903, she was the largest merchant ship under the German flag. Seized by the United States Government on April 6, 1917, the ship was renamed *Agamemnon* and used as a troop transport, then later as a mail ship.
**Est: $1,700-$2,000.**

444

446

447

448

## J. ROSETTI

**444. La Raphaëlle.** 1908.
47 x 62³/₈ in./119.4 x 158.4 cm
Imp. I. Lang, Paris
Cond B+/Slight tears at folds.
Ref: PAI-XXXVII, A37
The latest technological innovation is used to promote one of France's oldest Bonal liqueurs. Actually, it would appear as if this Wright-style aircraft is being used to pilfer a bottle of Raphaëlle from a rather agitated waiter. Seems to me as if this rather dubious achievement is one best left off of the lexicon of manned flight's proudest moments. *This is the first known French poster to depict a Wright flyer.*
**Est: $1,500-$1,800.**

## AUGUSTE ROUBILLE (1872-1955)

**445. Paris-London Journal.** 1897.
19¹/₂ x 25³/₄ in./49.5 x 65.3 cm
Imp. F. Appel, Paris
Cond A–/Slight tears at folds.
Who needs a paddle when the power of the quill compels you? Connecting the two European nations with erudite integrity, this fine-looking Art Nouveau allegorical representation of the Paris-London illustrated journal requires no more than the colors of representative flags to make her message definitive. The bilingual literary magazine was available on all the newsstands of both England and France, naturally and *naturellement. Rare!*
**Est: $1,500-$2,000.**

## FERNANDE ROUSSEAU (?-1963)

**446. Boulogne s. Mer.**
39¹/₄ x 54 in./99.7 x 137.1 cm
Imp. d'Art Moderne, Paris
Cond B+/Unobtrusive tears and stains in margins.
Ref: PAI-XIV, 437
The style is old-fashioned, the approach formal, yet somehow the shipboard vista makes a pleasing image to promote travel to a seaside resort on the Channel coast. The colors are restrained, but clear and bright. Rousseau died in Belgium in 1963, but whether she was Belgian by birth has not been determined.
**Est: $1,400-$1,700.**

## RICHARD RUMMELL (1848-1924)

**447. French Line/The "France".** ca. 1920.
40⁵/₈ x 26³/₄ in./103 x 68 cm
Albert J. Leon, NYC
Cond A–/Unobtrusive tears at edges.
Ref: PAI-XXXI, 155 (var)
The majesty of the big luxury liner as it glides past the New York skyline is impressively depicted, with small tugs and other vessels paying homage. An excellent maritime poster in all respects. Rummell grew up in Brooklyn and remained active in New York City all his life. This particular version of the poster comes with an imprint of an Italian travel agency with an office in San Francisco applied atop Rummell's graphics.
**Est: $3,500-$4,000.**

## VIKTOR RUTZ (1913- )

**448. Eichhorn.**
35¹/₄ x 50 in./89.7 x 127 cm
Paul-Bender, Zollikon-Zürich
Cond A–/Slight creasing at paper edges/P.
Nothing beats a great pair of legs. Decades before those words became the catch-phrase for a brand of nylons, Rutz showed that it was much more than a slogan—it was the truth, plain and simple, at least where Eichhorn stockings were concerned. In celebrating 100 years of quality hosiery, Rutz takes a nearly identical approach as Birkhäuser (*see* No. 104)—present the public with what practically every woman wants to look like and what virtually every man wants to at the very least ogle. If it ain't broke, don't fix it. Rutz (also known as Victor Ruzo) turned to graphic art after starting out as a fashion and retail illustrator in Zurich. He did the bulk of his work—200-odd posters that earned prizes Europe-

**451**

**449**

**450**

wide—in the early-1940s. In 1946, he moved to Vevey and began concentrating on painting; since 1960 he has lived in Montreux.
**Est: $1,000-$1,200.**

**449. Stalden.** 1947.
35$^{1}$/2 x 50$^{3}$/8 in./90.3 x 127.8 cm
Klaus Felder, Vevey

Cond A–/Unobtrusive tears at paper edges/P.
Ref: Enfant dans l'Affiche, p. 89
Thoughts of Willy Wonka can't help but come to mind when one gets a look at this Rutz design for Stalden preserves. Certainly the disproportion is meant to convey the big fruit-and-sugar deliciousness of the product, but isn't it far more fun to take the promotion at face value, with a quartet of tots literally can-diving to their sweet-teethed delight. A delightfully sticky overstatement.
**Est: $1,000-$1,200.**

## C. SCHAAF

**450. Hollandsche Spoor/Den Haag Nÿmegen.**
25$^{5}$/8 x 33$^{7}$/8 in./65 x 86 cm
Drukkerij Senefelder, Amsterdam
Cond A.
In another Schaaf poster for this Dutch rail service, the artist relied on an overburdened traveler boarding a train to make its promotional impact (*see* PAI-XXVI, 531). Here, he takes an altogether opposite approach: the oncoming rush of express travel, with the lettering placed in a rather clever manner that makes it appear as if they're streaking away from the viewer. The Hollandse Spoor line was significant as it was the first railway in the Netherlands to offer west-to-east service; this particular poster promotes travel from The Hague to Nÿmegen with a single stop in Rotterdam.
**Est: $1,200-$1,500.**

## A. SCHINDELER

**451. Voyage Autour du Monde/Round the World.**
ca. 1890.
50$^{5}$/8 x 37$^{3}$/8 in./128.5 x 95 cm
Lith. Viellemard, Paris
Cond A.
Ref: PAI-XIII, 402
This is one of the most magnificent travel posters ever created. It advertises a 'Round-the-World tour by ship and railroad. The globe gives us part of the itinerary: from the right, the ship comes through the Red Sea and Mediterranean, by railway from Marseilles to Le Havre, then by ship to New York, where the railroad, shown at the bottom of the design, takes you to San Francisco either by way of Chicago or New Orleans, and then the ship again across the Pacific.
**Est: $20,000-$25,000.**

452

## WALTER SCHNACKENBERG (1880-1961)

**452. Peter Pathe/Maria Hagen.** 1918.
35¹/₂ x 48³/₄ in./90.4 x 124 cm
O. Consée, München
Cond A–/Unobtrusive tears, largely at paper edges.
Ref: Schnackenberg, (no folio); Plakate München, 419;
    PAI-XL, 488
This gifted German artist could be one of the poster
collector's favorites, if only there were some posters of
his to collect. He did only a few, and all of those are
so rare that most poster enthusiasts never come across
them. His designs are a quaint amalgam of caricature

and fantasy which he himself called "suggestive dreams."
With an unerring instinct for color, and an exquisitely
refined taste of subtle irony, he created a body of
work that is uniquely individualistic—small but choice.
Schnackenberg created several posters for this duo of
Munich ballet performers, of which this is the most
traditionally expressive.
**Est: $17,000-$20,000.**

**453. Peter Pathe/Maria Hagen.** ca. 1918.
35¹/₂ x 48¹/₂ in./90.1 x 123 cm
O. Consée, München

Cond B/Restored tears and losses, largely at paper edges.
Ref: Schnackenberg (no folio); Plakate Muenchen, 419;
    Takashimaya, 151; PAI-XXVIII, 525
In another poster for the Munich-based balletic duo,
Schnackenberg concocts a rather startling design for
an act they dubbed "Light and Shadows"—a variant of
the "Beauty and the Beast" theme. Schnackenberg's
poster is rather expressionistic, yet at the same time,
tenderly conceived—an intriguing, excellent example
of graphic language at its best.
**Est: $20,000-$25,000.**

PETER PATHE

MARIA HAGEN

Schmackenberg

KUNSTANSTALT O.CONSÉE MÜNCHEN

**455**

**456**

## SEM (Georges Goursat, 1863-1934)

**454. Alcazar d'Eté/Paulus.** 1891.
32¹/₄ x 47³/₄ in./82 x 121.2 cm
Imp. Chaix, Paris (not shown)
Cond B–/Slight tears and stains at folds and edges.
Ref: Spectacle, 827; PAI-IX, 469
The Alcazar d'Eté announces a revue featuring one of
the most popular singers of the 1880s and 1890s,
Paulus, the pseudonym of Jean-Paul Habans. The concept of the poster shows the the influence of Chéret: the
prominent central figure in a dynamic pose, very little
background and distinctive lettering woven skillfully
into the design. The career of caricaturist Sem started
modestly enough in his home town of Perigueux where
he published his first collection of local celebrity portraits
in 1895. Only after doing the same for Bordeaux in
1897 and Marseilles in 1898 did he venture to Paris
where he charmed the city folk with his talent. Hardly
anyone of note escaped being captured for posterity.
**Est; $1,200-$1,500.**

**455. Scala/A Fleur de Peau.**
31⁵/₈ x 46⁷/₈ in./80.2 x 119 cm
Affiches Devers, Paris
Cond B+/Slight tears at folds.
It's impossible to overlook the fact that Sem may have
drawn a touch of inspiration from Cappiello's earlier
work in his design for this bit of entertaining fluff in two
acts and twelve scenes playing at the Scala music hall.
But if you're going to artistically borrow, why not borrow
from the best?! And though this advertisement for the
"I'm Ticklish" revue may share a few similar conceptual
elements with the somewhat better known artist, one aspect definitely sets it apart—the unapologetic fun flowing freely throughout the design is pure, unfiltered Sem.
**Est: $1,500-$2,000.**

**456. La Revue du Casino de Paris.**
35³/₄ x 49⁵/₈ in./91 x 126 cm
Atelier/Imp. Sem, Paris
Cond B/Restored tears, largely at folds.

**454**

One of the more curious music hall posters that you're
ever likely to see. Certainly its standard-issue title doesn't
give anything away, but this Scala diversion was obviously devoted to humorous representations of ethnic
and cultural diversity. And though the lanky fellow in
the kimono is a caricaturistically accurate representation in of the *Gui Men Dan* roles in Chinese opera, it's
difficult to know what to make of the enrapt leprechaun
who's drinking him/her in. Wondrous and strange.
**Est: $1,500-$2,000.**

**457**

**457. Bénédictine.**
48¹/₂ x 77¹/₂ in./123.2 x 197 cm
Imp. de la Bénédictine
Cond B–/Tears and stains at folds. Framed.
Ref: PAI-XXXII, 497
This liqueur, an elixir concocted by the monks of the
Fecamp Abbey by combing local wine, native herbs
and imported ingredients such as ginger and cardamom

**458**

**459**

**460**

—a secret blend they maintained for three centuries—is given a sophisticated delivery by Sem, clearly putting forth the idea that fine spirits aren't just for the clergy anymore, but anyone with a properly refined palate.
**Est: $1,700-$2,000.**

**458. Folies-Bergere/Footitt.**
34¹/₂ x 49⁷/₈ in./87.7 x 126.7 cm
Imp. J. Messean, Paris
Cond B–/Restored tears, largely at folds.
Sem promotes a Folies-Bergère appearance by this famed Auguste clown with a surprisingly Kabuki-esque portrait. Though there's some discrepancy in terms of spelling (we've uncovered three different variants on the name "Footit" that all refer to the same performer), it's safe to assume that this white-faced cutup is none other than George Footit (1864-1921), one half of the celebrated clown duo, Footit et Chocolat, and that the poster comes from sometime after 1910, at which point both performers embarked on rather uneventful solo careers. Their partnership began in 1889 at the Nouveau Cirque and their routine was pure knockabout slapstick. Footit, a Manchester, England, native had been performing as a clown and acrobat since the age of twelve, beginning with Sangers' Circus in London. His partner in crime, Chocolat—nee Rafael Padilla (1868-1917)—was not a black-face performer at all, but a Cuban native and former slave turned performer. They ascended to the pinnacle of the Folies-Bergère in 1905. After their split, Footit tried to open a circus of his own, and later a bar, but both ventures failed.
**Est: $1,200-$1,500.**

**459. La Lampe Osram.**
44 x 60⁵/₈ in./111.8 x 154 cm
Affiches Devambez, Paris
Cond B+/Unobtrusive folds.
Ref: PAI-XXV, 498
Seeing as Sem was a caricaturist by vocation as well as avocation, he naturally gravitated to the Salon des Humoristes, and served as its president for a time. His

posters, usually for cabarets and places of amusement, always exude a good-natured but slightly skewed view of the world. For example, take this poster for Osram light bulbs. You have to appreciate the moxie of this third-rate master of ceremonies (or possibly magician) as he "politely" calls our attention to the advertised product. The ironic contrast of the words being used compared to the effort being expended makes this a classic of humorous brevity. Osram is one of the two largest lighting manufacturers in the world today and is part of Siemens AG. Their name is derived from the element *osmium* and *wolfram* (the German word for "tungsten"), as both these elements were commonly used for lighting filaments at the time the company was founded. Osram owns the brand Sylvania for use in the United States, Canada and Mexico.
**Est: $2,000-$2,500.**

**460. Max Dearly.**
28³/₈ x 68¹/₂ in./72 x 174 cm
Imp. Via Decor, Paris
Cond B/Slight tears and stains at seam and edges.
This 2-sheet portrait of Max Dearly (1874-1943) based on an original Sem design (the poster bears a "d'après" designation) makes it immediately clear that the seasoned music-hall veteran was a pretty smooth operator. What it doesn't show us right up front is that he was responsible for imaking two major contributions to the Parisian nightlife scene. First off, after observing a fight between a tough night club patron and his moll, Dearly decided to turn the row into a routine. The result was the famous "apache" dance. The faux-Native American label found its way into popular French slang via Western dime novels and short films with the term "apache" coming to denote a streetwise Parisian tough guy. The dance craze that ensued consisted basically of one of these "thugs" essentially "roughing-up" his partner. And his second contribution? Why, it was his choice of partners, a dancer that was appearing with him at the Moulin Rouge at the time—Mistinguett.
**Est: $1,700-$2,000.**

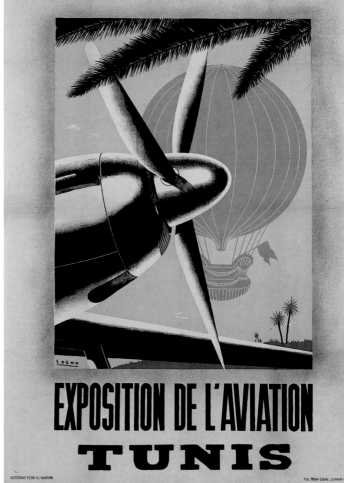

**463**

**464**

## SEM (cont'd)

**461. Max Dearly/La Vérité Toute Nue.**
31¼ x 45¾ in./79.5 x 115.3 cm
Imp. H. Chachoin, Paris
Cond A.
There's an old French proverb that states, "La Verité sort du puits"—"The Truth comes out of a well." Or, less literally, if you dig down deep enough, you're bound to get to the bottom of things. We've already seen this adage serve as the inspiration for a specialty bicycle chain polish (see PAI-XL, 25). Now the saying appears to have been Sem's muse in his promotion for Dearly's "immense success" playing at the Théâtre du Gymnase. Titled "The Naked Truth," we see the performer emerging from a well, dressed in nothing more than cuffs and collar, utterly enamored with the reflection that he sees in his handheld mirror. Regardless of what the entire "Truth" may have been, Sem's witty promotion provides ample delight in and of itself without further extrapolation.
**Est: $1,200-$1,500.**

**462. Cannes.** 1930.
28¼ x 39¾ in./ 71.7 x 101 cm
Imp. Draeger, Paris
Cond A–/Slight tears at paper edges.
Ref: Affiches Azur, 118; Mer s'Affiche, p. 113;
   Karcher, 452; PAI-XXXI, 645
As noted in *Affiches d'Azur* (p. 93), the three chief themes in posters for Cannes were elegance, sports and flowers. This poster has all three: orange blossoms, a golfer, and the slogan "The City of Elegant Sports." Elegant, too are the colors—serene deep blues, rose, orange. The orange branch and the unusual placement of the title across the middle recur in a companion poster by Sem of the same year (subtitled "The City of Flowers and Elegant Sports").
**Est: $1,700-$2,000.**

**461**

## KENNETH DENTON SHOESMITH
## (1890-1939)

**463. Anchor Line/Glasgow & New York.**
23¾ x 38¾ in./60.2 x 98.5 cm
Thos. Forman & Sons, Nottingham
Cond B+/Restored tears, largely near bottom text area.
Ref: PAI-XXXVII, 57
Not to cast any aspersions on Mr. Shoesmith's talents,

**462**

but it would appear as if a bit of inspiration for this Anchor Line promotion may have been drawn from a similar R. S. Pike design for the *Leviathan* (see PAI-XXXVIII, 497). This free interpretation, however, creates a monumental advertisement for one of two Anchor Line turbine steamer ships: the *Tuscania* or the *California*, both of which possessed two-tiered promenade decks, as opposed to the other Anchor ships that had only a single promenade deck. A powerful image!

**465**

**466**

**467**

A pupil of Fred Taylor and a sailor by training, Shoesmith was a brilliantly talented English painter, posterist and decorative artist. Graphically speaking, he is best known for his work executed for the British railway and maritime industries.
**Est: $2,500-$3,000.**

## JACQUES SOGNO

**464. Exposition de l'Aviation/Tunis.** 1942.
31⁵/₈ x 46¹/₂ in./80.4 x 118.3 cm
Imp. Mont-Louis, Clermont-Ferrand & Paris
Cond B/Restored paper loss at top and bottom text
areas; image and colors excellent.

Nostalgia meets reality; practicality meets the fantastical in this Sogno poster for an air expo taking place in the Tunisian capital during the winter of 1942. Though the palm trees and the baking golden sun are certainly as evocative and fundamental to the design as the foreground propeller and the ornate hot air balloon, it's important to remember that Tunisia was still a French protectorate at this point in history and that the Battle of Tunisia—the series of World War II battles that took place in Tunisia in the North African Campaign between Axis and Allied forces—loomed on the horizon. With that in mind, it's probably no coincidence that the foreground plane looms so large as contemporary French air power was certainly a dominant theme of the event.
**Est: $1,500-$1,800.**

## THÉOPHILE-ALEXANDRE STEINLEN (1859-1923)

**465. Tournée du Chat Noir.** 1896.
38¹/₈ x 53⁷/₈ in./96.7 x 136.7 cm
Imp. Charles Verneau, Paris
Cond B–/Restored tears, largely at folds and edges.
Ref: Bargiel & Zagrodski, 22; Crauzat, 496;
    DFP-II, 787; Wagner, 63; Timeless Images, 51;
    Lautrec/Montmartre, 104; PAI-XLIII, 548
That darn cat is at it again in the promotional service of the Chat Noir cabaret. The design was no doubt meant as a satirical comment on Mucha's posters, with Steinlen's well-traveled cat's long tail replacing the long tresses in Mucha's images and the halo here having the inscription "Mont-Joye-Montmartre." *This is the larger format.*
**Est: $8,000-$10,000.**

**466. Lait pur Stérilisé.** 1894.
37 x 52¹/₂ in./93.9 x 133.4 cm
Imp. Charles Verneau, Paris
Cond B/Unobtrusive folds; restored tears at edges.
Ref: Bargiel et Zagrodzki, 16. A1; Crauzat, 491;
    Wine Spectator, 112; Maitres, 95; DFP-II, 783;
    Abdy, p. 97; Weill, 63; Gold, 56; PAI-XLI, 533A

Steinlen arrived in Paris from his native Switzerland in 1882; his first poster dates from 1885 and, in a long and extremely prolific career that saw him illustrate about 100 books and over 1,000 issues of periodicals, as well as create paintings, lithographs and bronzes, he produced about fifty posters. Abdy makes this point: "Steinlen was one of the four or five great poster artists of his time; all his lithographic work is distinguished by a freshness and vigour which makes it powerful, and a simplicity and sympathy which makes it appealing . . . The subject of his posters are those dearest to his heart, his pretty little daughter Colette, and his beloved cats" (p. 94). All the warmth, humanity and affection for which he is so loved comes through gloriously in this poster for the newly-marketed "lait stérilisé" that was touted over the "lait ordinaire" at that time. Charles Knowles Bolton, writing a year after its publication, proclaimed that this "is perhaps, the most attractive poster ever made. No man with half a heart could fail to fall in love with the child." Louis Rhead himself commented: "When I saw it in Paris last year . . . it seemed to me the best and brightest form of advertising that had appeared." That judgment remains valid today. *This is the medium format.*
**Est: $20,000-$25,000.**

**467. Le Rêve.** 1890.
23³/₈ x 30⁷/₈ in./59.4 x 78.2 cm
Imp. Gillot, Paris
Cond A. Framed.
Ref: Bargiel et Zagrodzki, 10; Crauzat, 529; DFP-II, 779;
    French Opera, 28; Dance Posters, 18; PAI-XLII, 467
For the ballet, "Le Rêve" ("The Dream"), Steinlen indulges in his showier side, calling for a design that "shows the giant fan from Act I that is opened by a magical arrow shot. At the top is the golden goddess Isanami, who leads the heroine behind the fan into a dream experience" (French Opera, p. 28). In 1891, this poster was offered by Sagot to poster collectors at a price of five francs; by 1895, the price had more than doubled, with Arnould selling it for twelve francs. Obviously, this trend has continued on this fanciful, rare Steinlen gem.
**Est: $1,200-$1,500.**

Clinique Chéron

MÉDECIN VÉTÉRINAIRE SPÉCIALISTE
8 RUE des MOULINS AVENUE DE L'OPÉRA PARIS
SANATORIUM . PENSION
Téléphone 141.06

Steinlen

468

"LA RUE" CHARLES VERNEAU, IMP.
114, RUE OBERKAMPF, PARIS

For several fine illustrated works by Steinlen, see Nos. 534, 537, 545, 546 in the Books & Periodicals section.

## STEINLEN (cont'd)

**468. Clinique Cheron.** 1905.
$53^5/8$ x 76 in./136.2 x 193 cm
Imp. Ch. Wall, Paris
Cond A–/Slight stains at edges.
Ref: Bargiel & Zagrodzky, 45; Crauzat, 511; DFP-II, 799;
    Wagner, 66; Suntory, p. 30; Gold, 39; PAI-XXX, 96
This large, life-size poster for a veterinarian is one of Steinlen's most beautiful, and today, one of the rarest. The fine grouping of affectionate animals makes for a most appealing image. It also shows Steinlen's gift for effective poster design: His composition forces us to look at the advertising message as our eyes go from the cats above to the dogs below.
**Est: $40,000-$50,000.**

**469. Affiches Charles Verneau/"La Rue."** 1896.
$118^1/2$ x $92^1/2$ in./301 x 235 cm
Imp. Charles Verneau, Paris
Cond B+/Slight tears, largely at seams and edges.
Ref: Bargiel et Zagrodzki, 20; Weill, 64; Crauzat, 495;
    Timeless Images, 50; DFP-II, 786;
    Wine Spectator, 110; PAI-XLI, 536
"One of Steinlen's finest lithographic achievements was a huge, six-sheet poster for Affiches Charles Verneau.

The bustling street scene is alive with an assortment of colorful Montmartre types, prominent among them the artist's daughter, Colette, with a hoop, being carefully led by her mother, Emilie. Note how Steinlen shows the working class side by side with the smartly dressed bourgeois, giving them equal dignity—one of his most endearing traits" (Wine Spectator, 110). *L'Estampe et l'Affiche* concluded its ecstatic review of this poster by declaring "One can't applaud it enough" (1897, p. 20). One also can't see it enough; possibly because of its large size, it's extremely rare and most poster enthusiasts know it only from reproductions. It must be seen "in the flesh" to be appreciated; only then is its breathtaking power felt by the viewer. What a magnificent tour de force!
**Est: $70,000-$90,000.**

**470. Exposition de Peintures/Th.-A. Steinlen.** 1903.
$35^1/2$ x $52^3/4$ in./89.7 x 134.1 cm
Imp. Ch. Wall, Paris
Cond A–/Slight tears along folds.
Ref: Bargiel & Zagrodzki, 44; PAI-XXXIX, 473
A rarely seen poster for Steinlen's own second exhibition. There are two subjects that were dear to Steinlen's heart: cats, used in the poster for his first exhibition (*see* PAI-XLIII, 544) and humanitarian causes, depicted here. In this later poster, Steinlen gives us a compassionate view of an intense worker, but there's an added dimension here of an almost helpless disorientation in the face of relentless industrialization.
**Est: $1,700-$2,000.**

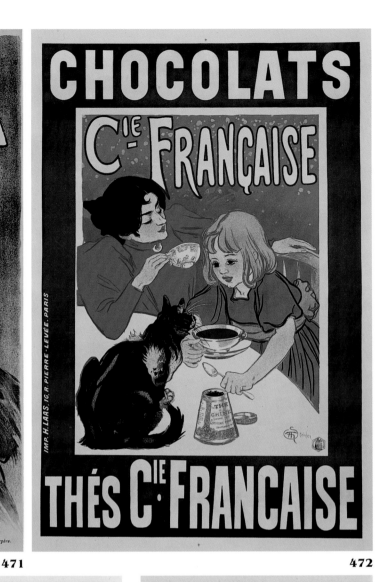

471

472

473

## STEINLEN (cont'd)

**471. Mothu et Doria.** 1893.
36⅝ x 48½ in./93 x 123 cm
Impressions Artistiques, Paris
Cond B+/Unobtrusive folds.
Ref (All Var but PAI): Bargiel & Zagrodzki, 12A.2;
    Crauzat, 490; DFP-II, 780; Maitres, 46; PAI-XXXVII, 511
A gentleman rather disdainfully proffers a light to a
lowly ruffian on the street in this poster for a pair of
singers. We get just the right hint of the social tensions
of the period. *This is the rare black-and-white proof
of the design.*
**Est: $4,000-$5,000.**

**472. Chocolats/Thés Cie Française.** 1895.
31 x 46¼ in./78.6 x 117.5 cm
Imp. H. Laas, Paris
Cond A–/Unobtrusive folds. Framed.
Ref: Bargiel et Zagrodzki, 19C; Crauzat, 494 (var);
    DFP-II, 784 (var); Wagner, 62 (var);
    Timeless Images, 49 (var); Maitres, 170 (var);
    PAI-XXV, 506
*This is a very rare version with enlarged text border.*
A charming domestic scene advertises a tea importer.

The cat was obviously expecting a dish of milk that
would be used in the making of cocoa, the company's
other most popular product. The girl is Steinlen's
daughter, Colette, and the woman is his wife, Emilie.
More than any other poster artist, Steinlen entices us
with a heartfelt charm and sympathetic treatment of
subjects. In fact, this design was so irresistible that
the client used it with several text variations; this is
one of the least known versions.
**Est: $25,000-$30,000.**

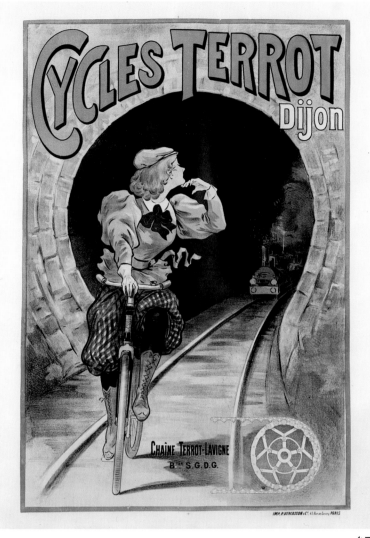

474

475

476

**473. Chansons de Femmes.** 1897.
Each Plate: 12⁷/₈ x 19³/₄ in./32.6 x 50.2 cm
Imp. Eugene Verneau, Paris
Ref: Crauzat, 183
*Fifteen hand-signed plates, all in excellent condition;*
*slight staining on cover; in presentation box.*
Initially, these fifteen "Songs of Women" were accompanied with a text by French composer Paul Delmet (1862-1904), who wrote some of the most celebrated songs of the Belle Epoque, including "Envoi de fleurs," "la Petite Église" and "Vous êtes si jolie." But then the fifteen plates were separately issued, published by

Enoch of Paris, with wide margins in a numbered edition of 100 copies—this particular set being #4—the cover simply decorated with the monograms of Enoch and Steinlen, to which the "Table of Contents" ("*Tables des Matières*") was added with the titles of the plates. As one might expect from the sympathetic Steinlen, these varied portraits and scenes featuring an array of different women from various social strata amply demonstrate what a keen observer of the human condition the artist was, an illustrator of complexities who set his visions to paper without judgment or condescension. Also, it should come as no big surprise that cats are featured in five of the fifteen plates.
**Est: $12,000-$15,000.**

## FRANCISCO TAMAGNO (1851-?)

**474. Liebig.**
48 x 78 in./122 x 198.2 cm
Affiches Camis, Paris
Cond B/Tears and stains at folds and edges; resoration
      in margins.
In the name of Liebig beef extract, Tamagno has presented the public with both brawny (*see* PAI-XXIII, 495) and boyish (*see* PAI-XXXV, 476) chefs. Here, however, he decides to take a turn for the allegorical in a 2-sheet design featuring a fleshy Byzantine embodiment of the product—whose appearance (attire aside) would seem to be more along the lines of the demographic for which Liebig was intended—and her bovine acquaintance. When inventor Justus Liebig introduced this beef extract in 1852, it bore the claim "between 30 and 50 kilograms of beef chunks go into every kilogram of Liebig." Relieved of the time consuming task of making their own *glace de viande*, essential for enriching sauces and stews, grateful French cooks snapped the stuff up and continue to do so today.
**Est: $3,000-$4,000.**

**475. Cycles Terrot/Dijon.** 1898.
47¹/₂ x 62¹/₂ in./120.6 x 158.7 cm
Imp. P. Vercasson, Paris
Cond B/Recreated margins; unobtrusive tears near
      borders; image and colors excellent.
Ref: DFP-II, 808
Attitude is everything in the several Terrot bicycle posters Tamagno created at the turn of the century. In all of them a young lady makes it to the top of a hill way ahead of the competition (*see* PAI-XXII, 32 & PAI-XIX, 53), effortlessly outdistancing an airplane (*see* PAI-XXVI, 545) or, as seen here, beating a locomotive coming on at full speed. And no matter what the competition, she never neglects to let them know in no uncertain—if not precisely ladylike—terms who's the champ.
**Est: $2,000-$2,500.**

**476. Jouets/Etrennes.**
39 x 51¹/₈ in./99 x 130 cm
Imp. Affiches-Camis, Paris
Cond B+/Unobtrusive folds.
With a newly-acquired doll that isn't much smaller than herself hugged to her bosom, this little whirlwind looks like she's ready to make a mad dash for home in order to not waste one second of precious potential playtime. It would appear as if at some point the name of a store promoting its toys and gifts was a part of Tamagno's creation, but for some reason it has been obscured by the central blue/green splash of color. It's hard to imagine why since the promotion's infectious enthusiasm would seem to be an advertiser's dream come true.
**Est: $2,000-$2,500.**

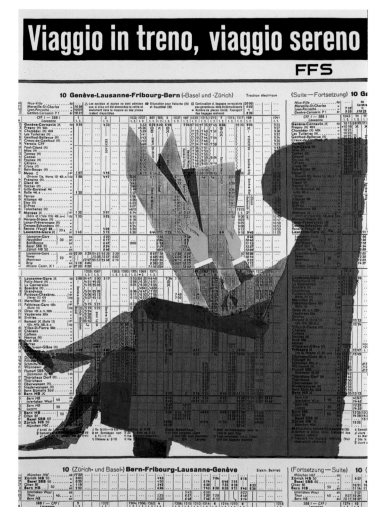

**477**

**479**

**478**

## ALEARDO TERZI (1870-1943)

**477. Mele.** 1910.
38³/₄ x 55¹/₂ in./98.5 x 141 cm
G. Ricordi, Milano
Cond A–/Unobtrusive folds.
Ref: Mele, 59

The half-dozen posters that Terzi created for the Naples department store are among the best in that consume haven's output and all are rare today. This gathering of smartly clad children convened beneath the store's name surely procured their outfits there, but it's the relationships more than the rendered pint-size couture that make the design fascinating, from the enamored lass at left to the attentive sister at right. Not to mention the central tike whose undivided attention belongs to the puppy at her feet, who, truth be told, appears to be a rolling toy rather than a living canine. Positively brilliant. Considered one of the masters of early poster design in Italy, Terzi was born in Palermo on the island of Sicily, but by 1900 we find him doing drawings for the Rome daily *La Tribuna Illustrata*. From then on, he dedicated himself to posters, first for the printer Instituto d'Arte Graphiche in Bergamo, later for Ricordi in Milano and others. His draftsmanship, as well as his feeling for colors, is impeccable, his designs always pictorially fascinating. *Rare!*
**Est: $4,000-$5,000.**

## THEODORO (1896-1973)

**478. La Syphilis.** ca. 1926.
31¹/₄ x 47 in./79.5 x 119.5 cm
Imp. Kaplan-L. Legras, Paris
Cond A.
Ref: Health Posters, 325 (var); Phillips I, 570

A marvelous document: syphilis, says the poster, is a social plague and its victims are countless. It then goes on to enumerate the myriad effects of the far-reaching malady—that many have the disease without knowing it; that it's one of the principal causes of sickness and death among the newborn; that a good number of chronic illnesses originate with syphilis. However, the silver lining is that, happily, syphilis is curable. The design urges all those contracting the disease to seek immediate treatment in order to prevent its transmittal to others. The poster is sponsored by the French National League Against the Venereal Peril. The message is serious, and no doubt still timely, but it's the image of the kissing couple against the "God'll-getchya" grinning skull that makes it memorable. *This is the larger format.*
**Est: $1,200-$1,500.**

## HANS THÖNI (1906-1980)

**479. FFS/Viaggio in trenno.** 1958.
35¹/₂ x 50³/₈ in./90.1 x 127.8 cm
J. C. Müller
Cond A/P.
Ref (All Var): Margadant, 293; Swiss Posters, 58.12; PAI-XXXV, 477

What an inspired way of showing that Swiss trains get you to your destination on time and in comfort. Placing the passenger in a comfortable arm chair against the timetable is more than clever; it creates a superb collage effect that makes its point with immediacy and impact. In this Italian-language version of the poster, the text proclaims: "Travel in train, travel serene."
**Est: $1,400-$1,700.**

## HENRI DE TOULOUSE-LAUTREC 1864-1901)

**480. La Chaîne Simpson.** 1896.
47⁵/₈ x 33⁵/₈ in./121 x 85.3 cm
Imp. Chaix, Paris
Cond B+/Slight tears at folds. Framed.
Ref: Wittrock, P19C; Adriani, 189; Wagner, 147; DFP-II, 839; Bicycle Posters, 28; Dodge, p. 172 (var); Ailes, p. 30; PAI-XL, 66

**480**

In her excellent biography of Lautrec, Julia Frey indicates that "Henry, the frustrated athlete, was compulsively familiar with the vocabulary and technical aspects of a variety of sports in which he could participate as a spectator: horse and bicycle racing, wrestling, navigation and yachting, bullfighting. He watched them all with the same intensity that he watched a line of dancers or a circus bareback rider, attracted by the beauty of the movement, but also by the smells, sounds and excitement of the spectacle" (Frey, p. 353). His "insider" knowledge of the cycling field shows up abundantly in this poster for the French agent of the Simpson bicycle chain company. In the foreground is the champion cyclist Constant Huret; in the background are Tristan Bernard, the sports impresario who was a close friend of Lautrec, with Louis Bougle, the French agent who adopted the name "Spoke." A touch of levity is added by what seems to be a "bicycle-built-for-ten" in the upper left corner; in fact, it's two five-seaters, known at the time as "quints."
**Est: $70,000-$80,000.**

**481. Aux Ambassadeurs.** 1894.
14¹/₄ x 17¹/₈ in./36.2 x 43.4 cm
Cond A. Framed.
Ref: Wittrock, 58; Adriani, 70; PAI-XXXVII, 530A
*1 of 100 signed copies.*
This delicate print—its full title was *Aux Ambassadeurs chanteuse au café-concert*—was the second of Lautrec's three contributions to *L'Estampe originale*. Little is known of the background of this image or the identity of the singer. Lautrec titled it after the most elegant of the outdoor café-concerts, located on the Champs-Elysées near a number of embassies. This may well have been a marketing ploy to associate the relatively expensive series with Paris' most upscale district.
**Est: $50,000-$60,000.**

**481**

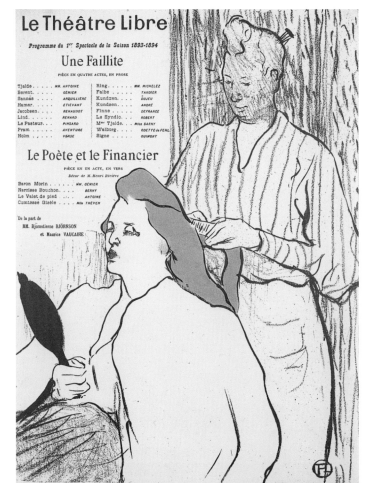

**482**

**483**

## TOULOUSE-LAUTREC (cont'd)

**482. Divan Japonais.** 1893.
23³/₈ x 30³/₈ in./59.3 x 77.3 cm
Imp. Edw. Ancourt, Paris (not shown)
Cond B–/Slight tears in image; trimmed bottom and left edge; image and colors excellent. Framed.
Ref: Wittrock, P11; Adriani, 8; DFP-II, 824; Maitres, 2; Wagner, 3; Modern Poster, 5; Wine Spectator, 42; Lautrec/Montmartre, 164; PAI-XLIII, 561
"Of all the female entertainers Lautrec celebrated in his posters, Jane Avril and Yvette Guilbert were the two with whom he maintained the longest friendships. He portrayed them both together in one of his most brilliant posters, *Divan Japonais* . . . Although Guilbert was the performer at this rather shabby cabaret when it opened in the spring of (1893), Lautrec made the half-Italian Avril the focal figure in his composition. Under a shock of red-orange hair topped with a pagoda-shaped hat and towering plume, her black, silhouetted figure dominates the frontal plane as she assumes a regal pose and an attitude of hauteur. Neither she nor her companion, Edouard Dujardin, the distinguished founder of the Symbolist *Revue Wagnerienne*, deign to look at Guilbert on stage, whom Lautrec has portrayed as acephalous, probably as a witty response to her complaint that he caricatured her and made her ugly" (Wagner, p. 21).
**Est: $30,000-$40,000.**

**483. Le Théâtre Libre.** 1893.
9¹/₄ x 12¹/₂ in./23.5 x 31.7 cm
Imp. Eugène Verneau, Paris
Cond B+/Slight restorations. Framed.
Ref: Wittrock, 15; Adriani,40-III; PAI-XLI, 563
Originally published as a lithograph in color, without lettering, and released with the title "La Coiffure," the poster shows one of the women from the Rue des Moulins brothel having her hair done. In the state seen here, it's being used as a program for the Théâtre Libre in order to promote the 1893-94 winter season. This experimental theater's audience was necessarily limited: "The only people who could attend (Antoine's) plays were the two-hundred patrons who bought season tickets. Naturally, they included the élite of the intellectual avant-garde" (Frey, p. 368).
**Est: $3,000-$4,000.**

**484. Etude de Femme.** 1893.
11 x 14 in./28 x 35.5 cm
Cond A. Framed.
Ref: Wittrock, 11; Adriani, 33
*One of 100 numbered impressions (#46), hand-signed by the artist; on vellum with Kleinmann blind stamp lower-left.*
Though the treatment used here is rather similar to the one the artist called into play to promote a collection of songs titled "Les Vieilles Histoires" (The Old Tales), this design was created to promote another little ditty entitled "Study of a Woman" that wasn't a part of that suite. Lautrec doesn't stray far from that title in his execution either, presenting us with a woman disrobing as she makes her way to bed. There's surprisingly little information provided in terms of narrative—is she turning in for the night or joining a lover awaiting her arrival on the unseen side of the bed? It's up to the viewer to fill in the blanks, with Lautrec providing just the right amount of realism to imbue the scene with humility and humanity.
**Est: $2,500-$3,000.**

**485. Napoleon.** 1895.
18¹/₄ x 23⁷/₈ in./46.3 x 60.6 cm
Cond A. Framed.
Ref: Wittrock, P1C; Adriani, 135; DFP-II, 841; Wagner, 20; Abdy, 89; PAI-XXXI, 683
*From the hand-signed edition of 100 copies (#70).*
"In the summer of 1895 a competition was held by the art-dealers Boussard, Valadon et Cie. for a poster to advertise a biography of Napoleon by William Milligan Sloan, which was to be published in the *Century Magazine* in New York in 1896. No doubt encouraged by Maurice Joyant, a friend from his youth and director of Boussod and Valadon, Lautrec entered the competition . . . Although the handling of the motif should actually have appealed to the specially selected jury—the successful society painters Detaille, Gér'me and Vibert, and the Napoleon scholar Frédéric Masson—the design was not judged worthy of a prize. From the 21 entries, Lucien Métivet, a minor illustrator and former fellow student of Lautrec's in the Atelier Cormon, won the prize. The rejection of Lautrec's work is all the more astonishing since Lautrec, no doubt with the jury in

**484**

mind, produced a composition in full sympathy with the elevated traditional image of the great man, and aimed to give an accurate representation of the historic facts, even down to the details of the uniforms. After vain attempts to sell the design elsewhere, the artist decided to have an edition printed at his own expense" (Adriani, p. 190).

Ebria Feinblatt's appreciation of this image is right on the spot: "Lautrec's *Napoleon* occupies a distinctive place in his oeuvre as his only poster on a historical theme. Omitting any glorifying attributes, Lautrec presented his famous subject directly and humanly; there is dignity and restraint in the hint of Napoleon's pride and melancholy. Yet it was probably this very simplicity and absence of panoply that was responsible for Lautrec's failure to win first prize" (Wagner, p. 28).
**Est: $120,000-$150,000.**

485

486

487

488

489

## TOULOUSE-LAUTREC (cont'd)

**486. Le Deuxième Volume de Bruant/Mirliton.** 1893.
$23^{1}/_{4}$ x 31 in./59 x 78.7 cm
Imp. Chaix, Paris
Cond B+/Slight tears and stains, largely at paper edges.
    Framed.
Ref: Wittrock, P10C; Adriani, 57-IV; DFP-II, 832;
    PAI-XL, 509
In one version of this poster, we see the *chansonnier*
with text announcing the opening of his new cabaret
(*see* PAI-XLII, 495). In this one, the sale of a songbook
by Bruant, illustrated by Steinlen, is promoted and we're
reminded that we can hear it all at the Mirliton. Both
are distinguished by Bruant's insolent stance: the point
made is that we can recognize the famous performer
not only despite his turning his back to us, but *because*
of it. Who else would have the audacity to be so rude?
**Est: $12,000-$15,000.**

**487. Bruant au Mirliton/Bock 13 Sous.** 1893.
$22^{1}/_{2}$ x $31^{3}/_{8}$ in./57 x 79.7 cm
Imp. Chaix, Paris
Cond B+/Unobtrusive folds; slight tears at edges. Framed.
Ref: Wittrock, P10A; Adrianni, 57-II; DFP-II, 831;
    PAI-XXVI, 552
And this is the third and rarest version of the previous
image. It is also likely that it's the first. Sharing billing
with Bruant is the fact that you can get a glass of beer
for just thirteen sous. Yet another good reason to visit
the Mirliton.
**Est: $20,000-$25,000.**

**488. Sagesse.** 1893.
10 x $13^{1}/_{2}$ in./25.5 x 34.3 cm
Cond A.
Ref: Wittrock, 9; Adriani, 31
*One of 100 numbered impressions (#70), hand-signed
by the artist; on vellum with Kleinmann blind stamp
lower-left.*
This expression of "Wisdom" was the eighth title in
the "Vieilles Histoires" suite. And from what Lautrec is
showing us, you'd have to imagine that it's the woman
with her back to the viewer that's the wise one in his
design, unless the moonfaced gentleman is far shrewder
than his anxious appearance would seem to indicate.

"Henri Gabriel Ibels had persuaded the music publisher
Gustave Ondet, who lived in the building which housed
the Ancourt printing works at 83 Rue de Faubourg
Saint-Denis, to have his titles designed by well-known
artists. In addition to Ibels himself, Ondet asked Lautrec,
Henri Rachou and others to design title pages . . .
These were poems by Jean Goudezki set to popular
romance melodies by Désiré Dihau. Lautrec designed
the cover and titles 2, 4, 5, 8 and 9 in the first series
published by Ondet, which consisted of ten songs in
all at 2 francs each" (Adriani, p. 59).
**Est: $4,000-$5,000.**

**489. La Dépêche/Le Tocsin.** 1895.
$21^{1}/_{4}$ x $28^{1}/_{2}$ in./54 x 72.2 cm
Cond A.
Ref: Wittrock, P19A; Adriani, 143-I; PAI-XL, 511
Arthur Huc, art collector and editor of the Toulouse
newspaper *La Dépêche*, had already used one of
Lautrec's earlier posters successfully in 1892; this time
he is advertising a serialization of the novel, "The
Warning Bell" by Jules de Gastyne in his publication,
seen here before the addition of letters. Toulouse-
Lautrec strikes the perfect note for the gothic romance,
with the pale heroine followed by a dejected dog strol-
ling through the gloom of the night, with the forbid-
dingly austere walls of a castle behind her. Adriani
makes it clear that this blue-ink first-state version before
lettering was intended for the poster collecting market
(p. 203). Frey says that "the poster he did in December
1895 . . . was somber and nocturnal, reflecting what
seemed to be his own mood" (Frey, p. 416).
**Est: $6,000-$7,000.**

**490. May Belfort.** 1895.
$23^{3}/_{4}$ x $31^{1}/_{4}$ in./60.3 x 79.4 cm
Kleinmann, Paris
Cond A. Framed.
Ref: Wittrock, P14B; Adriani, 136-IV; DFP-II, 837;
    Wagner, 16; PAI-XXXIX, 491
"In the poster Belfort is framed by long black curls
under an enormous cap, her hands hiding most of a
yellow-eyed kitten. Lautrec presents her on a diagonal
plane, her brilliant orange-red dress slanting to the left,
her shoulder brought forward in the picture plane to

place her in a frontal position. The flat sweep of her
gown below the frilled, green-splattered sleeves is, taken
by itself, merely a red sail or banner" (Wagner, p. 27).
Julia Frey's excellent biography gives some interesting
background to this: "May Belfort, whom Henry represented in at least ten works, had gained a reputation
for corrupt innocence by appearing onstage dressed as
a baby holding a black kitten in her arms, and 'miaow-
ing or bleating' her popular song, 'Daddy Wouldn't Buy
Me a Bow-Wow,' whose lines had a double meaning
which was not lost in the French-speaking audience:
'I've got a pussycat, I'm very fond of that.' Henry, enthu-
siastic, later wrote letters to friends trying to find a mate
for the cat, and even got a cat himself" (Frey, p. 382).
**Est: $40,000-$60,000.**

**491. La Revue Blanche.** 1895.
$37^{1}/_{4}$ x $51^{1}/_{8}$ in./94.7 x 130 cm
Imp. Edw. Ancourt, Paris
Cond A. Framed.
Ref: Wittrock, P16B; Adriani, 130-II; PAI-XLII, 491
When Toulouse-Lautrec chose to advertise the art and
literary magazine "La Revue Blanche" by using a portrait
of Misia Natanson, wife of coeditor Thadée Natanson,
it was because the brainy, redheaded beauty was the
real mover behind the throne. Her house was the mecca
of the literati, and it was she who coaxed some of the
major celebrities of the day—Catulle Mendès, Paul
Valéry, Léon Blum, Octave Mirbeau, Claude Débussy,
André Gide, Colette and Toulouse-Lautrec himself—to
contribute to the publication's success. The original
design for this poster had a small remarque printed at
left which made it clear that Misia was being shown
skating. In her biography of the artist, Frey writes that
"many people feel (this poster) is (Toulouse-Lautrec's)
strongest individual work . . . The strength of this work
comes in large part from the fact that, as in many of
Henry's posters, the figure is cut off by the lower edge
just below the knees . . . The entire poster is like a little
joke, as if Henry were amusing himself by proving that
he could show an ice skater without ever showing her
skates" (p. 408). *A rare variant of the poster before
the addition of letters that was issued in a limited
edition of 50.*
**Est: $50,000-$60,000.**

492

493

**492. La Vache Enragée.** 1896.
22³/₈ x 30³/₄ in./57 x 78.2 cm
Imp. Chaix, Paris
Cond B+/Tear at right paper edge. Framed.
Ref: Wittrock, P27A; Adriani, 175; Abdy, p. 85; DFP-II, 844; Wagner, 26;
    PAI-XLII, 488
*Rare first state, before letters.*
This poster was created to advertise Willette's magazine, *La Vache Enragée*,
which lasted for only a single year. Wittrock, who rates the rarity of this
state as "uncommon," also indicates that "the image in the poster was
drawn by Toulouse-Lautrec in imitation of the style of A. Willette" (p. 808).
This is one of the few Lautrec posters with movement: the runaway cow is
the centerpiece of a remarkable caricature depicting sheer panic in some,
curious complacency in others—an obvious reflection of the world that
swirled around the artist.
**Est: $25,000-$30,000.**

**493. Elles.** 1896.
17³/₈x 23 in./44 x 88.4 cm
Cond A. Framed.
Ref: Wittrock, 155-III; Adriani, 177-IV; DFP-II, 842; PAI-XLII, 489
This image of a woman taking her hair down advertises the portfolio of ten
lithographs of Lautrec's scenes of Paris brothels as well as their exhibition
at the gallery of *La Plume* magazine. The ladies' occupation could not be
openly named any more than it could be depicted. They are simply called
"Elles" (Those Women), and their business is indicated merely by a gentleman's hat on the bed. Adriani calls Lautrec's *Elles* series "one of the high-
points of nineteenth-century art" (p. 222).
**Est: $35,000-$40,000.**

**494. Jane Avril.** 1899.
14 x 21¹/₈ in./34.7 x 53.5 cm
H. Stern, Paris
Cond B+/Unobtrusive creases. Framed.
Ref: Wittrock, P29B; Adriani, 354-II; Abdy, p. 80; DFP-II, 851; Wagner, 30;
    PAI-XXVI, 559
"It is very fitting, however, that one of Toulouse-Lautrec's finest posters
should be the last one he made for Jane Avril. It is dated in February of
1899, and in March he entered a clinic for the first time. This fascinating
work is a true child of the Art Nouveau age . . . It shows the constant flirta-
tion with the macabre that is part of Art Nouveau. Snakes were portrayed
a great deal in the jewelry of the period . . . So Toulouse-Lautrec's final
portrayal of Jane Avril is not as a Japanese geisha from Bing, but as a girl
stifled by the art of her time. She liked the poster very much, but her impresario refused it, and it was never shown." (Abdy, pp. 80-81). Adrianni
calls this "one of Lautrec's most compelling colour posters . . . For (this
poster) the artist was able to use a process which enabled different colours
to be applied in one printing, provided they were arranged in the order of
rotation of the machine, and here only three printings were needed for
the four colours used" (p. 411).
**Est: $70,000-$80,000.**

JANE
Avril

H.Stern, Paris.

1899

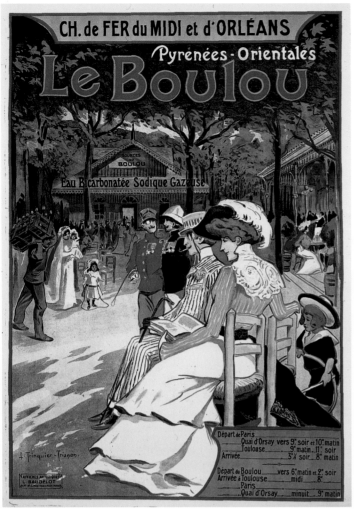

496

497

498

495

## ADOLPH TREIDLER (1886-1981)

**495. Bermuda.**
24¹/₈ x 39¹/₂ in./61.2 x 100.3 cm
Cond A–/Slight stains at edges.
Not to be pushy, but it's hard to overlook the fact that this Treidler silk-screen design—fairly bursting at the lithographic seams with romantic overtones—would

make a perfect wedding gift. I'm just sayin'. Treidler was the "in-house" graphic artist for the Furness Lines, creating a number of stylish posters for Furness ocean travel to Bermuda. And even though there's not a ship to be seen, it's quite likely that this snuggling twosome may have arrived at their island destination courtesy of either the *Queen of Bermuda* or the *Ocean Monarch*. Known as the "Honeymoon Ships," their Saturday afternoon sailings made them especially popular with the "Just Married" set.
**Est: $1,400-$1,700.**

## A. TRINQUIER-TRIANON

**496. Le Boulou.**
29¹/₄ x 40⁷/₈ in./74.4 x 103.7 cm
Affiches L. Baudelot, Paris
Cond A–/Unobtrusive folds.
Ref: PAI-XXX, 666
The bustle of Trinquier-Trianon's verdant advertisement for the Central and Orleans Railways' service to the southern French resort situated in the foothills of the Albères mountains shows that Le Boulou was the place for everyone with a strong interest in naturally carbonated mineral water—society folk, children and soldiers.

**499**

Primarily society folk. A splendid nod to an opulence of travel long since faded from our ever-shrinking world. Apart from the posters he left behind, nothing is known about the artist.
**Est: $2,000-$2,500.**

**497. Royat.**
30 x 42¹/₂ in./76.3 x 108 cm
Imp. Courmont Frères, Paris
Cond B+/Slight tears and creases at folds and edges.
Royat, a destination renowned for its thermal and spring-

fed superiority, is given a gloriously romanticized treatment by Trinquier-Trianon for the P.L.M. railway. Located scant kilometers from Auvergne's capital, Clermont-Ferrand, Royat is situated in the heart of south-central France's Massif Central, whose core consists of the extinct volcanic mass of the Auvergne Mountains. This design more than capably reflects the region's unusual and beautiful scenery, marked by hot mineral springs, deep river gorges and rolling pastureland. In order to round out the spa completely, the artist gives us a woman enjoying cup after cup of Royat's *l'eau fortifiante*, whose restorative qualities have apparently transformed her into a classic vision of healthful living.
**Est: $1,500-$2,000.**

### ABEL TRUCHET (1857-1918)

**498. Concerts Fcis Touche.**
23¹/₈ x 15¹/₂ in./58.6 x 39.3 cm
Cond A.
Francis Touche was an instructor at the Paris Conservatory, not to mention a popular cellist and conductor at the turn-of-the-twentieth century. Perhaps most remarkably, he created the "Concerts Francis Touche" at 25 Boulevard de Strasbourg, a concert venue where Parisians could attend classical performances nightly, on Sundays and feast days, as well as daily matinees. Interestingly, the poster indicates that the Concerts Touche also could supply chamber music for "séances." Now, seeing as that word translates as both "meeting" and "seance," Truchet's somber execution makes it a bit ambiguous as to which gathering the term applies. "Truchet was primarily a painter, but he also mastered the techniques of illustration, etching, and lithography and produced a few posters of undoubted merit. He found his inspiration among the habitués of Montmartre, and this is a fine example of the results" (Gold, p. 139).
**Est: $2,000-$2,500.**

### SUZANNE VALADON (1865-1938)

**499. L'Aide Amicale aux Artistes.** 1927.
30³/₄ x 47 in./78 x 119.5 cm
Affiches Gaillard, Paris

Cond B+/Unobtrusive tears at folds and edges.
Ref: PAI-X, 425 (var)
The poster announcing the 4-A Ball of May 20, 1927 passes along its information grace of a lovely model who has taken over the artist's palette in order to give color to the occasion with flowers and golden patches being strewn hither and yon. A rather whimsical poster by Suzanne Valadon, mother of Maurice Utrillo. The artist had an eventful career in which she herself was a model for a while, posing for illustrious painters such as Chavannes, Renoir and Degas, and befriending many of the artists on the Montmartre scene, including Toulouse-Lautrec, with whom she briefly lived in 1896.
**Est: $1,700-$2,000.**

### JOHANN G. VAN CASPEL (1870-1928)

**500. De Hollandsche Revue.** 1899.
40¹/₂ x 28³/₄ in./103 x 73 cm
Senefelder, Amsterdam
Cond A–/Vertical fold. Framed.
Ref: Van Caspel, 17; Dutch Poster, 88;
    Livre d'Affiche, 100; PAI-XLII, 503
A line of readers, engrossed to a man in their copies of the *Hollandsche Revue*, a literary journal published by DeErven Loosjes in Haarlem. A masterful drawing, fascinating for its authentic historical feel, detail and characters. Although Van Caspel designed show cards, book covers, calendars and book plates in addition to several posters of note, "one of his most interesting posters was executed for the 'Dutch Review,' representing a well-known Amsterdam rendezvous, the reading room at Krasnapolsky's. It is treated in the style of some American artists, reminding one of J. J. Gould's manner, with more elaborate details . . . To conclude, J. G. van Caspel is an *affichiste* with a great future . . . His name, although not yet famous beyond Holland, must be remembered by lovers of art, and the Senefelder Printing Co. must be congratulated to have retained such a brilliant artist" (*The Poster*, May 1899. pp. 213-214).
*One of the most magnificent posters ever created in Holland. A true international masterpiece!*
**Est: $17,000-$20,000.**

**503**

**505**

## ROGER DE VALERIO (1896-1951)

**501. Cherry Chevalier.** ca. 1930.
46¹/₂ x 63 in./118.2 x 160 cm
Imp. Devambez, Paris
Cond A.
Ref: Célébrités, 218; PAI-XLII, 501
How surprising is it that Maurice Chevalier would lend his name to a liqueur aimed directly at a female demographic? The answer, of course, is that it's no surprise whatsoever. Because after all, candy is dandy, but liquor is quicker. And de Valerio gives us some classic Chavalier: boater at a rakish tilt, jaunty walk, come-hither pout, not to mention a brimming basket of cherries. De Valério, borne in Lille, worked in Paris—principally at the Devambez and Perceval agencies, whose clients included Air France, Citroën and Chrysler. He also designed more than 2,000 sheet-music covers for music publisher-producer Salabert.
**Est: $1,200-$1,500.**

## EUGENE VAVASSEUR (1863-?)

**502. Poteries Culinaires.**
22³/₄ x 31³/₄ in./57.8 x 80.6 cm
Imp. Imbert, Grasse
Cond A.
The text that accompanies Vavasseur's artwork for this culinary stoneware made from Vallauris clay—the Riviera town, three miles northeast of Cannes, is well-known for its ceramics—is in place for one singular purpose: to validate the product. Thank goodness for Vavasseur's kitchen staff, which provides an absolutely necessary levity that makes it clear that cooking with Vallauris is a joy. Vavasseur was well known for his invention of humorous characters, as well as contributing drawings to such periodicals as *La Caricature*, *La Silhouette* and, under the pseudonym Ripp, to *L'Eclipse*, *La Gaudriole* and *La Revue Illustrée*.
**Est: $800-$1,000.**

## P. VERJEZ

**503. Bal des Etudiants/Bordeaux.** 1906.
49⁵/₈ x 78 in./126 x 198 cm
Imp. J. Bière, Bordeaux
Cond B/Slight tears at folds and edges.
The inmates are running the asylum in this splashy Verjez cartoon-style promotion for a Bordeaux student gala. Not that the rendered local gendarme seem terribly concerned—they appear to be turning a blind eye to the shenanigans and taking a "Kids will be kids" attitude. But maybe they should be a tad more concerned seeing as this assemblage of revelers is essentially a hedonistic cavalcade in the flesh, from *commedia* drunkards to classic buffoons to a breast-bearing hooligan with no respect for the law. Which really looks like an awful lot of fun. Hopefully for the students that needed to let off some pent up 1906 midwinter steam the event lived up to the Verjez hype.
**Est: $2,000-$2,500.**

## MARCEL VERTÈS (1895-1961)

**504. Dancing.** 1923.
17³/₄ x 24¹/₂ in./45.3 x 62.3 cm
Editions Pellet, Paris
Cond A–/Slight staining in background/P.
This rakish hoofer and his twiglike partner provide the promotional moves for "Dancing," a Vertès collection of twelve graceful lithographic plates that romantically and athletically celebrate the art of tripping the light fantastic. Vertès, a highly talented painter and illustrator, was born in Budapest. After an initial stint designing political posters in his home town following World War I, he settled in Paris, chronicling the city life during the Roaring Twenties. Later, he would relocate once more, this time to the United States. *Hand-signed and numbered (#90/300).*
**Est: $1,500-$2,000.**

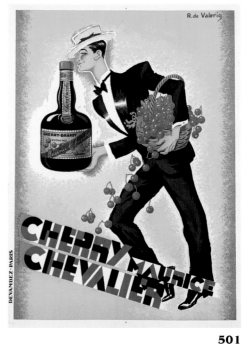

**501**

## VISTOR/TRIP

**505. Aero-Holland.**
23¹/₄ x 32⁵/₈ in./59.1 x 82.8 cm
Kuhn en Zoon, Rotterdam
Cond B/Unobtrusive tears and stains at edges and bottom text area.
The skies over their Ypenburg airstrip look rather idyllic—a few low-lying clouds hover over the scene, but there's visibility for miles and certainly nary a hint of turbulence—as an Aero-Holland Douglas DC-3 soars to an unnamed destination. Sadly, the lofty ideal being promoted here didn't quite play itself out for the Dutch

**502**

**504**

aux Sceptiques

**506**

**507**

**508**

emprunt 1974

**509**

airline based out of a suburb of The Hague: founded in 1948, Aero-Holland would never recover from the November 20, 1949 Hurum air disaster when one of their planes crashed to the southwest of Oslo, killing thirty-five of the thirty-six people onboard. Though they would struggle along for a few years following the incident, Aero-Holland ceased operations in 1953.
**Est: $1,200-$1,500.**

## GEORGES VILLA (1883-?)

**506. Aux Sceptiques.** 1921.
31¹/₂ x 47¹/₄ in./80 x 120 cm
Ateliers Georges Villa, Paris
Cond B/Tears and stains along folds.
Ref (All Var): Air France, p. 17; Looping the Loop, 88; PAI-XXXII, 604
Following the bitter experience of World War I, the French wanted air power, and the government set up a special propaganda department to sway public opinion to its cause. Here, the skeptics who doubt the vision of the plan are compared cartoon-wise to their earlier counterparts—embodied by the fictional character named Joseph Prudhomme—who didn't think the trains would ever catch on. This is the streamlined version of the image, with very little text for a maximum of visual impact. Seven years later, Villa would create another

poster that shows Prudhomme's ghost watching in wonder as his bumbling son hurries to catch a flight (*see* Looping the Loop, 88).
**Est: $1,700-$2,000.**

**507. Les Ailes.** 1922.
30¹/₄ x 45¹/₂ in./76.9 x 115.6 cm
Cond B+/Unobtrusive tears at folds and edges.
Ref: Looping The Loop, 14; PAI-XXXV, 100
Georges Villa contributed a series of posters for the French Aeronautic Propaganda Department, overflowing with clever wordplay and impetuous graphics. Though several of the designs feature the short-visioned—and completely fictional—skeptic Joseph Prudhomme (*see* previous poster, PAI-XXXIV, 595 & Looping the Loop, 88), Villa takes a more inspirational approach towards fostering "the Spirit of Flight in France . . . by portraying the mythical Icarus, whose wings, according to legend, were melted by the sun. The caption reads: 'In the following centuries, the air seemed to be an unreachable domain . . . Finally the human being flies away'" (Looping The Loop, p. 159).
**Est: $1,500-$1,800.**

## BERNARD VILLEMOT (1911-1989)

**508. Wagons Lits Cook.** 1953.
24³/₄ x 39 in./62.9 x 99 cm
Hubert Baille, Paris
Cond A.
Ref: PAI-XXIII, 509
"Everywhere and always at your service" is well-documented in this rare Villemot image. The neatly-organized design has an accommodating agent offering hotel, plane, steamship and train arrangements while his world-map double reinforces the company's far-flung reach.
**Est: $1,400-$1,700.**

**509. Emprunt 1974.**
22³/₄ x 30³/₄ in./58 x 78 cm
Dufournet
Cond A.
Villemot's poster for a state-guaranteed national bond drive to provide economic assistance to the hotel industry, commercial sector and industrial complex is far from heavy-handed. However, his colorful stick figures and their symbolic burdens make it very clear that there's work to be done.
**Est: $800-$1,000.**

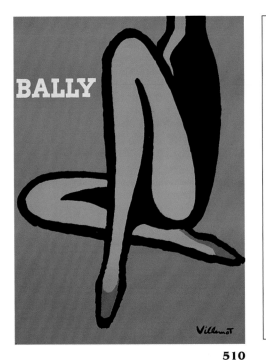

**510**

**511**

MAROC · ALGÉRIE · TUNISIE

**512**

**513**

**514**

## BERNARD VILLEMOT (cont'd)

**510. Bally.** 1967.
35¹/₂ x 50¹/₄ in./90.2 x 127.8 cm
A. Trüb, Aarau
Cond A/P.
Ref: Schweizer Plakate, 368; Villemot, p. 87 (var);
    Villemot A-Z, p. 115 (var);
    Villemot/La Femme, p. 65; PAI-XXVII, 611
For thirty years, Villemot was one of the finest French posterists, unsurpassed at setting the right mood with just a few simple lines and bold colors. This represents the very first poster which he executed for Bally shoes, one of his longest-standing clients. Villemot spoke of the advertisement fondly: "The poster appeared on the walls at the beginning of September. These two legs attracted the eye with the power of the graphics, seducing it with the draftsmanship and color . . . The poster isn't only capable of selling the product at a precise moment . . . Moreover, I arrived at this conclusion: The poster needs to be known by the non-buyers. Take shoes for example . . . This poster is going to be seen by passer-bys that have no need to replace their shoes, who don't have money for that . . . The message of the poster needs to confirm the make's image, one day transforming the non-buyer into a client for this brand. Jean-Pierre Rocher (Head of Publicity at Bally) understood that very well. He wanted to create a 'Bally image,' memorized (by the public) as we now say" (Villemot, p. 86). A successful design, described by *Vendre* of October, 1967, as "a high-class work."
**Est: $1,200-$1,500.**

**511. Bally.** 1986.
47¹/₄ x 62³/₄ in./120 x 159.4 cm
Imp. IPA, Champigny
Cond B+/Slight tears at folds.
Ref: Villemot A-Z, p. 114;
    Villemot/La Femme, p. 69 (var); PAI-IX, 533b
In this poster for Bally flats and heels, Villemot uses hues that glow with profound intensity and a seated model that appears to be little more than a disassembled mannequin to forcibly grab our attention and focus it on the brand-name. The irrepressible artist could always be counted on to come up with something fresh, carefully calculated to create a riveting impression.
**Est: $1,200-$1,500.**

**512. Air France/Maroc-Algérie-Tunisie.** 1952.
24¹/₂ x 39 in./62.2 x 99 cm
Imp. Hubert Baille, Paris
Cond A.
Ref: Air France, p. 51; Villemot, p. 139; PAI-XXI, 453 (var)
Among the many posters that Villemot did for Air France, this is one of the two he created for destinations in North Africa. With his characteristically evocative brushstrokes, he captures the blocky architecture—old and new—and the exotic street life, as a tiny Air France jet flies overhead.
**Est: $1,200-$1,500.**

**513. Contrex: Two Hand-Signed Proofs.** 1974 & 1979.
Each: 19¹/₂ x 25³/₄ in./49.5 x 65.5 cm

Cond A–/Slight tears at edges.
Ref (Both Var): Villemot, checklist Nos. 273 & 279;
    PAI-XXIX, 671
The Villemot sparkle is evident in these two hand-signed limited edition artist's proofs for one of his favorite clients: Contrex—where nudity is dressed as simplicity, purity and health. *From editions of 200—#180 and #14. respectively.*
**Est: $2,000-$2,500.** (2)

**514. Vichy.** 1956.
24¹/₈ x 39¹/₈ in./61.2 x 99.5 cm
Imp. Courbet, Paris
Cond B+/Restored tears at edges.
Ref: Villemot A-Z, p. 89
No matter where you come from, no matter what pastimes you prefer to pursue, Vichy is the perfect resort for you to visit. And even though a camera case may have been lashed to it in advance, the glowing front-and-center chair gives off the impression that a place

**515**

**517**

**516**

**518**

But nothing compares to this ecstatic 2-sheet image of a beachside couple, guzzling Perrier as they devour one another, giving-off an aurora borealis of passion as they do. Crazy! This is the rarest and most spectacular of all the designs that he executed for the brand.
**Est: $2,500-$3,000.**

**516. Division Leclerc/100 km.** 1986.
$15^3/_4$ x $23^5/_8$ in./40 x 60 cm
Imp. IPA, Paris
Cond A.
Athleticism meets heroism in this Villemot promotion for a 100-kilometer foot race being run from Paris to Rambouillet and back again, which derives its name from the French 2nd Armored Division, commanded by General Maréchal Leclerc. The Division Leclerc played a critical role in Operation Cobra—the Allied breakthrough from Normandy during the latter phases of World War II—but is most celebrated for the role the unit played in the liberation of Paris.
**Est: $700-$900.**

**517. Vichy/Celestine.** ca. 1975.
108 x $26^3/_4$ in./274.2 x 68 cm
Imp. Lalande-Courbet, Wissous
Cond A.
Ref: Villemot/Femme, p. 22 (var)
In this very long 2-sheet poster, Villemot calls a flip-flopped couple executed in—what else—various shades of cool blue into play to promote Vichy Celestine mineral water, so-named for the mineral's pale-blue color. What a healthful, enjoyable way to while away the afternoon. *Rare!*
**Est: $1,200-$1,500.**

**518. Foire Gastronomique/Dijon.** 1971.
$31^1/_2$ x 47 in./80 x 119.2 cm
Imp. Bedos, Paris
Cond A.
Villemot's poster for this Dijon Gastronomic Fair leads the viewer to believe that the theme of this Fair leaned towards the Italian. Red wine aside, is there any other motif more universal for Italian eateries, from pizzerias to purveyors of gourmet fare, than the red-and-white checkered tablecloth? "What allows one to recognize a Villemot poster without a shadow of hesitation is the powerful drawing, that seeks to be natural, spontaneous . . . and significant enough in itself to the point of not needing any slogan" (Villemot, p. 120).
**Est: $1,200-$1,500.**

has been saved for whoever happens to be looking at the poster at any given moment. Absolute genius.
**Est: $1,400-$1,700.**

**515. Perrier/c'est fou!** 1984.
92 x $61^3/_8$ in./233 x 155.7 cm
Lalnde-Courbet, Wissous

Cond B+/Unobtrusive folds.
Ref: Villemot, p. 130; Villemot A-Z, p. 108;
Villemot/La Femme, p. 62; PAI-XXII, 543
Villemot created memorable poster campaigns for several potables—Contrex and Vichy mineral waters, sunny Orangina—and his series for Perrier beginning in 1967 is virtually a textbook of modern poster art.

**519**

**520**

## JACQUES VILLON (1875-1963)

**519. L'Anti-Bélier/A Cruchon.** 1899.
16¹/₂ x 22⁵/₈ in./42 x 57.5 cm
Imp. Malfeyt, Paris
Cond A. Framed.
Ref: PAI-XL, 522

Villon was an important figure in the history of modern art and a quintessential figure in the bohemian scene of fin-de-siècle Paris. A cubist painter, illustrator and printmaker, he created only some six posters—all graced by his superb drawing and observation of character. And this exceedingly rare poster for the Cruchon salon is no exception: this primping sophisticate is the very picture of satisfied self-indulgence. What isn't nearly as clear is what particular service or product is being offered—the term "Anti-Bélier" doesn't hold meaning anymore in a cosmetological sense. However, if it's broken down, the term would seem to indicate that it meant one of two things: either it referred to a hair detangler ("bélier" is a wool bearing mammal and unruly hair sometimes draws sheep-like comparison) or possibly to the perfume pump set in front the woman (the word "atomizer" didn't yet exist and current usage of "antibélier" is associated with industrial pumping). Despite its ambiguous product, the poster is simply exquisite, a gorgeous homage to beauty for beauty's sake.
**Est: $25,000-$30,000.**

## JOHANN VON STEIN (1896-1965)

**520. Rotterdam Lloyd.**
17³/₄ x 28¹/₈ in./45 x 71.5 cm
Ned. Rotogravure, Leiden
Cond A.
Ref: PAI-XLI, 533

A sleek Art Deco design frames the steamship *Baloeran* of the Rotterdam Lloyd Line, a Dutch shipping company that sailed worldwide, but placed its primary focus on the Dutch East Indies and the Far East. Launched in 1930, the *Baloeran* was captured by the Germans in Rotterdam a decade later. Converted to a hospital ship and renamed *Strassburg*, she would be beached near Ijmuiden, North Holland, after being mined, where the wreck would be destroyed by British torpedo boats. A rather ignoble end for such a majestic-looking liner. Stein achieved a solid reputation with his meticulously crafted posters for the Nederlandse Rotogravure Maatschappij, a renowned printer

**521**

**523**

**524**

**522**

based in Leiden. His clear lines and geometric neatness come from the same Art Deco font of inspiration as Cassandre's designs of the 1930s.
**Est: $4,000-$5,000.**

## EDOUARD VUILLARD (1868-1940)

**521. Douze Lithographies en Couleurs.** 1899.
17 x 23 in./43.2 x 58.4 cm
Cond A–/Slight stains at edges/P.
Ref: Color Revolution, 188
"A painter, printmaker , and photographer, Vuillard moved to Paris in 1877 . . . Vuillard was soon drawn into the group of young artists who called themselves the Nabis and adopted a bold style inspired in part by the works of Paul Gaugin. In contrast to his fellow Nabis, who prized a more mystical and abstract approach to art, Vuillard remained firmly grounded in the world around him, in particular the domestic tableaux within the homes of his family and closest friends" (Lautrec/Montmartre, p. 277). That sense of abstraction wed with domesticity is on display in the poster Vuillard designed to promote an album of twelve color lithographs—for which this also served as the cover art—named "Landscapes and interiors," of which this is obviously the latter. Incredibly esoteric, the civility of the interior seems to be in direct opposition to the dank color scheme, a stylistic alternative that appears to widen the gulf betwixt the man reading in his chair and the woman performing an identical activity across the room in the company of her cat. Domestic, yet distant; together, yet worlds apart. *Pencil-signed by the artist.*
**Est: $2,500-$3,000.**

## WILLIAM WELSH (1889-?)

**522. The Oriental Institute/University of Chicago.**
12¹/₂ x 22 in./31.7 x 55.8 cm
Cond B+/Slight tears at folds.
Founded in 1919 by James Henry Breasted, the Oriental Institute, a part of the University of Chicago, is an internationally recognized pioneer in the archaeology, philology and history of early Near Eastern civilizations. Though a number of the institute's attractions are pointed out textually in the lower half of Welsh's design, it's the upper half that provides the promotional heft, with its bust of Nefertiti—the Great Royal Wife of Pharaoh

Akhenaten whose name roughly translates as "the beautiful (or perfect) woman has come"—and a human-headed winged bull known as a "lamassu"—excavated from Khorsabad.
**Est: $1.000-$1,200.**

**523. Pullman/Winter Resort.** 1934.
18³/₄ x 26¹/₄ in./47.7 x 66.8 cm
Charles Daniel Frey Co., Chicago
Cond B+/Slight stains and creases, largely at edges.
Ref: PAI-XXXIV, 603
This is what I think of when a winter resort pops to mind —snuggly warm and fashionably earth-toned clothing, an abundance of the frozen white stuff, curious, yet civil wildlife and a photo-worthy hoar-frosted bush trapped somewhere between a snowflake and a fantastic out-cropping of coral. As evidenced here, Welsh's svelte way-farer had an easygoing, nearly Disneyesque affinity with the indigenous animals of the regions through which she passed. Kentucky-born Welsh was trained through-out the United States and in Paris as well. Accomplished and lauded as both a painter and an illustrator, his work can be seen in numerous museums.
**Est: $2,000-$2,500.**

## JEAN D'YLEN (1866-1938)

**524. Miss Blanche Cigarettes.** 1927.
40³/₈ x 67¹/₂ in./102.5 x 171.5 cm
Imp. Vercasson, Paris
Cond B+/Slight tears at folds.
Ref: D'Ylen (listing)
The circle of addiction goes 'round and 'round, but rarely has it been manifested with such seductive élan as in this d'Ylen creation for Miss Blanche cigarettes. From her hidden, smoldering secret to the nicotinic halo that surrounds her, this agape redhead combines guilty pleasure and angelic appearance in perfect proportion. It's interesting to note that the d'Ylen listing refers to this lady in white as "Miss Blanche tennis woman" and that the "Cigarettes" at poster's bottom is a tip-on.
**Est: $3,000-$4,000.**

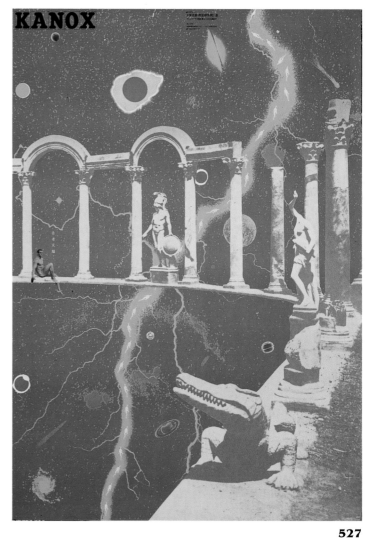

**526**

**527**

**525**

**528**

**529**

## JEAN D'YLEN (cont'd)

**525. Fiorino/Asti Spumanti.** 1922.
45⁵/₈ x 63 in./115.8 x 160 cm
Imp. Vercasson, Paris
Cond A–/Unobtrusive tears near folds.
Ref: D'Ylen, 22; PAI-XLII, 521
After several years as a designer of jewelry, d'Ylen became a full-time posterist in 1919 and signed an exclusive contract with Vercasson in 1922. He may have
owed the job offer to the fact he was a sincere admirer
and disciple of Cappiello, who was the previous star of
the Vercasson shop, and thus the firm was assured of
an uninterrupted flow of designs of unbridled exuber-
ance which had been Cappiello's trademark. A fine ex-

ample is this poster for Fiorino Asti Spumante, calling
upon exaggerated size, a sense of abandon and an ex-
pansive black background to deliver the Fiorino message.
**Est: $1,700-$2,000.**

## TADANORI YOKOO (1936- )

**526. Kyotomo/Some no Kimono.** 1978.
28¹/₂ x 40¹/₂ in./72.5 x 103 cm
Cond A/P.
Ref: Yokoo/Graphic Works, 1496
Chances are that if you hadn't read the title of this
piece, you wouldn't single it out as a poster promoting

the dyed kimonos available at the Kyotomo shop. Apart
from the Cubist garter-wearer down-right, there aren't
even that many feminine elements in the poster. But it
is a feast for the eye, a kaleidoscopic deconstructionist
playground composed of geometric mish-mash—but
between the mish and the mash there appear to be
very carefully chosen images: a view of the beach from
a verandah, a locomotive, playing cards, electric gui-

**530**

**531**

tars, a bottle of wine, an arrow-pierced heart, a face, the word "year." The text in the ad mentions that Kyotomo also "deals with dressing." And why would they do that? Because most modern women can't do it, that's why. If they need to wear a kimono for some formal event, they will go to a beauty salon or a shop like this one to have someone (or several someones) help dress them.
**Est: $1,000-$1,200.**

**527. Kanox.** 1979.
$28^5/8$ x $40^3/4$ in./72.7 x 102.6 cm
Cond A–/Slight tear at top paper edge/P.
Ref: Yokoo/Graphic Works, 1649; Yokoo's Posters, 128
"Yokoo's designs often seem the result of some sort of benign madness . . . No other graphic designer has combined, so apparently effortlessly and successfully, visual motifs from a vast variety of epochs and cultures . . . His interest in history and particularly the history of art of both western and eastern cultures yields an unrivaled eclecticism of sources. What makes this eclecticism so remarkable is that the motifs somehow coexist harmoniously on the page, revealing something about themselves that is distinct to their combination and ultimately startling in their new context" (Yokoo's Posters, p. 5). All the elements of this visionary artistry fall into perfect place in his design for Kanox, a Japanese production company involved with television, radio, film, stage and commercial advertising. There's no specific product per se on display, however Yokoo's combination of classic architecture, statuary and contemporary nudity, all set adrift in a trippy, surrealist galaxy makes it known in a glance that the production company is willing and able to work outside the box.
**Est: $1,000-$1,200.**

**528. UCLA Asian Performing Arts Institute.** 1981.
$28^1/2$ x $40^1/2$ in./72.5 x 102.7 cm
Toppan Printing Co.
Cond A/P.
Ref: Yokoo/Graphic Works, 1873; Yokoo's Posters, 26;

PAI-XVII, 527 (var)
One of a series of twelve posters made by Japan's leading graphic artists for the 1981 Asian Performing Arts Festival held at the University of California in Los Angeles. Each of the posters were intended to promote a specific element of the festival. For the presentation of *nihon buyo*—a term that literally translates as "Japanese dance," but more fully and accurately can be described as a traditional Japanese performing art consisting of a mixture of dance and pantomime based on the tradition of classical techniques—Yokoo creates a lush garden into which the names of the cities (Los Angeles, New York and Washington D.C.) where the festival will be making stops have been inconspicuously placed. Immediately perceived as a dazzling young graphic artist in the early 1960s, Tadanori Yokoo quickly garnered medals at Tokyo's prestigious Art Directors Club and went on to be honored with solo exhibitions and awards too numerous to recount in both his native Japan and on the international scene. His unique pop posters have won him the kind of cult status among his countrymen normally associated with rock stars.
**Est: $1,000-$1,200.**

## P. H. YORKE

**529. Aberdeen & Commonwealth Line/Australia.**
$23^3/4$ x $39^3/8$ in./60.5 x 100 cm
Howard, Jones, Roberts & Leete, London
Cond A.
Ref: PAI-XXXIII, 616 (var)
What ho, stalwart Scottie! When last we saw you standing watch, brave terrier, you were ensuring the safety of the Aberdeen & Commonwealth's precious human cargo as they made their way through the waters of the Indian and icy Atlantic oceans on their voyage to jolly old England (*see* PAI-XXXIII, 616). This time out, you appear to be fulfilling the same function for a return trip to "The Land Down Under." And judging from your diminutive, yet regal bearing, salty pooch, could there be any

question that the "One Class" service provided by the A & C line could be referring to anything but "First Class?"
**Est: $1,700-$2,000.**

## KEES VAN DONGEN (1877-1968)

**530. Bal à l'Opéra des Petits Lits Blancs.** ca. 1920.
43 x $62^7/8$ in./109.1 x 159.8 cm
Imp. Françaises Réunis, Paris
Cond B+/Slight tears and stains at folds and edges.
Ref: PAI-XI, 194
A painter and portraitist, van Dongen was described as a sensitive ironist, a penetrating moralist and a magician of nuances. He was born in Rotterdam and studied art there; but, by 1900 he settled in Paris, becoming a French citizen in 1929. He contributed to illustrated journals, painted landscapes and many fine portraits, and, infrequently did posters. His fine hand is evident in this work for the famous annual charity ball for a children's hospital: even with a minimum of detail, each recognizable face gets an intense visualized treatment. *This is the larger format.*
**Est: $3,000-$4,000.**

## ZIG (Louis Gaudin, ?-1936)

**531. Casino de Paris/Mistinguett/Paris Qui Brille.** 1931.
$15^1/2$ x $35^1/2$ in./39.5 x 90 cm
Central Publicité, Paris
Cond B/Unobtrusive tears along folds; restored tears at right margin.
Ref: Folies-Bergère, 67; Delhaye, p. 35; PAI-XLII, 524
In this poster for the revue "Paris Adazzle" at the Casino de Paris, Zig depicts Mistinguett perched on a stool, with the city at her feet, displaying most of her visible assets. Setting off all that skin: long red gloves, oodles of dripping jewelry and an insouciant little hat. *This is the smaller format.*
**Est: $1,700-$2,000.**

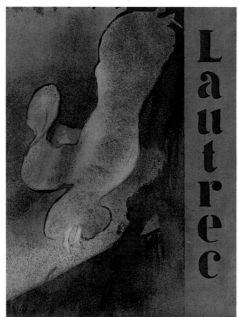

**532**

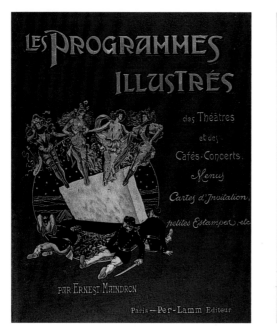

**533**

**534**

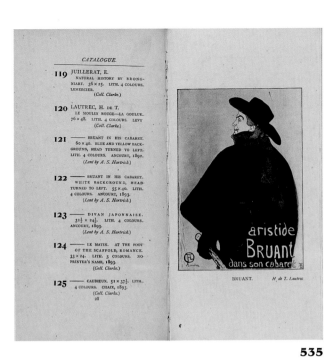

POSTERS

EDITED BY
EDWARD
BELLA

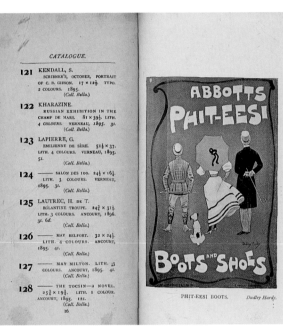

**535**

**536**

**537**

of the time. Along with forty pages of introductory text, the sixty plates—most in color—contained herein include works by the best-known artists of the day, including: Ibels, Misti, Grasset, Rochegrosse, Chéret, Willette, Roubille, De Feure, Toulouse-Lautrec, Casal, Choubrac, Guillaume and Roedel.
Est: $1,500-$1,800.

**534. Gil Blas.** 1891-1902.
10⁵/₈ x 15 in./27 x 38 cm
Ref: PAI-XL, 540 (var)
*Bound in four leather volumes; excellent condition.*
The eleven years chronicling this Paris weekly contain short stories, social commentary, music and poetry, but most importantly, approximately 1,000 illustrations, more than 300 of which are color illustrations by Steinlen. Featured artists include Balluriau, Guillaume, Guydo, Grün, Bernard, Redon, Poulbot, Bac, Picasso, Sandy Hook, van Dongen and other designers well-known to poster collectors. In short, a veritable gold mine of Belle Epoque graphic richness.
Est: $6,000-$8,000.

**535. Posters, Edited by Edward Bella.** 1894.
4³/₄ x 8³/₄ in./12 x 22 cm
*Overall very good condition; hardcover binding; some cover wear and slight staining.*
*Illustrated exhibition catalogue for the first exhibition organized by Bella at the Royal Aquarium in London, 1894-95. Forty-eight pages with nineteen poster illustrations.*
A wonderful appreciation of the new museum of the street by Joseph Thatcher Clarke contains the following sentiment: "What painter of genius has not been, and will not ever be, glad to thus openly display his work to the passerby; delighted to behold his novel idea, his bold design, his brilliant colour, resplendent in the sunshine of high noon? Thus does modern art address itself, like the epic of old, to the crowded market-place." But this catalogue not only gushes over the art of the poster, it also lists the price of every poster in the appendix. Not surprisingly, the most expensive (eighty shillings) is Lautrec's Moulin Rouge. However, most posters were under ten shillings. A total of 258 posters are listed.

*Make no mistake: this is the exhibition that kicked-off the poster revolution of the 1890s. A must for the serious collector!*
Est: $2,500-$3,000.

**536. Posters, Edited by Edward Bella.** 1896.
4³/₄ x 8³/₄ in./12 x 22.2 cm
Ref: PAI-XXIX, 681
"As promised in the first catalogue, I have endeavored to glean from such parts of the world as are endowed with the doubtful blessing of publicity, specimens as such of their posters indicating artistic thought in their production and finish, in order to give the exhibition a more international character." Thus begins the "Editorial Note" in the illustrated exhibition catalogue for the Royal Aquarium of London's Second Exhibition in 1896, with twelve color reproductions and eighteen black-and-white illustrations, as well as an embossed cover with a design by Alexandre Charpentier. It's also important to note that Bella's prices are indicated for each available poster in the exhibition. Some examples are: Toulouse-Lautrec—Salon des Cent (3 shillings) and La Revue Blanche (7 shillings); Mucha—Gismonda (12 shillings); Cheret—Théâtre de l'Opéra/Carnaval 1896 (3 shillings), Theatrophone (30 shillings) and Pastilles Géraudel (4 shillings); Penfield— Harper's (4 & 12 shillings).
Est: $2,000-$2,500.

**537. Des Chats: Dessins sans paroles, par Steinlen.** 1898.
11³/₄ x 16³/₈ in./29.7 x 41.5 cm
Printed by Imp. Charles Verneau; published by Flammarion, Paris
Ref: Crauzat, 598; PAI-XLII, 466
*Hardcover binding; slightly trimmed with water stains at some paper edges.*
"This album, in addition to its color lithograph cover, contains 26 inset plate compositions, wordless cartoons published in the newspaper 'Le Chat Noir' and reproduced in black by the Gillot process" (Crauzat, pp. 159-60). Steinlen indulges his love of cats in a variety of pleasing and sometimes frightening situations.
Est: $1,000-$1,200.

**532. Henri de Toulouse-Lautrec, 1864-1901, by Maurice Joyant.**
Each: 8⁵/₈ x 10⁵/₈ in/22 x 27 cm
Published by H. Fleury, Paris; in two volumes.
Ref: PAI-XLIII, 598 (var)
Vol. I: "Peintres." 1926
Vol. II: "Dessins-Estampes-Affiches." 1927.
*Deluxe edition of this famed two-volume set.*
*In overall excellent condition in original softcover binding; slight damage to spine and binding.*
Volume I is one of 175 (#30) numbered copies printed on japan paper to which three original dry-point etchings in two states each are added. Volume II is one of 200 numbered copies (also # 30) on japan, and contains three dry-point etchings, each in two states, as well as four original lithographs in two states. No one knew Lautrec better than Joyant and it shows in the care and detail of presentation.
Est: $5,000-$6,000.

**533. Les Programmes Illustrés, by Ernest Maindron.** 1897.
9⁷/₈ x 12¹/₂ in./25.2 x 31.6 cm
Published by the Librairie Nilsson-Per Lamm, Paris
Ref: PAI-XLI, 589
*Hardcover binding; in overall excellent condition.*
A hardcover compendium presenting reproductions of some of the most beautiful menus, invitations, business cards and announcements of the Belle Epoque. Little could he have known how off the mark his thoughts were, as today we look back at the technical virtuosity these posterists displayed with the limited technology

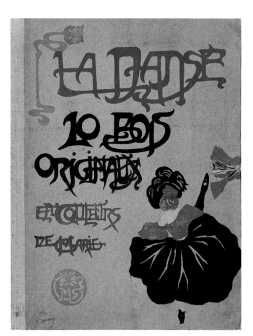

538

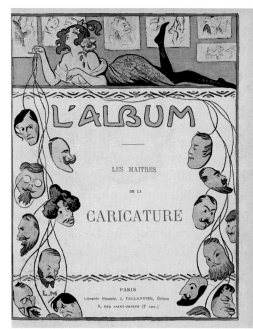

539

540

**541**

**542**

**544**

**543**

## BOOKS AND PERIODICALS (cont'd)

**538. La Danse: 10 Bois Originales en Couleurs de G. Marie.**
Each: 14¹/8 x 19 in./36 x 48.3 cm
*Loose prints in hardcover portfolio; overall excellent condition.*
*An edition of ten numbered and signed copies—this being #9/10.*
Gustave Marie was best known for his magazine illustrations and as an editor for the short-lived magazine, *L'Art et la Scène*. Here, in this edition of ten hand-colored woodblock engravings—with each print hand-signed by the artist—Marie dedicates himself to the dance, indicating in his own hand which style he is setting down in the lower-left corner of each. From the innocent to the barely dressed, as well as the other interpretations that dwell somewhere in the middle, Marie does an impressive job of capturing the individual character of each physical manifestation of artistic expression.
**Est: $4,000-$5,000.**

**539. L'Album/Le Maitre de la Caricature.**
1901 & 1902.
9¹/2 x 12 in./24 x 30.5 cm
Published by Montgredien, Paris
Ref: PAI-XL, 536 (var)
*Overall excellent condition; most covers are before the addition of top title text.*
A hardcover bound volume—containing all eighteen monthly numbers of the publication—of a magazine that gave each issue over to a single artist who was given full freedom of expression—hence its name. Most of these artists were also top posterists—Albert Guillaume, Ferdinand Bac, H. Gerbault, Caran d'Ache, Charles Léandre, Benjamin Rabies, Jean-Louis Forain, Abel Faivre, Steinlen, René Hermann-Paul, Grün, Paul Balluriau, Adoph Willette, Lucien Metivet and others. Each edition is full of humorous and bawdy Belle Epoque illustrations, as well as many colorful 2-page spreads and interesting biographical sketches of each artist. *Special deluxe edition.*
**Est: $2,000-$2,500.**

**540. Das Moderne Plakat, by Jean-Louis Sponsel.**
1897.
8¹/2 x 10⁷/8 in./21.2 x 27.7 cm
Verlag von Gerhard Kuhtmann, Dresden
Ref: PAI-XLIII, 610
*In overall excellent condition; slight wear on hardcover binding.*
A country-by-country survey of posters, published in Germany in 1897. Its wide scope required a total of 316 pages and 318 illustrations, including fifty-two plates in color. Coming a year after Mandron's 1896 classic, this monumental work is further proof of the worldwide *affichomanie* ("poster craze") of the period. A rare and valuable reference for the serious collector.
**Est: $4,000-$5,000.**

**541. Les Contemporains Célèbres.** 1904.
10 x 12³/4 in./25.2 x 32.4 cm
Published by Publications Octave Beauchamp & G. de Malherbe, Paris
Ref: Cappiello/Rennert, p. 13; PAI-XLII, 161
A volume published by Lefèvre-Utile and Octave Beauchamp, Paris, and distributed by G. de Malherbe, containing portraits, biographies, signed testimonials and some of Cappiello's finest caricatures of contemporary celebrities. You might be asking yourself just what do Sarah Bernhardt, Anatole France, Réjane, Granier, Massenet, Bartholdi and the Queen of Madagascar have in common? The answer is quite simple: They all love Lefèvre-Utile biscuits, of course.
**Est: $1,700-$2,000.**

**542. Catalogue d'Affiches Illustrées/Ed. Sagot.** 1891.
6¹/4 x 9³/4 in./15.9 x 24.7 cm
Ref: PAI-XXXVII, 554
*In presentation case; cover and some edges are worn.*
Sagot was the principal poster dealer in Paris during the 1890s and this, his first poster catalogue, launched the poster craze of that epoch. A total of 2,233 posters are offered, with wonderful commentary on many of them. Prices range mostly from 1 franc to 10 francs (a few maquettes are priced as high as 100 francs). Cover by Chéret, who is represented by 569 of his posters for sale. *1 of only 550 printed copies.*
**Est: $1,000-$1,200.**

**543. Les Arts et les industries du Papier en France —1871-1894, by Marius Vachon.** 1894.
10 x 13 in./25.2 x 33 cm
Published by Librairies-Imprimeries Réunies, Paris.
Ref: PAI-XLII, 538
*Hardcover; in overall excellent condition.*
The printing processes of the 19th century are explained and illustrated in the 248 pages of this hardcover publication with many historic photos of printing plant interiors, such as Imprimerie Chaix, Dupont and Camis (the last two shown here), with an additional bonus of some impressive color proofs of their technological prowess.
**Est: $1,400-$1,700.**

**544. L'Assiette au Beurre/A Nous l'Espace!** 1901.
9¹/2 x 12¹/4 in./24.2 x 31 cm
*In excellent condition; hardcover binding.*
*L'Assiette au Beurre* was surely the most hard-hitting of all the political and social satire journals of the period. However, this special edition does away with the critique in order to cast a hopeful eye to the future and the emerging field of aviation. With drawings by Guillaume, this issue features fifteen full-page illustrations and three triple-page spreads all anticipating the wonders of flight.
**Est: $1,000-$1,200.**

**545**

## BOOKS AND PERIODICALS (cont'd)

**545. Histore du Chien de Brisquet.** 1899.
9¹/₄ x 11⁵/₈ in./23.5 x 29.5 cm
Published by Editions d'Art Edouard Pelletan, Paris
*The ultimate deluxe edition of Steinlen's work: one of twenty-five copies (#16) on grand velin containing an original hand-signed Steinlen design, with double suites of others, from a total edition of 127. Includes a dedication from Steinlen and the author to the publisher's daughter.*
Fine Moroccan leather binding with gilt floral back, borders and top. All plates in three states and all signed in pencil by the artist. Steinlen brings his animal master into full play for Nodier's classic tale of a beloved and devoted mongrel. That this book cost 350 francs in 1899 (four times the cost of Lautrec's Moulin Rouge!) attests to its desirability and value from Day One.
**Est: $4,000-$5,000.**

**546. L'Oeuvre Gravé et Lithographié de Steinlen.**
1913.
10 x 13 in./25.5 x 33 cm
Ref: PAI-XLI, 542
*222-page book by E. de Crauzat published in an edition of 500 copies (this is No. 138) by Société de Propagation des Livres d'Art. Preface by Roger Marx. Contains three original dry-point etchings. Total of 745 works are detailed, with full index; overall excellent condition; hardcover binding.*
Ever since its publication in 1913, the *Crauzat* book has been *THE* catalogue raisonné of the prolific, diverse French posterist. The sweep of the publication is incredible, containing every illustration and engraving executed by the artist up to that point. It provides a rare opportunity to see Steinlen's visionary insights placed alongside one another, be they politic or commercial, from song sheet covers to the purely artistic.
**Est: $2,000-$2,500.**

**547. 70 Dessins de Cappiello.** 1905.
11 x 15 in./28 x 38 cm
Published by Libraire H. Floury, Paris
Ref: Cappiello/Rennert, p. 7; PAI-XLII, 156
*Overall excellent condition with slight stains at edges; in hardcover binding.*
*1 of 1500 numbered copies.*
This is a delightful collection of insightful character studies of prominent people from the world of turn-of-the-century Paris theater, politics and public life. All told, the volume contains sixty-four pages of caricatures, printed by lithography and pochoir.
**Est: $1,500-$1,800.**

**548. Le Grand Prix Automobile de Monaco: Histoire d'une Legende 1929-1960.** 1992.
19¹/₈ x 13¹/₄ in./48.5 x 33.6 cm
Editions Automobilia, Monaco

**546**

**547**

**548**

**549**

**550**

BAL TABARIN

MAURICE CHEVALIER

DE LA NOIRE A LA BLANCHE

**551**

Librairie
Centrale des Beaux-Arts
13, Rue La Fayette
Paris

Combinaisons
ornementales
par MM.
M.P. Verneuil
G. Auriol
et
Mucha

**552**

but some simply bear the name of the function that they fulfilled—"Dance Beats."
**Est: $1,700-$2,000.**

**550. Les Robes de Paul Poiret.** 1908.
11³/4 x 12³/4 in./30 x 32.4 cm
Société Générale d'Impression, Paris
Ref: PAI-XXXV, 518
*Ten pochoir-printed designs by Paul Iribe in a hard-cover binding; plates in very good condition; some staining on cover, title page and at edges.*
*#55 of 250 copies.*
Paul Poiret (1879-1944) was born to a cloth merchant family in Paris. He established his own business, La Maison Poiret, during 1904. Poiret brought vitality and vibrant color back to women's fashion which had been decimated by the First World War. A pioneer in the use of oriental influences, he liberated women from their corsets and gave them high Empire waistlines, flowing kimono tunics and bellowing harem pants, but ironically constrained them with his restricting hobble skirts. His exotic embroideries and aigrette-adorned turbans were bright, exciting satellites of fashion.
**Est: $4,000-$5,000.**

**551. Music-Hall, by Leon-Paulo Fargue.** 1948.
10¹/4 x 12⁷/8 in./26 x 32.7 cm
Published by Les Bibliophiles du Palais.
*Fine hardcover binding; excellent condition; 156 pages.*
*#32 of an edition of 200 copies.*
Contains fifty-four lithographs of music-hall performers by Luc-Albert Moreau (1882-1948). In addition to a great appreciation of the history of the French music-hall, each chapter features top performers, such as Little Tich, Grock, Mistinguett, Maurice Chevalier, Josephine Baker and Barbette, not to mention a myriad of assorted jugglers and circus performers. Focus is also placed on the music-hall experience, both textually and graphically. Moreau was a widely-acclaimed painter and printmaker, specializing in sporting and entertainment subjects.
**Est: $1,700-$2,000.**

**552. Combinaisons ornementales.**
10 x 8⁵/8 in./25.3 x 22 cm
Ref: PAI-XXXVII, 553
*Excellent condition; in original hardcover binding; loose sheets all within a presentation carton.*
"The necessity of the decorator to vary ad infinitum the applications of the ornamentations that are asked of him have led curious spirits to seek a practical means, simple and rapid to arrive at this result." Of course these curious spirits just happened to be members of the Libraire Centrale des Beaux-Arts. And their job became considerably less challenging once they enlisted the services of Verneuil, Auriol and Mucha to demonstrate, over the course of sixty plates, just how easy it was to create harmonious compositions once a "kaleidoscope method" was applied.
**Est: $1,500-$2,000.**

*Overall excellent condition.*
Juan Manuel Fangio (1911-1995), considered by many to be the greatest driver of all time, provided the preface for a tome dedicated to this glamorous, legendary test of skill offset by Mediterranean splendor. This book (#265 out of a printing run of 999) chronicles the first three decades of the event with ample photographs and illustrations, placing the thrill of the race directly into the hands of the race enthusiast. *Text in French.*
**Est: $1,500-$1,800.**

**549. Tanztee und Tonfilm: Eight Issues.** 1930.
9³/4 x 12¹/4 in./23.8 x 31 cm
Published by Alrobi Musik Verlag, Berlin
If only every life could be as breezy and wonderful as those portrayed on Herzig's cover designs for this publication. His swank, elegant Art Deco masterpieces adorn each issue of "Tea Dances and Talkies," which contained forty-eight pages of sheet music for the era's popular dance tunes—approximately twenty song sheets per edition. As you may expect, the titles vary,

# BIBLIOGRAPHY

The following is a list of books used in the preparation of this catalogue. In the interest of brevity, these works have been abbreviated in the Reference ("Ref:") section of the description of each lot. The abbreviations can be found below accompanied by the work's full title, publisher's name, city and date of publication. It should be noted that we have made no reference to the many magazines and annuals which are essential tools in this area, such as *The Poster, Estampe et Affiche, La Plume, Arts et Metiers Graphiques, Vendre, Das Plakat, Gebrauchsgraphik* and *Graphis Posters.*

NOTE: References to prior PAI books are limited to the last auction in which the poster was offered. We refer readers to our book, *Poster Prices IX,* which gives the complete record of each poster offered at the first 40 PAI sales.

**Abdy**
*The French Poster,* by Jane Abdy. Clarkson N. Potter. New York, 1969.

**Absinthe**
*Absinthe: History in a Bottle,* by Barnaby Conrad III. Chronicle Books, San Francisco, 1988.

**Absinthe Affiches**
*L'Absinthe: Les Affiches,* by Marie-Claude Delahaye. Musée de l'Absinthe, Auvers-sur-Oise, 2002.

**Adriani**
*Toulouse-Lautrec: The Complete Graphic Works,* by Götz Adriani. The catalogue raisonné, featuring the Gerstenberg collection. Thames & Hudson, London, 1988.

**Affiche Réclame**
*Quand l'Affiche Faisait de la Réclame!* Editions de la Réunion des Musées Nationaux, Paris. 1991.

**Affiches Azur**
*Affiches d'Azur—100 Ans d'Affiches de la Côte d'Azur et de Monaco,* by Charles Martini de Chateauneuf. Editions Gilletta, Nice, 1992.

**Affiches Etrangères**
*Les Affiches Etrangères Illustrées,* by M. Bauwens, T. Hayashi, La Forge, Meier-Graefe & J. Pennel. Boudet, Paris, 1897.

**Affiches Riviera**
*Affiches de la Riviera,* by Annie de Montry, Françoise Lepeuve & Charles Martini de Chateauneuf. Editions Gilletta, Nice-Matin, 2001.

**Affiches Suisses**
*Objets-Realisme-Affiches Suisses: 1905-1950.* Catalogue of the exhibition held at the Bibliothèque Forney, Paris, 1982. Text by Eric Kellenberger.

**Affichomanie**
*L'Affichomanie.* Catalogue of the exhibition on the subject of the Postermania of the period 1880-1900 held at the Musée de l'Affiche, Paris, 1980. Text by Alain Weill.

**Ailes**
*Voici des Ailes, affiches de cycles.* Catalogue from the exhibition at the Musée d'Art et d'Industrie, Saint-Étienne, May 3-September 22, 2002.

**Air France**
*Air France/Affiches/Posters 1933-1983,* by Jérôme Peignot. Fernand Hazan, Paris, 1988.

**Alimentaires**
*Un Siecle de Reclames Alimentaires,* by F. Ghozland. Editions Milan, 1984.

**Alpes**
*Les Alpes à l'Affiche,* by Yves Ballu. Editions Glenat, Grenoble, 1987.

**Art & Auto**
*L'Art et Automobile,* by Hervé Poulain. Les Clefs du Temps, Zoug, 1973.

**Art Deco**
*Art Deco Graphics,* by Patricia Frantz Kery. Harry N. Abrams, New York, 1986.

**Art et Biscuits**
*L'Art et les Biscuits: La publicité de la firme Lefèvre-Utile de 1897 à 1914.* Edited by Georges Herscher. Editions du Chêne, Paris, 1978.

**Auto Posters**
*100 Years of Auto-Posters,* by Dominique Dubarry. Maeght Editeur, Paris, 1991.

**Auto Show I**
*1er Salon de l'Affiche Automobile.* Catalogue of the exhibition, compiled by Jacques Perier, and sponsored by the Automobile Club de France, Paris, October 1978.

**Ballet Suedois**
*Les Ballets Suedois dans l'Art Contemporain.* Editions du Trianon, Paris, 1931.

**Bargiel et Zagrodzki**
*Steinlen-Affichiste. Catalogue Raisonné,* by Réjane Bargiel and Christophe Zagrodzki. Editions du Grant-Pont, Lausanne, 1986. (Distributed in the United States by Posters Please, Inc., New York City).

**Baumberger**
*Otto Baumberger 1889-1961.* Catalogue of the exhibition of Baumberger posters held at the Museum für Gestaltung Zurich, May-July 1988, and subsequently in Basel and Essen.

**Beaumont**
*L'Affiche Belge,* by A. Demeure de Beaumont. Chateau de Daussinanges, Clairac, France, 1897.

**Belgische Affiche 1900**
*De Belgische Affiche 1892-1914,* by Yolande Oostens-Wittamer. Koninklijke Bibliotheek Albert I, Brussels, 1975.

**Belle Epoque 1980**
*La Belle Epoque.* Catalogue of the loan exhibition from the Wittamer-De Camps collection, featuring the works of Combaz, Léo Jo and Livemont. Text by Yolande Oostens-Wittamer. International Exhibitions Foundation, 1980-81.

**Benezit**
*Dictionnaire des Peintres, Sculpteurs, Dessinateurs et Graveur,* by E. Benezit. Libraire Gründ, Paris, 1976.

**Bernhardt/Drama**
*Sarah Bernhardt: The Art of High Drama,* by Carol Ockman and Kenneth Silver. Catalogue of the exhibition at the Jewish Museum, New York, 2005-2006. Yale University Press, New Haven, 2005.

**Berthon & Grasset**
*Berthon & Grasset,* by Victor Arwas. Academy Editions, London; Rizzoli, New York, 1978.

**Bibliothèque Nationale**
*Inventaire du fonds francais,* prints from 1800 in the collection of the Bibliothèque Nationale de France, published in 15 volumes, from 1930 to 1985 (but ending with the letter "M").

**Bicycle Posters**
*100 Years of Bicycle Posters,* by Jack Rennert. Harper & Row, New York, 1973.

**Boissons**
*Les Boissons/Un Siècle de Réclames,* by F. Ghozland. Editions Milan, Toulouse, 1986.

**Bouvet**
*Bonnard: The Complete Graphic Work,* by Francis Bouvet. Rizzoli, New York.

**Broders**
*Voyages: Les Affiches de Roger Broders,* by Annie de Montry and Françoise Lepeuve. Syros-Alternatives, Paris, 1991.

**Broders Travel**
*Roger Broders/Travel Posters,* by Alain Weill and Israel Perry. Queen Art Publishes, New York, 2002.

**Broido**
*The Posters of Jules Chéret: 46 Full Color Plates and an Illustrated Catalogue Raisonné,* 2nd ed., by Lucy Broido. Dover Publications, New York, 1992.

**Brown & Reinhold**
*The Poster Art of A. M. Cassandre,* by Robert K. Brown and Susan Reinhold. E. P. Dutton, New York, 1979.

**Cappiello**
*Cappiello.* Catalogue of the exhibition at the Galerie Nationale du Grand Palais, Paris, 1981.

**Cappiello/Rennert**
*The Posters of Leonetto Cappiello,* by Jack Rennert. Poster Art Library, Posters Please, Inc., New York, 2004.

**Cardinaux**
*Emil Cardinaux (1877-1936).* Catalogue of the exhibition at the Museum für Gestaltung Kunstgewerbemuseum, Zurich, August-October, 1985.

**Cassandre/BN**
*A. M. Cassandre–Oeuvres Graphiques Modernes 1923-1939.* Catalogue of the exhibition at the Bibliothèque Nationale de France in Paris, 2005.

**Cassandre/Suntory**
*Cassandre: Every Face of the Great Master, 1901-1968.* Catalogue of the exhibition held at the Suntory Museum, Osaka, June-August, 1995.

**Cassandre/Tokyo**
*A. M. Cassandre.* Catalogue of the exhibition held at the Tokyo Metropolitan Teien Art Museum, 1991.

**Célébrités**
*Célébrités à l'Affiche,* by A. C. Lelieur and R. Bachollet. Edita, Lausanne, 1989.

**Chocolate Posters**
*Chocolate Posters,* by Israel Perry and Alain Weill. Queen Art Publishers Inc., New York, 2002.

**Cinéma Français**
*Affiches du Cinéma Français,* by J. M. Borga & B. Martinand. Editions Delville, Paris, 1977.

**Cirque**
*Le Cirque Iconographie.* The circus poster catalogue of the Bibliothèque Nationale, Paris, 1969.

**Colin**
*100 Posters of Paul Colin,* by Jack Rennert. Images Graphiques, New York, 1977.

**Colin Affichiste**
*Paul Colin: Affichiste,* by Alain Weill & Jack Rennert. Editions Denoel, Paris, 1989.

**Collectionneur**
*Collectionneur d'Affiches,* edited by Laurence Prod'homme. Editions Apogé, Musée de Bretagne, 1996.

**Color Revolution**
*The Color Revolution.* Catalogue of the exhibition at Rutgers University Art Gallery, Boston Public Library and Baltimore Museum of Art. Edited by Philip Denis Cate and Sinclair Hamilton Hitchings. 1978.

**Cosmetiques**
*Cosmetiques: Etre et Paraitre,* by F. Ghozland. Editions Milan, Toulouse, 1987.

**Crauzat**
*L'Oeuvre Gravé et Lithographié de Steinlen,* by E. de Crauzat. Société de Propogation des Livres d'Art, Paris, 1913. Reprinted by Alan Wofsy Fine Arts, San Francisco, 1983.

**Dance Encyclopedia**
*The Dance Encyclopedia,* edited by Anatole Chujoy. A.S. Barnes & Co., New York, 1949.

**Dance Posters**
*100 Years of Dance Posters,* by Walter Terry & Jack Rennert. Avon Books, New York, 1973.

**Deco Affiches**
*Affiches Art Deco,* by Alain Weill. Inter-Livres, Paris, 1990.

**Delhaye**
*Art Deco Posters and Graphics,* by Jean Delhaye. Academy Editions, London, 1977.

**DFP-I**
*Das Frühe Plakat in Europa und den USA.* Volume I. British and American Posters. Edited by Ruth Malhotra and Christina Thon. Mann Verlag, Berlin, 1973.

**DFP-II**
*Das Frühe Plakat in Europa und den USA.* Volume II. French and Belgian Posters. Edited by Ruth Malhotra, Marjan Rinkleff and Bernd Schalicke. Mann Verlag, Berlin, 1977.

**DFP-III**
*Das Frühe Plakat in Europa und den USA.* Volume III. German Posters. Edited by Helga Hollman, Ruth Malhotra, Alexander Pilipczuk, Helga Prignitz and Christina Thon. Mann Verlag, Berlin, 1980.

**Dodge**
*The Bicycle,* by Pryor Dodge. Flammarion, Paris-New York, 1996.

**Dubout**
*Affiches Dubout.* Editions Michele Trinckvel, Lausanne, 1985.

**Dutch Poster**
*A History of the Dutch Poster 1890-1960,* by Dick Dooijes and Pieter Brattinga. Scheltema & Holkema, Amsterdam, 1968.

**Enfant dans l'Affiche**
*L'Enfant dans l'Affiche,* by Jean-Charles Giroud and Michel Schlup. Association des Amis de l'Affiche Suisse, Neuchatel, 1998.

**Ferrari**
*Piloti, Che Gente,* by Enzo Ferrari. Conti Editore, Bologna, 1985.

**De Feure**
*Georges De Feure: Maitre du Symbolisme et de l'Art Nouveau,* by Ian Millman. ACR Editions, Courbevoie (Paris), 1991.

**Fit to Print**
*Fit to Print–The Newspaper and the Poster,* by Marc Davidson. The News-Journal Corporation, Daytona Beach, Florida, 2004.

**Folies-Bergère**
*100 Years of Posters of the Folies Bergère and Music Halls of Paris,* by Alain Weill. Images Graphiques, New York, 1977.

**French Opera**
*French Opera Posters 1868-1930,* by Lucy Broido. Dover Publications, New York, 1976.

**Frey**
*Toulouse-Lautrec: A Life,* by Julia Frey. Viking Penguin, New York, 1994.

**Fuller/Goddess of Light**
*Loie Fuller: Goddess of Light,* by Richard Nelson Current and Marcia Ewing Current. Northeastern University Press, Boston, 1997.

**Futurismo e Publicità**
*Il Futurismo e la Publicità,* by Claudia Salaris. Lupetti Editore, Milano, 1986.

**Gallo**
*The Poster in History,* by Max Gallo. American Heritage Publishing, New York, 1974.

**Gold**
*First Ladies of the Poster: The Gold Collection,* by Laura Gold. Posters Please Inc., New York City, 1998.

**Golf**
*L'Affiche de Golf/Golf Posters,* by Alexis Orloff. Éditions Milan, Toulouse, 2002.

**Grün**
*Jules-Alexandre Grün: The Posters/Les Affiches,* by Alain Weill and Israel Perry. Queen Art Publishers, New York, 2005.

**Health Posters**
*Posters of Health,* by Marine Robert-Sterkendries. Therabel Pharma, Brussels, 1996.

**Hillier**
*Posters,* by Bevis Hillier. Weidenfeld and Nicholson, London, 1969; Stein & Day, New York, 1969; Spring Books, The Hamlyn Publishing Group, New York, 1974.

**Ives**
*Pierre Bonnard/The Graphic Art,* by Colta Ives, Helen Giambruni and Sasha M. 1989-1990. Harry N. Abrams, New York, 1989.

**Josephine**
*Josephine Baker: The Hungry Heart,* by Jean Claude Baker and Chris Chase. Random House, New York, 1993.

**Karcher**
*Memoire de la Rue–Souvenirs d'un imprimeur et d'un afficheur.* Illustrated book of the archives of the Karcher printing firm of Paris with introduction by Alain Weill. WM Editions, Paris, 1986. (Distributed in the U.S.A. by Posters Please, Inc., New York, with a translation of text and the addition of an index).

**Kauffer**
*E. McKnight Kauffer: a designer and his public,* by Mark Haworth-Booth. Gordon Fraser, London, 1979.

**Keller**
*Ernst Keller Graphiker 1891-1968 Gesamtwerk.* Catalogue of the exhibition at the Kunstgewerbemuseum, Zurich, 1976.

**Lautrec/Montmartre**
*Toulouse-Lautrec and Montmartre.* The book of the exhibition at the National Gallery of Art, Washington, D.C., and the Art Institute of Chicago. Text by Richard Thomson, Phillip Dennis Cate and Mary Weaver Chaplin. Princeton University Press, Princeton, NJ, 2005.

**Lendl/Paris**
*Alphonse Mucha: La Collection Ivan Lendl.* Catalogue of the exhibition at Musée de la Publicité, Paris, 1989. Text by Jack Rennert. Editions Syros/Alternatives, Paris.

**Leupin**
*Herbert Leupin: Plakate, Bilder, Graphiken,* by Karl Lüönd and Charles Leupin. Friedrich Reinhardt, Basel, 1995.

**Lingerie**
*Rayon Lingerie.* Catalogue of the 1992 exhibition at the Bibliothèque Forney, Paris.

**Litfass-Bier**
*Litfass-Bier: Historische Bierplakate-Sammlung Heinrich Becker.* Edited by Gerhard Dietrich. Plakat/Konzepte, Hannover, 1998.

**Livre de l'Affiche**
*Le Livre de l'Affiche,* by Réjane Bargiel-Harry and Christophe Zagrodzki. A publication of the Musée de la Publicité, Paris. Editions Alternatives, Paris, 1985.

**Loie Fuller**
*Loie Fuller: Magician of Light.* Catalogue of the exhibition at the Virginia Museum, Richmond, 1979.

**Looping the Loop**
*Looping the Loop: Posters of Flight,* by Henry Serrano Villard and Willis M. Allen, Jr. Kales Press, San Diego, California, 2000.

**Loupot**
*Charles Loupot.* Catalogue of the exhibition at the Musée de l'Affiche, Paris.

**Loupot/Zagrodzki**
*Charles Loupot: L'Art de l'Affiche,* by Christophe Zagrodzki. Le Cherche-Midi, Paris, 1998. (Exclusive American distributor: Posters Please Inc., N.Y.C.)

**Maindron**
*Les Affiches Illustrées, 1886-1895,* by Ernest Maindron. G. Boudet, Paris, 1896.

**Maitres**
*Les Maitres de l'Affiche 1896-1900,* by Roger Marx. Imprimerie Chaix, Paris 1896-1900. Reprinted as "Masters of the Poster 1896-1900," by Images Graphiques, New York, 1977, and "The Complete 'Masters of the Poster,'" by Dover Publications, New York, 1990.

**Mangold**
*Burkhard Mangold (1873-1950).* Catalogue of the exhibition at the Kunstgewerbemuseum, Zurich, 1984.

**Margadant**
*Das Schweizer Plakat/The Swiss Poster, 1900-1983,* by Bruno Margadant. Birkhaus Verlag, Basel, 1983.

**Marx**
*Bonnard: Lithographie,* edited by Claude Roger-Marx. Monte Carlo, 1952.

**Masters 1900**
*Masters of the Poster 1900,* by Alan Weill. Bibliothèque de l'Image, Paris, 2001.

**Matter**
*Herbert Matter/FotoGrafiker/Sehformen der Zeit,* edited by Walter Binder, Adrian Battig and Armin Hofmann. Verlag Lars Muller, Baden, 1995.

**Mauzan**
*The Posters of Mauzan–A Catalogue Raisonné,* by Mirande Carnévalé-Mauzan. Exclusive North American distribution by Posters Please, Inc., New York, 2001.

**Mauzan Affiches**
*Mauzan: Affiches/Oeuvres Diverses,* by A. Lancellotti. Casa Editrice d'Arte Bestettie Tumminelli, Milan, ca. 1928.

**Mauzan/Treviso**
*Manifesti di A. L. Mauzan,* by Antonio Mazzaroli. Editrice Canova, Treviso, 1983.

**Mele**
*I Manifesti Mele.* Catalogue of the exhibition at the Museo Diego Aragona Pignatelli Cortes, Napoli, 1988. Curator: Mariontonietta Picone Petrusa. Arnoldo Mondadori Editore, Milano, 1988.

**Mer s'Affiche**
*La Mer s'Affiche,* by Daniel Hillion. Editions Ouest-France, Rennes, 1990.

**Modern Poster**
*The Modern Poster,* by Stuart Wrede. Catalogue of the exhibition at the Museum of Modern Art, New York, 1988. New York Graphic Society/Little Brown and Co., Boston, 1988.

**Moderno Francés**
*El Cartel Moderno Francés.* Catalogue for the Colin, Carlu, Loupot and Cassandre exhibition at the Museo Nacional Centro de Arte Reina Sofia, Madrid, 2001.

**Mouron**
*A. M. Cassandre,* by Henri Mouron. Rizzoli, New York, 1985.

**Mucha/Art Nouveau**
*Alphonse Mucha: The Spirit of Art Nouveau.* Catalogue of the touring exhibition organized by Art Services International, Alexandria, Virginia, 1998. Edited by Victor Arwas, Jana Brabcová-Orliková and Anna Dvorák.

**Müller-Brockmann**
*History of the Poster,* by Josef and Shizuko Müller-Brockmann. ABC Edition, Zurich, 1971 (in German, French and English).

**Murray-Robertson**
*Grasset: Pionnier de l'Art Nouveau,* by Anne Murray-Robertson. Bibliothèque des Arts, Paris/Editions 24 Heures, Lausanne, 1981.

**Musée d'Affiche**
*Musée d'Affiche.* Catalogue for the inaugural exhibition titled *Trois Siècles d'Affiches Françaises,* Paris, 1978.

**Olympics**
*L'Olympisme par l'Affiche/Olympism through Posters.* International Olympic Committee, Lausanne, 1983.

**PAI—Books of the auctions organized by Poster Auctions International, Inc.**

**PAI-I**
*Premier Posters.* Book of the auction held in New York City, March 9, 1985.

**PAI-II**
*Prize Posters.* Book of the auction held in Chicago, November 10, 1985.

**PAI-III**
*Poster Impressions.* Book of the auction held in New York City, June 1, 1986.

**PAI-IV**
*Prestige Posters.* Book of the auction held in New York City, May 3, 1987.

**PAI-V**
*Poster Pizzazz.* Book of the auction held in Universal City, California, November 22, 1987.

**PAI-VI**
*Poster Splendor.* Book of the auction held in New York City, May 1, 1988.

**PAI-VII**
*Poster Potpourri.* Book of the auction held in New York, November 13, 1988.

**PAI-VIII**
*Poster Treasures.* Book of the auction held in New York, May 7, 1989.

**PAI-IX**
*Poster Palette.* Book of the auction held in New York, November 12, 1989.

**PAI-X**
*Elegant Posters.* Book of the auction held in New York, May 20, 1990.

**PAI-XI**
*Poster Passion.* Book of the auction held in New York, November 11, 1990.

**PAI-XII**
*Poster Panache.* Book of the auction held in New York, May 5, 1991.

**PAI XIII**
*Poster Jubilee.* Book of the auction held in New York. November 10, 1991.

**PAI-XIV**
*Poster Extravaganza.* Book of the auction held in New York May 3, 1992.

**PAI XV**
*Rarest Posters.* Book of the auction held in New York, November 8, 1992.

**PAI-XVI**
*Poster Parade.* Book of the auction held in New York, May 2. 1993.

**PAI-XVII**
*Poster Classics.* Book of the auction held in New York, November 14, 1993.

**PAI-XVIII**
*Winning Posters.* Book of the auction held in New York, May 1, 1994.

**PAI-XIX**
*Prima Posters.* Book of the auction held in New York, November 13, 1994.

**PAI-XX**
*Poster Panorama.* Book of the auction held in New York, May 7, 1995.

**PAI-XXI**
*Timeless Posters.* Book of the auction held in New York, November 12, 1995.

**PAIXXII**
*Positively Posters.* Auction held in New York City, May 5, 1996.

**PAIXXIII**
*Poster Delights.* Auction held in New York City, November 10, 1996.

**PAI-XXIV**
*Poster Pleasures.* Auction held in New York City, May 4, 1997.

**PAI-XXV**
*Sterling Posters.* Auction held in New York City, November 9, 1997.

**PAI-XXVI**
*Postermania.* Auction held in New York City, May 3, 1998.

**PAI-XXVII**
*Poster Ecstasy.* Auction held in New York City, November 8, 1998.

**PAI-XXVIII**
*Poster Vogue.* Auction held in New York City, May 2, 1999.

**PAI-XXIX**
*Posters for the Millennium.* Auction held in New York City, November 4, 1999.

**PAI-XXX**
*Poster Allure.* Auction held in New York City, May 7, 2000.

**PAI-XXXI**
*Poster Power.* Auction held in New York City, November 12, 2000.

**PAI-XXXII**
*Dream Posters.* Auction held in New York City, May 6, 2001.

**PAI-XXXIII**
*Swank Posters.* Auction held in New York City, November 11, 2001.

**PAI-XXXIV**
*Poster Pride.* Auction held in New York City, May 5, 2002.

**PAI-XXXV**
*Posters Perform.* Auction held in New York City, November 10, 2002.

**PAI-XXXVI**
*Posters Persuasion.* Auction held in New York City, May 4, 2003.

**PAI-XXXVII**
*Poster Holiday/The Wright Stuff.* Dual-auction held in New York City, November 9, 2003.

**PAI-XXXVIII**
*Poster Style.* Auction held in New York City, May 2, 2004.

**PAI-XXXIX**
*Poster Intoxication.* Auction held in New York City, November 14, 2004.

**PAI-XL**
*Posters Excel.* Auction held in New York City, May 1, 2005.

**PAI-XLI**
*Matchless Posters.* Auction held in New York City, November 13, 2005.

**PAI-XLII**
*Posters Charm.* Auction held in New York City, May 7, 2006.

**PAI-XLIII**
*Posters Va-Va-Voom.* Auction held in New York City, November 12, 2006.

**Paradis**
*Paradis à vendre: Un siècle d'affiches touristiques suisses,* edited by Jean-Charles Giroud and Michel Schlup. Patrick Cramer Editeur, Geneva, 2005.

**Perier**
*Ils s'envolèrent.* Catalogue of the exhibition held at LeBourget from the collection of Jacques Perier on the 100th Anniversary of the Fédération Aéronautique Internationale in October 2005. Text by Jacques Perier.

**Peters**
*America on Stone,* by Harry T. Peters. Doubleday, Doran and Co., Garden City, New York, 1931.

**Petite Reine**
*La Petite Reine: Le Vélo en Affiches à la fin du XIXeme.* Catalogue exhibition of bicycle posters of the end of the 19th century held at Musée de l'Affiche, Paris, May to September, 1979.

**Phillips I**
*A Century of Posters 1870-1970.* The catalogue of the Phillips Auction held November 10, 1979, in New York. Text by Jack Rennert.

**Phillips II**
*Poster Classics.* The catalogue of the Phillips Auction held May 10, 1980, in New York. Text by Jack Rennert.

**Phillips III**
*The World of Posters.* The catalogue of the Phillips Auction held November 14, 1980, in New York. Text by Jack Rennert.

**Phillips IV**
*Poster Pleasures.* The catalogue of the Phillips Auction held April 11, 1981, in New York. Text by Jack Rennert.

**Pierrot**
*Les 100 plus belles images de Pierrot,* by Daniel Bordet. Editions Dabecom, Paris, 2003.

**Plakat Schweiz**
*Das Plakat in der Schweiz,* by Willy Rotzler, Fritz Schärer and Karl Wobmann. Edition Stemmle, Zurich, 1990.

**Plakate München**
*Plakate in München 1840-1940.* Catalogue of the exhibition of Munich posters at the Münchner Stadtmuseum, 1975-76.

**Purvis**
*Poster Progress.* Introduction by Tom Purvis. Edited by F.A. Mercer & W. Gaunt. The Studio, London and New York, ca. 1938.

**Rademacher**
*Masters of German Art,* by Hellmut Rademacher. October House, New York, 1966 (Original German edition published in 1965 by Edition Leipzig).

**Reims**
*Exposition d'Affiches Artistiques Françaises et Etrangères.* The catalogue of the November 1896 exhibition held in Reims. Reissued in a numbered edition of 1,000 copies by the Musée de l'Affiche in 1980.

**Rennert/Weill**
*Alphonse Mucha: The Complete Posters and Panels,* by Jack Rennert and Alain Weill. G. K. Hall, Boston, 1984.

**Richmond**
*The Technique of the Poster,* by Leonard Richmond. Sir Isaac Pitman & Sons, London, 1933.

**Roberts**
*Any color so long as it's black: the first fifty years of automobile advertising,* by Peter Roberts. David & Charles, Devon, England, 1976.

**Rogers**
*A Book of the Poster,* by W. S. Rogers. Greening & Co., London, 1901.

**Russian & Soviet Artists**
*A Dictionary of Russian & Soviet Artists 1920-1970,* by John Miller. Antiques Collectors' Club Ltd., Woodbridge, Suffolk, 1993.

**Salon des Cent**
*Le Salon des Cent: 1894-1900. Affiches d'artistes*, by Jocelyne Van Deputte. Catalogue of the exhibition held at the Musée Carnavalet, Paris, 1995.

**Salon des Cent/Neumann**
*Les Affiches du Salon des Cent.* Catalogue of the exhibition sponsored by the Foundation Neumann in Paris at the Musée de Pont-Aven and the Musée des Arts decoratifs de Bordeaux in 2000-2001.

**Schnackenberg**
*Schnackenberg: Kostüme, Plakate und Dekorationen*, by Oskar Bie. Musarion Verlag, Munich, 1920.

**Schweizer Hotel**
*Schweizer Hotelplakate 1875-1982*, by Karl Wobmann. Biregg Verlag, Luzern, 1982.

**Shell**
*The Shell Poster Book.* Introduction by David Bernstein. Hamish Hamilton, London, 1992.

**Sorlier**
*Chagall's Posters: A Catalogue Raissonné*, edited by Charles Sorlier, Crown Publishers, Inc., New York, 1975.

**Spectacle**
*Les Arts du Spectacle en France–Affiches Illlustrées 1850-1950*, by Nicole Wild. The catalogue of the Bibliothèque de l'Opera (part of the Bibliothèque Nationale), Paris, 1976.

**Swiss 1941-1965**
*Schweizer Plakatkunst.* The best Swiss posters of 1941-1965 with the Certificate of Honor of the Federl Department of the Interior. Visualis AG, Zurich, 1968.

**Swiss Posters**
*50 Years Swiss Posters*, selected by the Federal Department of Home Affairs. Published in 5 languages, including English. Kummerly & Frey, Bern, 1991.

**Swiss Winter Posters**
*A Century of Swiss Winter Sports Posters*, by Jean-Charles Giroud. Patrick Cramer Publisher, Geneva, 2006.

**Takashimaya**
*The Poster 1865-1969.* Catalogue of the exhibition which opened at the Takashimaya Art Gallery, Nihonbashi, Tokyo, April 18, 1985, and consisted largely of posters from the Deutsches Plakat Museum of Essen, Germany.

**Theaterplakate**
*Theaterplakate: ein internationaler historischer Überblick*, by Hellmut Rademacher. Edition Leipzig, Leipzig, 1990.

**Timeless Images**
*Timeless Images.* Catalogue of the touring exhibition of posters in Japan, 1984-85. Text by Jack Rennert; in English and Japanese. Exclusive American distributor: Posters Please, Inc., New York City.

**Toujours Plus Haut**
*Toujours Plus Haut: Affiches Aviation.* Catalogue of the aviation poster exhibition at the Centre de l'Affiche in Toulouse, France, 2004-2005. Edited by François-Régis Gastou. Chorus Editions, Toulouse, 2004.

**Train à l'Affiche**
*Le Train à l'Affiche: Les plus belles affiches ferroviaires française*, by Florence Camard and Christophe Zagrodzki. La Vie du Rail, Paris, 1989.

**Trouville/Deauville**
*Trouville Deauville a l'Affiche*, by Frederique Citera-Bullot. Editions Cahiers du Temps, Cabourg, 2000.

**V & A**
*The Power of the Poster*, edited by Margaret Timmer. Book of the exhibition at the Victoria & Albert Museum, London, 1998. V & A Publications, London, 1998.

**Van Caspel**
*Johann Georg Van Caspel–Affichekunstenaar (1870-1928).* Exhibition catalogue by Peter Van Dam, edited by Pim Reinders, organized by the author at the Amsterdams Historisch Museum, Amsterdam, 1990.

**Villemot**
*Les affiches de Villemot*, by Jean François Bazin. Denoël, Paris, 1985.

**Villemot/A to Z**
*Villemot–L'Affiches de A à Z*, by Guillaume Villemot. Éditions Hoëbeke, Paris, 2005.

**Villemot/La Femme**
*Villemot affiche la femme.* Catalogue of the exhibition at the Musée de Trouville, 2006-2007. Edited by Hélène Decaen Le Boulanger. Editions Cahiers du Temps, Cabourg.

**Wagner**
*Toulouse-Lautrec and His Contemporaries: Posters of the Belle Epoque from the Wagner Collection.* Book of the exhibition at the Los Angeles County Museum of Art, 1985.

**Wagons-Lits**
*125 Years International Sleeping Car Company*, by Albert Mühl and Jürgen Klein. The history in text and graphics of the Wagons-Lits company, with text in German, French and English. EK-Verlag GmbH, Freiburg, 1998.

**Weill**
*The Poster: A Worldwide Survey and History*, by Alain Weill. G.K. Hall, Boston, 1985.

**Wine Spectator**
*Posters of the Belle Epoque: The Wine Spectator Collection*, by Jack Rennert. The Wine Spectator Press, New York, 1990.

**Wittrock**
*Toulouse-Lautrec: The Complete Prints*, by Wolfgang Wittrock. 2 volumes. Sotheby's, London, 1985.

**Wobmann**
*Touristikplakate der Schweiz (Tourist Posters of Switzerland)*, by Karl Wobmann, introduction by Willy Rotzler. AT Verlag, Aarau, 1980.

**Word & Image**
*Word & Image.* Catalogue of the exhibition at the Museum of Modern Art, New York, edited by Mildred Constantine. Text by Alan M. Fern. New York Graphic Society, Greenwich, Connecticut, 1968.

**D'Ylen**
*Jean d'Ylen.* Catalogue of the exhibition at the Bibliothèque Forney, Paris, 1980.

**Yokoo/Graphic Works**
*Tadanori Yokoo-All About Tadanori Yokoo and his Graphic Work.* Kodansha, Tokyo, 1989.

**Yokoo's Posters**
*Tadanori Yokoo's Posters: IDEA Special Issue.* September 1994 special issue of IDEA Magazine, Tokyo.

# CONDITIONS OF SALE

The Conditions of Sale in this catalogue, as it may be amended by any posted notice during the sale, constitutes the complete terms and conditions under which the items listed in this catalogue will be offered for sale. Please note that the items will be offered by us as agent for the consignor.

Every potential buyer should read these Conditions of Sale and it will be agreed, acknowledged and understood by such buyer that said buyer has consented to each and every term and condition as set forth herein.

## 1. Authenticity and Terms of Guarantee.

For a period of five years from the date of this sale, Poster Auctions International, as agent, warrants the authenticity of authorship of all lots contained in this catalogue as described in the text accompanying each lot.

This warranty and guarantee is made only within the five year period and only to the original buyer of record who returns the purchased lot in the same condition as when sold to said buyer; and, it is established beyond doubt that the identification of authorship, as set forth in the description in this catalogue as may have been amended by any posted signs or oral declarations during tire sale, is not correct based on a reasonable reading of the catalogue and the Conditions of Sale herein. Any dispute arising under the terms in this paragraph will be resolved pursuant to final and binding arbitration at the American Arbitration Association.

Upon a finding by an Arbitrator in favor of buyer, the sale will be rescinded and the original purchase price, including the buyers premium, will be refunded. In such case, Poster Auctions International and the purchaser shall be deemed released of any and all claims that each may otherwise have had against the other arising out of the sale of such item.

The benefits of any warranty granted herein are personal to the buyer and are not assignable or transferable to any other person, whether by operation of law or otherwise. Any assignment or transfer of any such warranty shall be void and unenforceable. The purchaser refers only to the original buyer of the lot from Poster Auctions International and not any subsequent owner, assignee, or other person who may have or acquire an interest therein.

It is understood, in the event of disputed authenticity of authorship of any lot results in a rescission of the sale and restitution of the original price and premium paid by such purchaser, stated aforesaid, such restitution is buyer's sole remedy and Poster Auctions International disclaims all liability for any damages. incidental, consequential or otherwise, arising out of or in connection with any sale to the buyer.

Poster Auctions International has provided as much background information for each item listed in this catalogue as possible and has made reasonable efforts to insure the accuracy of the descriptions provided; but Poster Auctions International disclaims any warranty with regard to such descriptions and statements which accompany the listings in this catalogue, including but not limited to, the year of publication, the size, the condition, the printer, the references or any other background information or fact. Accordingly, buyer has due notice that any such information and/or descriptions cannot and will not be considered as material facts to this transaction and will root affect any sales herein.

## On the fall of the gavel, THE SALE IS FINAL.

## All items are sold AS IS.

The consignor warrants good title to the buyer. Poster Auctions International and the consignor make no representations or warranty that the buyer acquires any reproduction rights or copyright in items bought at this sale.

Any statements made by Poster Auctions International, whether in this catalogue or by its officers, agents or employees, whether oral or written, are statements of opinion only and not warranties or representations of material facts as to each arid every transaction herein.

## 2. Auctioneers Discretions.

Poster Auctions International has absolute discretion to divide any lot, to combine any of them, to withdraw any lot, to refuse bids and to regulate the bidding. Poster Auctions International reserves the right to withdraw lots at any time prior to or during the sale. The highest bidder acknowledged by the auctioneer will be the purchaser of the lot. Any advance made on an opening bid may be rejected if the auctioneer deems it inadequate. In the event of any dispute between bidders, or in the event of doubt as to the validity of any bid, the auctioneer shall have the final decision either to determine the successful bidder or to re-offer and re-sell the lot in dispute. If any dispute arises after the sale, the auctioneer's sale record shall be deemed the sole and conclusive evidence as to the purchaser of any lot or item.

## 3. Transfer of title and property.

Upon the fall of the auctioneer's hammer, title to the offered lot shall pass to the highest bidder, who may be required to sign a confirmation of purchase; and, shall be required to pay the full purchase price. The purchaser shall assume full risk and responsibility for the lot purchased upon the fall of the auctioneer's hammer. Poster Auctions International, at its option, may withhold delivery of the lots until funds represented by check have been collected or the authenticity of bank or cashier checks has been determined. No purchase shall be claimed or removed until the conclusion of the sale. In the event Poster Auctions International shall, for any reason whatsoever, be unable to deliver the lots purchased by the buyer, its liability shall be solely limited to the rescission of the sale and refund of the purchase price end purchaser's premium.

Poster Auctions International disclaims all liability for damages, incidental, consequential or otherwise, arising out of its failure to deliver any lots purchased. Poster Auctions International does not charge extra or sell separately any frame if a poster is so offered; but it is clear that it is the poster and not the frame which is being offered for sale. Poster Auctions International shall not be responsible for any damage to the frame or to any poster within the frame. Generally, framed posters offered for sale were received framed, photographed that way, and Poster Auctions International can make no warranty or representations regarding the condition of the poster in unseen areas of any such frame. All items are sold strictly as is and the purchaser assumes full risk and responsibility for the purchased lot upon the fall of the hammer, as stated aforesaid.

All lots shall be paid for and removed at the purchaser's risk and expense by noon of the second business day following the sale. Lots not so removed will, at the sole option of Poster Auctions International and at purchaser's risk and expense, be stored at Poster Auctions International's office or warehouse or delivered to a licensed warehouse for storage. Purchaser agrees, in either event, to pay all shipping, handling and storage fees incurred. In the case of lots stored at Poster Auctions International's own warehouse, the handling and storage fee will be an amount equal to 2% of the purchase price for each such lot, per month, until removed, with a minimum charge of 5% for any property not removed within thirty days from the date of the sale.

In addition, Poster Auctions International shall impose a late charge, calculated at the rate of 2% of the total purchase price per month, if payment has not been made in accordance with these Conditions of Sale.

Poster Auctions International may, on the day following the sale, remove all unclaimed lots to its offices or warehouse.

Unless purchaser notifies Poster Auctions International to the contrary, purchaser agrees that Poster Auctions International may, at its discretion, use purchaser's name as buyer of the item sold. If the purchaser fails to comply with one or more of these Conditions of Sale, then, in addition to any and all other remedies which it may have at law or in equity, Poster Auctions International may, at its sole option, cancel the sale without notice to the buyer. In such event, Poster Auctions International shall retain as liquidated damages all payments made by the purchaser, or sell the item and/or lots and all other property of the purchaser held by Poster Auctions International, without notice. Such liquidation sale shall be at standard commission rates, without any reserve. The proceeds of such sale or sales shall be applied first to the satisfaction of any damages occasioned by the purchaser's breach, and then to the payment of any other indebtedness owing to Poster Auctions International, including without limitation, commissions, handling charges, the expenses of both sales, reasonable attorneys fees, collection agency fees, and any other costs or expenses incurred thereunder. The purchaser hereby waives all the requirements of notice, advertisement and disposition of proceeds required by law, including those set forth in New York Lien Law, Article 9, Sections 200-204 inclusive, or any successor statue, with respect to any sale pursuant to this section.

## 4. Buyer's Premium

A premium of 15% will be added to the successful bid price of all items sold by Poster Auctions International. This premium shall be paid by all purchasers, without exception.

## 5. Order Bids

Poster Auctions International shall make reasonable efforts to execute bids for those not able to attend the auction; and act on the prospective purchaser's behalf to attempt to purchase the item desired at the lowest price possible, up to the limit indicated by purchaser in writing as if the purchaser were in attendance. Poster Auctions International shall not be responsible for any errors or omissions in this matter. Poster Auctions International reserves the right not to bid for any such purchaser if the order is not clear; does not arrive in sufficient time; the credit of the purchaser is not established prior to the sale; or, for any other reason in its sole discretion. An Order Bid Form shall be provided on request.

## 6. Sales Tax

Unless exempt by law, prior to taking pssession of the lot, the purchaser shall be required to pay the combined New York State and local sales tax, or any applicable compensating tax of another state, on the total purchase price.

## 7. Packing and shipping

Packing and/or handling of purchased lots by Posters Auctions International is performed solely as a courtesy for the convenience of purchasers. Unless otherwise directed by purchaser, packing and handling shall be undertaken at the sole discretion of Poster Auctions International. Poster Auctions International, at its sole discretion as agent of the purchaser, shall instruct an outside contractor to act on its behalf and arrange for or otherwise transport purchased lots. Charges for packing, handling, insurance and freight are payable by the purchaser. Poster Auctions International shall make reasonable efforts to handle purchases with care, but assumes no responsibility for damage of any kind. Poster Auctions International disclaims all liability for loss, or damages of any kind, arising out of or in connection with the packing, handling or transportation of any lots/items purchased.

## 8. Reserves.

All lots are subject to a reserve, which is the confidential minimum below which the lot will not be sold. Poster Auctions International may implement the reserve by bidding on behalf of the consignor. The consignor shall not bid on consignor's property.

## 9. Notices and jurisdiction.

(a)    All communications and notices hereunder shall be in writing and shall be deemed to have been duly given if delivered personally to an officer of PAI or if sent by United States registered mail or certified, postage prepaid, addressed as follows:

From:   Poster Auctions International
To:     _____(Seller)
        _____
        _____

From:   _____(Seller)
To:     Poster Auctions International
        601 W. 26th Street
        NewYork, NewYork 10001

or to such other address as either party hereto may have designated to the other by written notice.

(b)    These Conditions of Sale contain the entire understandings between the parties and may not be changed in any way except in writing duly executed by PAI and buyer.

(c)    These Conditions of Sale shall be construed and enforced in accordance with the laws of the State of New York.

(d)    No waiver shalt be deemed to be made by any party hereto of any rights hereunder, unless the same shall be in writing and each waiver, if any, shall be a waiver only with respect to the specific instance involved and shall in no way impair the rights of the waiving party or the obligations of the other party in any other respect at any other time.

(e)    The provisions of these Conditions of Sale shall be binding upon and inure to the benefit of the respective heirs, legatees, personal representatives and successors and assigns of the parties hereto.

(f)    The Conditions of Sale are not assignable by either party without written permission of the other party; any attempt to assign any rights, duties or obligations which arise under these Conditions without such permission will be void.

---

# DESCRIPTION OF THE POSTERS

I. Artist's name.
Unless otherwise indicated, the artist's name, mark or initials appear on the poster.

2. Year of the Poster.
The year given is that of the publication of the poster, not necessarily the date of the event publicized or the year that art for it was rendered.

3. Size.
Size is given in inches first, then centimeters, width preceding height. Size is for entire sheet, not just the image area.

4. Printer.
Unless otherwise indicated, the name of the printer is that which appears on the face of the poster. It should be kept in mind that frequently the establishment credited on the poster is, in fact, an agency, studio or publisher.

5. Condition of the Poster.
We have attempted a simplified rating of all the posters in this sale. It should be kept in mind that we are dealing in many cases, with 50 to 100-year-old advertising paper. The standards of the print collector cannot be used. Prints were, for the most part, done in small format, on fine paper, and meant to be immediately framed or stored in a print sleeve or cabinet. A poster, for the most part, was printed in a large format, on the cheapest possible paper, and was meant to last about eight weeks on the billboards.

Most important to the condition of a poster—not eight weeks but often eighty years later—is the image of the poster: is that image (the lines, the colors, the overall design) still clearly expressed? If so, it is a poster worth collecting.

While details of each poster's condition are given as completely and accurately as possible, blemishes, tears or restorations which do not detract from the basic image and impact should not seriously impair value.

All posters are lined, whether on linen or japan paper, unless otherwise indicated. But please note that posters received in frames are not inspected out of their frames and therefore no warranty can be made about them.

All photos are of the actual poster being offered for sale. A close look at the photo and a reading of the text should enable the buyer who cannot personally examine the item to make an intelligent appraisal of it.

The following ratings have been used:

Cond A   Designates a poster in very fine condition. The colors are fresh; no paper loss. There may be some slight blemish or tear, but this is very marginal and not noticeable. A+ is a flawless example of a poster rarely seen in such fine condition. A– indicates there may be some slight dirt, fold, tear or bubble or other minor restoration, but most unobtrusive.

Cond B   Designates a poster in good condition. There may be some slight paper loss, but not in the image or in any crucial design area. If some restoration, it is not immediately evident. The lines and colors are good, although paper may have yellowed (light-stained). B+ designates a poster in very good condition. B– is one in fairly good condition. The latter determination may be caused by heavier than normal light-staining or one or two noticeable repairs.

Cond C   Designates a poster in fair condition. The light-staining may be more pronounced, restorations, folds or flaking are more readily visible, and possibly some minor paper loss occurs. But the poster is otherwise intact, the image clear, and the colors, though possibly faded, still faithful to the artist's intent.

Cond D   Designates a poster in bad condition. A good part of such poster may be missing, including some crucial image area; colors and lines so marred that a true appreciation of the artist's intent is difficult, if not impossible. There are no D posters in this sale!

The above condition ratings are solely the opinion of Poster Auctions International, and are presented only as an aid to the public. Prospective purchasers are expected to have satisfied themselves as to the condition of the posters. Any discrepancy relating to the condition of a poster shall not be considered grounds for the cancellation of a sale.

Some other notes and designations relating to the condition of a poster:

Framed   Where a poster is framed, this is indicated. In many cases, we have photographed the poster in the frame and the dimensions given are those which are visible within the matting or edges of the frame.

Paper    All posters in this sale are linen- or japan-backed unless the designation "P" appears.

6. Bibliography.
An abbreviation for each reference (Ref) is given and can be found in the complete Bibliography. The reference is almost always to a reproduction of that poster. If a "p." precedes it, it means the reproduction or reference is on that page; if number only, it refers to a poster or plate number. Every effort has been made to refer to books that are authoritative and/or easily accessible.

7. Pre-Sale Estimate
These estimates are guides for prospective bidders and should not be relied upon as representations or predictions of actual selling prices. They are simply our best judgment of the fair market value of that particular poster in that condition on the date it was written.

# POSTER PRICES IX

The revised and expanded 272-page book, your index and price guide
to more than 24,000 posters offered by PAI at its first 44 auctions.

It is absolutely essential for any collector and we urge you to order it now.
The book will be shipped to subscribers on August 15, 2007.
Price: **$60** ($70 foreign).

*See next page for Order Form.*

# THE POSTER ENCYCLOPEDIA

These hardcover, auction catalogues form an essential encyclopedia for the poster collector. Each illustrates over 500 posters, with full annotations, bibliography, estimates and prices realized.

Price of individual volumes: **$50** each ($55 foreign).

**SPECIAL OFFER:** All 30 previous available catalogues for only **$950** ($1,100 foreign).

**ACT NOW!** With supplies of previous PAI catalogues rapidly dwindling, it's imperative that you take advantage of this special offer for the 30 remaining books still in print.

## POSTER AUCTIONS INTERNATIONAL, INC.
### 601 WEST 26TH ST., NEW YORK, N.Y. 10001
### TEL (212) 787-4000  FAX (212) 604-9175
www.posterauctions.com     Email: info@posterauctions.com

# WINNING POSTERS
## ABSENTEE BID FORM

Please bid on my behalf on the following lots up to the price shown. I understand that all bids are subject to the Conditions of Sale which are printed in the Catalogue.

Poster Auctions International will make every effort to execute bids for those not able to attend and act on the prospective purchaser's behalf to try to purchase the item desired at the lowest price possible up to the limit indicated by purchaser below as if the purchaser were in attendance, but Poster Auctions International cannot be responsible for any errors or omissions in this matter. Poster Auctions International may reserve the right not to bid for any such party if the order is not clear, does not arrive in sufficient time, or the credit of the purchaser is not established, or for any other reason in its sole discretion.

The purchase price will be the total of the final bid and a premium of 15% of the final bid together with any applicable sales tax. Unsuccessful bidders will not be informed but may telephone for sales results.

_____     Date _____
(Signed)

NAME _____

ADDRESS _____

City _____State _____Zip _____

TEL: Home: (      )_____ Office: (      )_____ FAX: (      )_____

E-mail address_____

BANK: Name _____Telephone (      )_____

   Address _____

   Account Number _____ Officer_____

Credit Card # _____ Expiration: _____

☐ ORDER BID

☐ TELEPHONE BID—Telephone number where you can be reached on Sunday, May 6

| Lot # | Artist | Title | BID (excluding premium) |
|-------|--------|-------|-------------------------|
| _____ | _____ | _____ | $ _____ |
| _____ | _____ | _____ | $ _____ |
| _____ | _____ | _____ | $ _____ |
| _____ | _____ | _____ | $ _____ |
| _____ | _____ | _____ | $ _____ |
| _____ | _____ | _____ | $ _____ |
| _____ | _____ | _____ | $ _____ |

CUT AT PERFORATED EDGE.

# YES, you CAN
## be with us on May 6.

If you cannot attend our New York sale in person, you can nonetheless take advantage of these rare offerings.

# BID by MAIL, FAX or PHONE
## with confidence.

Simply fill out the form on the reverse side of this page, indicating your maximum bid for each desired lot. It should be in our New York offices no later than Friday, May 4.

You may indicate an "either-or" bid if you want to purchase only a portion of the items on your wish list. You may also indicate a maximum total dollar amount. We execute your bid on your behalf at the lowest price possible.

To bid by telephone, simply fill in the lot numbers and indicate the phone number where we can reach you on Sunday, May 6. When your lot number comes up, we'll call you.

*Either way, you bid with confidence:* We execute your bid on your behalf at the lowest possible price.

**DON'T MISS OUT ON THE POSTER YOU WANT just because you can't be in New York.**

**REMINDER:** You can view all the posters at The International Poster Center, 601 W. 26th Street, New York City from April 20 to May 5. Hours: 9–5 Monday–Friday; 10–6 Saturday and Sunday.

*We are a bidder-friendly organization!*